C000144652

NERVA AND THE
ROMAN SUCCESSION CRISIS
OF AD 96–99

The imperial succession at Rome was notoriously uncertain, and where possible, hereditary succession was preferred, yet when Domitian was assassinated in AD 96, he had no sons and had executed several family members who might have succeeded him. The conspirators involved had arranged the elderly Nerva as his successor; but Nerva was also childless. He had to adopt the general Trajan in order to prevent a similar crisis on his own death, and it became clear that adoption was the only remedy for emperors, if military coups or civil wars were to be avoided.

John Grainger's detailed study looks at this period of intrigue and conspiracy. He explores how, why and by whom Domitian was killed, the rule of Nerva, and Trajan, who became a strong and respected emperor against the odds. Perhaps most significantly Grainger investigates the effects of this dynastic uncertainty both inside and outside the ruling group in Rome, asking why civil war did not occur in this time of political upheaval.

The last time a dynasty had failed, in AD 68, a damaging military conflict had resulted; at the next failure in AD 192, another war broke out; by the third century civil war was institutionalised, and was one of the main reasons for the eventual downfall of the entire imperial structure. Grainger argues that though AD 96 – 98 stands out as a civil war that did not happen, it was a perilously close-run thing.

John D. Grainger is a freelance historian and former teacher. He is the author or several books on ancient history, including *Seleukos Nikator* (Routledge 1991), *The League of the Aitolians* (1999) and *The Roman War of Antiochus the Great* (2002).

NERVA AND THE ROMAN SUCCESSION CRISIS OF AD 96–99

John D. Grainger

LONDON AND NEW YORK

First published 2003
by Routledge
2 Park Square, Milton Park, Oxon, OX14 4RN

Simultaneously published in the USA and Canada
by Routledge
711 Third Avenue, New York, NY 10017

Reprinted with corrections in 2004

Routledge is an imprint of the Taylor & Francis Group

© 2004 John D. Grainger

Typeset in Garamond by Bookcraft Ltd, Stroud, Gloucestershire

All rights reserved. No part of this book may be reprinted or reproduced or
utilised in any form or by any electronic, mechanical, or other means, now
known or hereafter invented, including photocopying and recording, or in
any information storage or retrieval system, without permission in writing
from the publishers.

British Library Cataloguing in Publication Data
A catalogue record for this book is available from the British Library

Library of Congress Cataloging in Publication Data
Grainger, John D., 1939–
Nerva and the Roman succession crisis AD 96–99/John D. Grainger.
p. cm.
Includes bibliographical references and index.
1. Nerva, Emperor of Rome, ca 30–98 2. Emperors–Rome–Biography.
3. Rome–History–Antonines, 96–192. I. Title.
DG293.G73 2002
937'.07'092–dc21   2002067991
[B]

ISBN 978-0-415-28917-7 (hbk)
ISBN 978-0-415-34958-1 (pbk)

CONTENTS

ILLUSTRATIONS

PLATES

TABLES

MAPS

ABBREVIATIONS

AE	*Année Épigraphique*
ANRW	*Aufstieg und Niedergang der Römischen Welt*
BAR	British Archaeological Reports
Bennett, *Trajan*	J. Bennett, *Trajan, Optimus Princeps, a Life and Times*, London, 1998
Birley, *Fasti*	A.R. Birley, *The 'Fasti' of Roman Britain*, Oxford, 1981
BMC III	H. Mattingly, *Coins of the Roman Empire in the British Museum, Part III: Nerva to Hadrian*, London 1936
CIL	*Corpus Inscriptionum Latinarum*
Dusanic and Vasic, 'Moesian Diploma'	S. Dusanic and M.B. Vasich, 'An Upper Moesian Diploma of AD 96', *Chiron 7*, 1986
Eck, 'Statthalter'	W. Eck, 'Jahres- und Provinzialfasten der senatorischen Statthalter von 68/70 bis 138/139 (I)', *Chiron 12*, 1983, 281–362
Garzetti, *Nerva*	A. Garzetti, *Nerva*, Rome 1950
HSCP	*Harvard Studies in Classical Philology*
ILS	*Inscriptiones Latinae Selectae*
Jones, *Domitian*	B.W. Jones, *The Emperor Domitian*, London, 1992
Jones, *Senatorial Order*	B.W. Jones, *Domitian and the Senatorial Order: a Prosopographical Study of Domitian's Relationship with the Senate, AD 81–96*, Philadelphia 1979
JRS	*Journal of Roman Studies*
Lambrechts	P. Lambrechts, *La Composition du sénat romain de l'accession au trone d'Hadrien à la mort de Commodus*, Ghent 1936
McCrum and Woodhead	M. McCrum and A.G. Woodhead, *Select Documents of the Principates of the Flavian Emperors, including the Year of Revolution, AD 68–96*, Cambridge, 1966
OGIS	W. Dittenberger, *Orientis Graeci Inscriptiones Selectae*
PIR	*Prosopographia Imperii Romani*
Pliny, *Letters*	Pliny the Younger, *Letters*
PBSR	*Papers of the British School at Rome*
Raepsaet-Charlier	M.T. Raepsaet-Charlier, *Prosopographie des femmes de l'ordre senatorial (Ier–IIe siècles)*, Louvain 1987
RIC	*Roman Imperial Coinage*

RMD I	M.M. Roxan, *Roman Military Diplomas 1954–77*, Institute of Archaeology Occasional Publication, London 1978
RMD III	M.M. Roxan, *Roman Military Diplomas, 1985–93*, Institute of Archaeology Occasional Publication, London, 1994
Roman Papers	R. Syme, *Roman Papers*, 7 vols, Oxford 1979–91
SEG	*Supplementum Epigraphicum Graecum*
SHA	*Scriptores Historiae Augustae*
Smallwood	E.M. Smallwood, *Documents illustrating the Principates of Nerva, Trajan and Hadrian*, Cambridge 1966
Syme, *Tacitus*	R. Syme, *Tacitus*, Oxford 1958
Vidman, *FO*	L. Vidman, *Fasti Ostienses*, Prague 1981
ZPE	*Zeitschrift für Papyrologie und Epigrafik*

PLATES

Plate 1 Domitian. A bust of Domitian which was recovered from the bed of the River Tiber. It is undamaged, and may be assumed to have been thrown into the river as part of the reaction against the emperor after his assassination. It is the sort of bust which would be in private possession, so one may conjecture a private gesture of hatred. The owner had, however, clearly gone to some expense to acquire it – it was no doubt a social and political requirement to display some devotion.

Source: Ny Carlsberg Glyptotek, Copenhagen; Cat. 664. Photo © Jo Selsing.

Plate 2   Nerva – ex Domitian. A statue of Domitian depicted as Jupiter, with the features recut as Nerva. Most of Nerva's statues began as Domitian, and were hastily altered. This was a commendable cost-cutting device, no doubt approved by the emperor himself, who was short of cash. It may also be a widespread recognition that Nerva would not last long, either because of his age, or because of the political uncertainty which lasted all through his reign.

Source: Ny Carlsberg Glyptotek, Copenhagen; Cat. 542. Photo © Jo Selsing.

Plate 3   Nerva – himself. One of the few portraits of Nerva which were not recut from heads of Domitian. It is nevertheless an image less close to death than the reality, yet still with lines of care and age and experience. Just what you would want your caring emperor to be.

Source: Ny Carlsberg Glyptotek, Copenhagen; Cat. 668. Photo © Jo Selsing.

Plate 4 Trajan. The emperor is seen in war-dress, stern and resolute. This was the image he was to project throughout his reign: the Roman warrior. It was a sharp contrast with the more peaceable depiction favoured by Domitian and the normally civilian aspect that Nerva showed.

Source: Ny Carlsberg Glyptotek, Copenhagen; Cat. 543. Photo © Jo Selsing.

TABLES

96

Ord.	C. Manlius Valens	C. Antistius Vetus
May	Q. Fabius Postuminus	T. Prifernius Paetus
Sep.	Ti. Catius Caesius Fronto	M. Calpurnius --icus

97

Ord.	Imp Nerva III	M. Verginius Rufus III
Mar.	Cn. Arrius Antoninus II	C? Calpurnius Piso
May	M. Annius Verus	L. Neratius Priscus
Jul.	L. Domitius Apollinaris	Sex. Hermetidius Campanus
Sep.	Q. Glitius Atilius Agricola	M. Cornelius Nigrinus Curiatius Maternus II
Nov.	P. Cornelius Tacitus	?

98

Ord.	Imp. Nerva IV	Imp. Traianus II
Jan.	Cn. Domitius Tullus II	
Feb.	Sex. Julius Frontinus II	
Mar.	L. Julius Ursus II	
Apr.	T. Vestricius Spurinna II	
May	C. Pomponius Pius	
Jul.	A. Vicirius Martialis	L. Maecius Postumus
Sep.	C. Pomponius Rufus Acilius [Prisc]us Coelius Sparsus	Cn. Pompeius Ferox Licinianus
Nov.	Q. Fulvius Gillo Bittius Proculus?	P. Julius Lupus

99

Ord.	A. Cornelius Palma Frontonianus	Q. Sosius Senecio
Mar.	Sulpicius Lucretius Barba	Senecio Memmius Afer
May	Q. Fabius Barbatus Valerius Magnus Iulianus	A. Caecilius Faustinus
Jul.	M. Ostorius Scapula	?
Sep.	?	?
Nov.	?	?

100

Ord.	Imp Trajan III	Sex. Julius Frontinus III
Jan.	L. Julius Ursus III	
Mar.	---cius Macer	C. Cilnius Proculus
May	L. Herennius Saturninus	L. Pomponius Mamilianus
Jul.	Q. Acutius Nerva	L. Fabius Tuscus
Sep.	C. Plinius Caecilius Secundus	C. Julius Cornutus Tertullus
Nov.	L. Roscius Aelianus Maecius Celer	Ti. Claudius Sacerdos Iulianus

Table 1 Consuls 96–100.

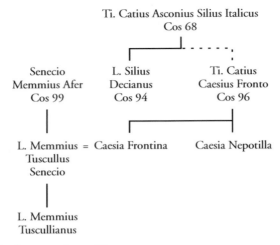

Ti. Catius Asconius Silius Italicus
Cos 68

Senecio	L. Silius	Ti. Catius
Memmius Afer	Decianus	Caesius Fronto
Cos 99	Cos 94	Cos 96

L. Memmius = Caesia Frontina   Caesia Nepotilla
Tuscullus
Senecio

L. Memmius
Tuscullianus

Table 2   The family connections of Fronto.

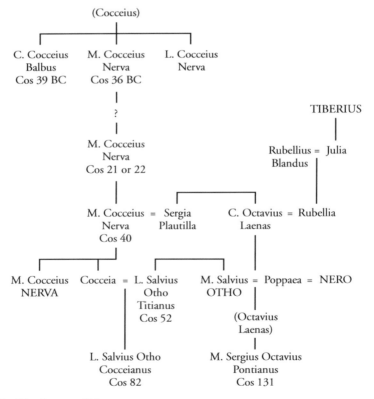

(Cocceius)

C. Cocceius	M. Cocceius	L. Cocceius
Balbus	Nerva	Nerva
Cos 39 BC	Cos 36 BC	

?

M. Cocceius
Nerva
Cos 21 or 22

TIBERIUS

Rubellius = Julia
Blandus

M. Cocceius = Sergia   C. Octavius = Rubellia
Nerva   Plautilla   Laenas
Cos 40

M. Cocceius	Cocceia = L. Salvius	M. Salvius = Poppaea = NERO
NERVA	Otho	OTHO
	Titianus	
	Cos 52	(Octavius
		Laenas)

L. Salvius Otho   M. Sergius Octavius
Cocceianus   Pontianus
Cos 82   Cos 131

Table 3   The descent of Nerva.

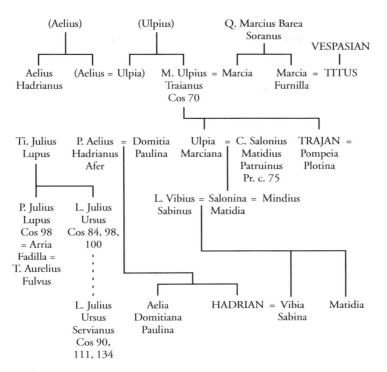

Table 4 The Ulpii.

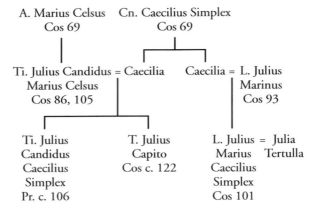

Table 5a The Asian network 1: The Narbonensian branch.

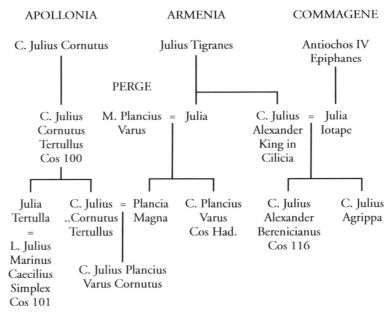

Table 5b The Asian network 2: the Asian branch – the Italian families.

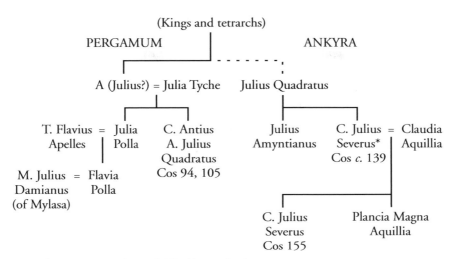

(Kings and tetrarchs)

PERGAMUM | ANKYRA

A (Julius?) = Julia Tyche   Julius Quadratus

T. Flavius = Julia   C. Antius   Julius   C. Julius = Claudia
Apelles | Polla   A. Julius   Amyntianus   Severus* | Aquillia
| Quadratus   Cos c. 139
M. Julius = Flavia   Cos 94, 105
Damianus   Polla
(of Mylasa)

C. Julius   Plancia Magna
Severus   Aquillia
Cos 155

* C. Julius Severus, according to OGIS 544, was related to:
1. Ti. Julius Aquila Polemaeanus – below.
2. C. Claudius Severus of Pompeiopolis.
3. C. Julius Alexander, king in Cilicia – Table 5b.
4. Julia Severa, wife of L. Servenius Capito of Akmoneia.
5. C. Julius Quadratus Bassus (Cos 105).

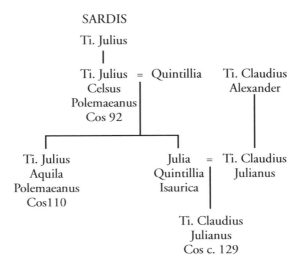

SARDIS

Ti. Julius
|
Ti. Julius = Quintillia   Ti. Claudius
Celsus   Alexander
Polemaeanus
Cos 92

Ti. Julius   Julia = Ti. Claudius
Aquila   Quintillia | Julianus
Polemaeanus   Isaurica
Cos110
Ti. Claudius
Julianus
Cos c. 129

Table 5c The Asian network 3: the Asian branch – the royal families.

MAPS

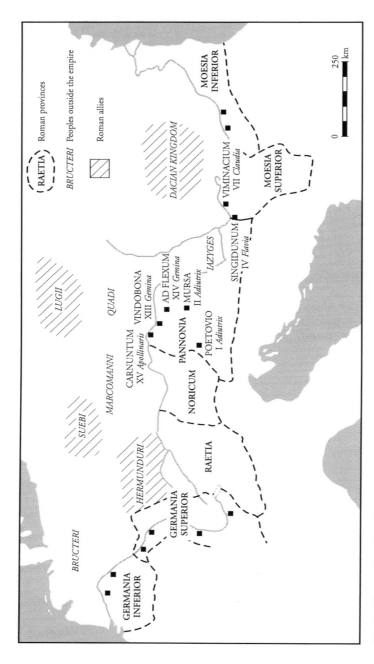

Map 1 The northern frontier.

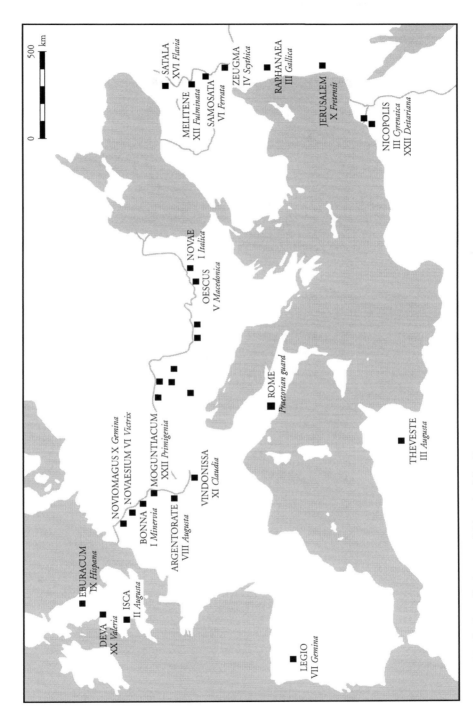

Map 2 Distribution of legions, AD 96 (see also Map 1).

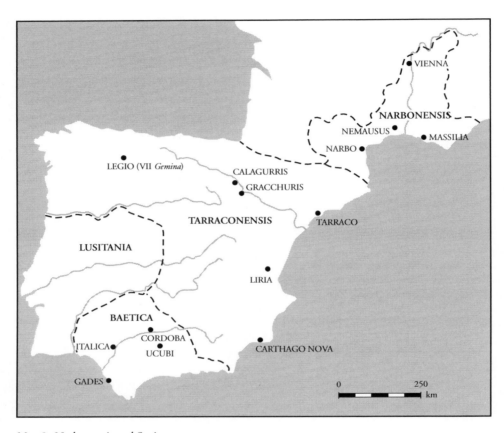

Map 3 Narbonensis and Spain.

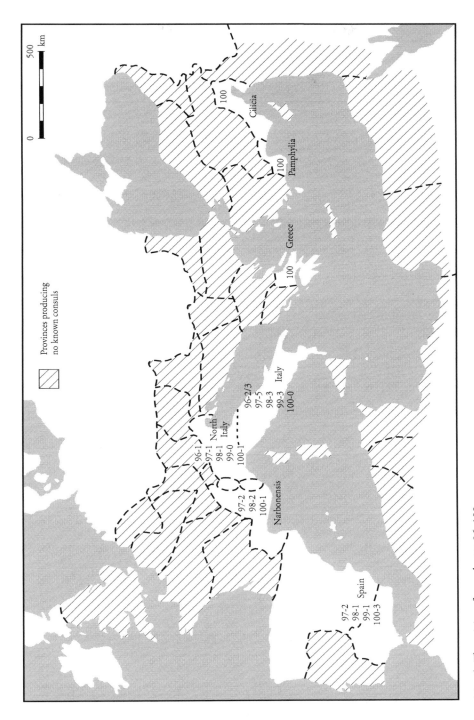

Map 4 The origins of consuls, AD 96–100.

Provinces producing
no known consuls

km
0   500

Cilicia 100

Pamphylia 100

Greece 100

Italy
96-2/3
97-5
98-3
99-3
100-0

North
Italy
96-1
97-1
98-1
99-0
100-1

Narbonensis
97-2
98-2
100-1

Spain
97-2
98-1
99-1
100-3

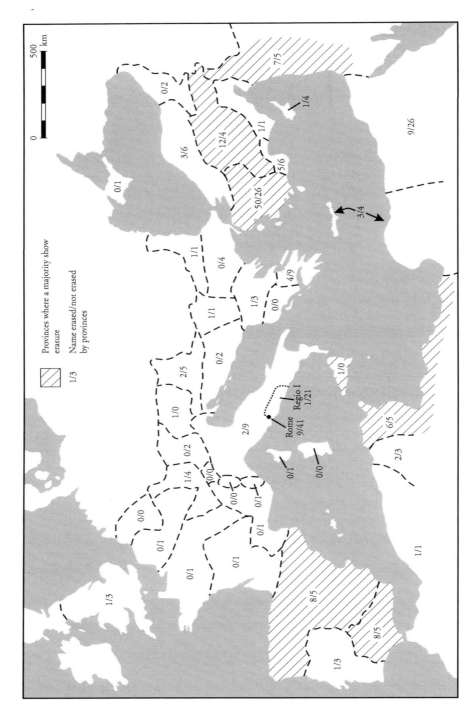

Provinces where a majority show erasure

Name erased/not erased by provinces

1/3

0

500 km

7/5

0/2

1/4

3/6

1/1

12/4

9/26

5/6

0/1

50/26

3/4

1/1

0/4

4/9

1/1

1/3

0/0

0/2

2/5

1/0

1/0

1/4

0/2

0/0

2/9

Rome
9/41

Regio I
1/21

1/3

0/0

0/0

0/1

0/0

0/1

0/1

0/1

6/5

0/1

2/3

8/5

1/1

1/3

8/5

Map 5 'Domitian' inscriptions.

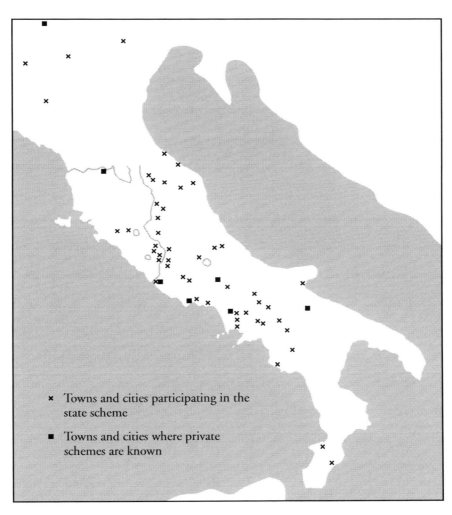

Map 6 The *'alimenta'* schemes

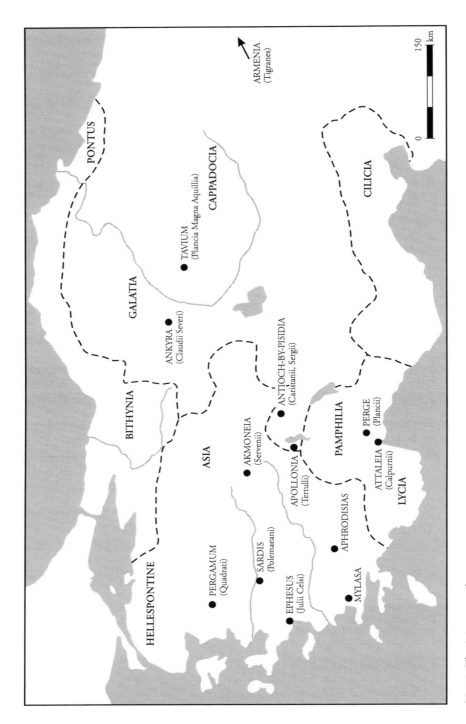

Map 7 The Asian network.

INTRODUCTION

A change of government is the most dangerous time for the stability of any state, apart from a physical invasion. Modern states tend to cope with it well enough, having had plenty of practice. Democracies are particularly competent at it, though their methods are various. In Britain, the change is virtually instantaneous, the new Prime Minister going into 10 Downing Street as the old one leaves; even so the police are especially alert during an election, and no doubt the armed forces have their plans. In the United States, there is a built-in period of ten weeks, originally longer, and originally intended to allow travelling time for legislators, electoral college members and the new President to get to the capital over non-existent roads; now it is called the 'transition', and allows participants to recover from the rigours of the election campaign, and the winner to choose his officials; and, as we saw in the election of 2000, it is also a useful device for sorting out electoral problems. In Europe, where parliamentary majorities are often rare, there is the institution of a 'caretaker government', put in place while the coalition negotiations go along.

Autocracies are different. The death of a ruler is a moment of infinite danger, providing opportunities for all kinds of mischief. As in democracies, the methods of avoiding such troubles are varied. Hereditary succession is one, and this method works so long as the line of succession is clear and generally accepted. Election is another method, though rare. Designating a successor in advance can work, as it has recently in Syria and North Korea, and this was the common Roman device, in the form of adoption. It was, however, a dangerous one: the adoptee might become too eager; the adopter might change his mind; and before the adoption took place there will have been competitors, who might not be capable in the event of accepting the decision which the adopter had reached, and may take measures to alter the decision. The moment of transition is the best moment for doing this. These difficulties are magnified when the ruler dies suddenly, and are increased still further, to the point of a likely civil war, when he is assassinated.

The imperial succession at Rome was notoriously uncertain, in large part because of the absence of any defined method, or rather because of the several possible methods which could be used. There were elective aspects to it, since the various offices which constituted the imperial power were formally offered by the Senate, but in fact it was hereditary, in accordance with the norms of the Roman aristocracy. In practice, none of the emperors in the first hundred years of the empire (BC 30 to AD 68) was able to pass the throne on to his son. Only one emperor, in fact, had a son to inherit, and that was Claudius, whose son Britannicus was a child and soon disposed of by his rivals. Further, only the first two emperors, Augustus and Tiberius, died certainly natural deaths, though murder was so common as the fate of the Julio-Claudian rulers that it was rumoured for those two as well. In the end, so lethal was membership of the imperial family that, when Nero died – by assisted suicide – there was effectively no member of the family left; that led to the civil wars of 68–70, in which four emperors or imperial heirs died by violence (not counting Nero), not to mention several tens of thousands of their subjects. In the Roman empire hereditary succession was therefore the preferred method, but it was normally moved on by assassination. Only when the possibility of inheritance within the imperial family failed did the aristocracy resort to violence beyond assassination to solve the problem.

The lesson of the events of 68–70 was learned. The winner of the civil wars, Vespasian, succeeded in establishing a new dynasty, in which the succession was hereditary in adult males. Both Vespasian and Titus died natural deaths: the first from old age, the second from illness, and Domitian reigned longer than any emperor since Tiberius. Yet the direct line of succession failed again, for Domitian, like the Julio-Claudians, had no sons and found it necessary to execute several members of his family, so that when he was assassinated the succession was once again uncertain. He had adopted two cousins, but both were teenage boys at his death, and the adoptions seem to have meant nothing to the rest of the aristocracy. The conspirators who organised the emperor's killing did have a new emperor, Nerva, in place at once, but Nerva was a ruler who was old and frail, and, once again, childless. Hence the problem of the successor to Domitian was only postponed and the issue remained wide open, until Nerva adopted as his heir the general Trajan – and even then Trajan had to work hard to establish himself. It may be thought that it was his very lack of a direct heir which commended Nerva to the conspirators, were it not for the fact that he was only the last in a line of men who had been approached, and some at least of these men will have had children. So adoption was the only available remedy, if either a military coup or civil war was to be avoided.

It was this sequence – assassination, succession, adoption – that constituted the 'Roman Succession Crisis' which I propose to investigate here. It was a crisis essentially about the question of who was to be emperor, and so had only limited effect outside Rome – but even so the provinces, from Syria to Germany, were affected. Hanging over the events of the reign of Nerva was the memory of the civil war of less than thirty years before, which all the participants could remember, and which constrained their actions. But at the same time the crisis had a major effect on the general history of the empire. In particular I contend that it redirected army energies away from the ambitious and intelligent plans of Domitian for conquest in the north and towards events in Rome, with the result that an emperor was chosen who had no understanding of the policy which Domitian had been pursuing, so that a promising process of conquest was aborted, and eventually displaced.

The problems which I will address, therefore, are how and why Domitian was killed, and by whom; the rule of Nerva; the choice of his successor; and the effects of all this inside and outside the ruling group. Why a civil war did not occur is also a problem which must be considered. The last time a dynasty had failed, in 68, a civil war had resulted; at the next failure, in 192, another civil war developed, and in the third century civil war became institutionalised, and so on, with regular civil wars in the fourth and fifth centuries, providing one of the major reasons for the eventual destruction of the whole imperial structure. The years 96–98 thus stand out as a civil war which did not happen. But it was close.

1

ASSASSINATION

The Emperor Domitian spent the morning of 18 September sitting in the court-room of the imperial palace in Rome, passing judgement on a variety of cases which came before him. This was one of his main imperial duties, and surely one which was more wearying than most. Between the fifth and sixth hours – that is to say, a little before noon – he left to go for a bath before his afternoon siesta. On the way he was intercepted by Parthenius, his senior *cubicularius*, or chamberlain, with the information that one of the freedmen in the household of his niece Domitilla, a man called Stephanus, had an important message for him, and that he had gone to the emperor's private bedroom with it.

The emperor obediently went off to see what Stephanus had to say, going to his small apartment deep in the centre of the palace. According to one source, Stephanus was somewhat under a cloud, having been charged with theft. Domitilla had been banished to exile on the island of Pandeteria the year before, soon after her husband, the emperor's cousin and designated successor T. Flavius Clemens, had been executed: Stephanus, who was still it seems employed in the palace, had presumably been taken into the emperor's household on Domitilla's banishment. He is said to have been eager to avenge her, and for the last week he had been going round with a bandage on his arm, under which he had concealed a dagger.

Domitian's death is supposed to have been foretold by more than one astrologer, to have been feared by the emperor himself, and to have been signalled by a wide variety of omens: all of these details are avidly recorded by the two historians whose detailed accounts of the emperor's murder have survived, Suetonius and Dio Cassius.[1] If all these events and signs had really happened, it is a truly astonishing thing that Domitian, reputed to be fearful, superstitious and a believer in omens and astrology, should have gone alone to a private meeting with the disaffected and vengeful Stephanus.

It is, however, one of the few certainties in this story that this is exactly what Domitian did. The fact that Stephanus was a freedman, a servant, and so of no social account, no doubt allowed the emperor to discount any threat from him he may have heard or thought of. Threats to the emperor usually came from outside the palace, from members of the Senate above all and, of course, the omens and predictions were only thought to be significant after the event. The emperor's fearfulness and superstition were either non-existent or exaggerated; in any case these beliefs were not important enough to him to override his normal human instincts to meet and converse with others, or to interfere with his everyday task of ruling and administering. Also, of course, the emperor must have been quite used to receiving such messages in private. He was certainly, as we shall see later, expecting to receive important information, though perhaps not from his niece's freedman. Yet Stephanus' message might well be important, especially if vouched for in some way by the high official Parthenius.

Stephanus' bandage had concealed a dagger, but this was only one of the preparations which had been made. They included locking the doors to the emperor's servants' quarters, whence help for the emperor could come, and disabling the emperor's own personal weapon of last resort. Other armed men had been stationed nearby to assist Stephanus if necessary.

Stephanus handed Domitian a list, which was said to contain the names of men who were forming a conspiracy against the emperor. Someone involved in all this had a taste for irony, surely, or perhaps it was the sort of information that was known to guarantee Domitian's total attention, or that of any other emperor for that matter. But then, with Domitian thus distracted, Stephanus took out his dagger and struck, though he only wounded the emperor. Domitian fought back, and the two grappled on the floor, watched by a frightened boy whose job it was to attend to the shrine of the household gods in the emperor's room. The boy responded to Domitian's frantic order and went for the emperor's own dagger, which was kept under his pillow. Its blade had been removed.

Stephanus' assault was clearly unsuccessful, and he was now unlikely to do more than wound the emperor. Domitian is said to have seized the dagger by the blade, severely cutting his fingers. Stephanus' efforts had therefore to be supplemented by the other men, who were held ready for just such a development. A freedman called Maximus, an officer called Clodianus, another chamberlain called Satur or Sigerius, and an unnamed gladiator are all listed as joining in a second attack, no doubt attracted to the scene by the continuing noise of the fight, which signalled the failure of Stephanus' attack. It was under the assaults of these men that the emperor finally died, having received at least eight stab-wounds. According to one account, Stephanus was forthwith murdered by Domitian's servants, who presumably now got through or round the locked doors; the fate of the others involved is not known. Stephanus may have been killed in revenge, or, of course, in order to silence him. He had clearly been an incompetent assassin. The altar boy survived, and is quoted as a source for these events by Suetonius.

The man who directed the emperor to the fatal meeting with Stephanus, the *cubicularius* Parthenius, was also the superior of Maximus and Sigerius in the hierarchy of the household servants. In Dio's account of the killing, Parthenius is said to have rushed into the room himself. He had thus kept himself at some distance from the deed so far, so it seems unlikely that he personally wielded a weapon, though he certainly confirmed the fact of the death of the emperor later. His arrival in the event of the emperor's survival, therefore, could have been in the guise of a rescuer – and he is surely to be suspected of ensuring the death of Stephanus, if that killing was not simply the servants' revenge. Parthenius was certainly deeply involved in the events, however, so deeply as to be identified by later sources as one of the emperor's murderers, even if he did not get blood on his hands.

The man who had been chosen to be the next emperor, Marcus Cocceius Nerva, was already in the palace. He heard a rumour that Domitian had survived the attack, and almost collapsed: Parthenius, who had verified the death, reassured him. Rumours in the palace were clearly flying with great speed. Word also spread outside, but in a more organised way. First of all, it went to the other conspirators, then to selected other men, but it does not seem to have spread much further beyond these until next morning, when a special meeting of the Senate was convened and informed.[2]

The senators greeted the news with a mixture of relief, annoyance, pleasure and fear, though pleasure was the dominant feeling recorded by Suetonius. The other reactions must be assumed, although, since some senators were committed Flavians, they seem reasonable; both indifference and annoyance were noted among the people of the city and in the army, and these feelings were surely shared by some at least of the senators. The one feeling which seems to have been absent was regret. Domitian had not been loved in the upper ranks of society in the city.

Elsewhere, however, closer to home, some did mourn. His body was retrieved from the public undertaker to whom it had been consigned – perhaps by Parthenius – by his former nurse, a freedwoman called Phyllis. (The story that the body was to be buried as a gladiator's is a reflection of Domitian's later equation with another assassinated emperor, the gladiator-mad Commodus.) Phyllis had the body cremated in the garden of her home on the Via Latina, and then she brought the ashes to the Temple of the Flavian Gens, where the ashes of his father and his brother were already interred. This was a temple built by Domitian himself, and completed only two years before (and which had been hit by lightning very recently – one of the disregarded, misunderstood, or later recollected omens). It had been built, suitably enough, on the site of the house owned by Vespasian before he was emperor, and where Domitian and his brother Titus had been born. Phyllis, lacking a prepared tomb for Domitian, or the resources to create one, put the ashes in that of his niece, Flavia Julia, whose nurse she had also been, and whom Domitian was reputed to have loved.

2

CONSPIRACY

In the two surviving descriptions of Domitian's assassination, by Suetonius and Dio Cassius, a total of seven men are named as being directly involved in the work. Parthenius the *cubicularius* is depicted as the prime mover and organiser; Stephanus was the agent of the killing, or at least was so designated; Maximus, Clodianus, the anonymous gladiator, Satur or Sigerius, and the *a libellis* Entellus were all involved as secondary agents either beforehand or assisting Stephanus. All these men were connected in some way with the palace – even the gladiator is said to be an 'imperial' gladiator; Clodianus is described as a *cornicularius*, and was no doubt one of the Praetorian Guards assigned to palace duty – he was also, like Stephanus, under suspicion of dishonesty, if not worse.[1] To the contemporary historians (Dio clearly used sources contemporary with the events)[2] the murder was seen as an inside job, a servants' plot confined to the palace; some of the killers were criminals.

Yet there are substantial discrepancies between the two accounts, and even more important contradictions within them. Of the men involved, four – Parthenius, Stephanus, Satur/Sigerius and Maximus – are named by both historians, but Entellus is only in Dio, and Clodianus and the gladiator only in Suetonius. It is through such discrepancies that the real conspiracy becomes visible. For these historians are reflecting, or transmitting, a particular version of the event, the story put about after the murder by those whose involvement rendered them targets for recrimination or revenge, in particular by the senators who, with some reason, later feared for their lives; this may be referred to as the 'official' version of events. For it turned out that in many areas of the empire, geographical or societal, Domitian was not nearly as unpopular as he had been among many of the senators and some of the staff at the palace.

It was thus convenient for the senators to unload the full responsibility on to the palace servants, who were inherently unable to shuffle it off on to anyone else – all the more so as some of them really had been involved, and some were suspected criminals. Yet the new story was inefficiently put together; perhaps because it was done in haste, perhaps because it was mainly designed to confuse. The murder was soon overtaken by events of more pressing moment, and the gaping seams in the stitched-up story were left unclosed. This sequence can be explained by the history of the next two years. The threat of vengeance came in the summer of 97, and was stifled finally by the death of Nerva and the accession of Trajan as sole emperor in January 98, after which it was no longer necessary to bother, and by then it had also become counter-productive to hunt for senatorial culprits or scapegoats. After all, the main beneficiaries were Nerva, now dead, and Trajan, the new emperor who was in full control of the army. So the cover story blaming Parthenius and the servants can be dated to the killing of Parthenius by the Praetorians in mid-97; after January 98 the story was no longer needed, and it was not necessary to plug the gaps. Even at the time many clearly disbelieved the story, notably the soldiers of the Guard, and perhaps Trajan himself,[3] and took measures to punish the guilty, and not all those who were punished were men of the palace. Through these gaps it is possible to discern the reality.

In the first place the conspiracy had taken some time to come to fruition. Stephanus had worn the bandage on his arm concealing the dagger for a week, but he only did this after he had volunteered his services to another group, defined by Suetonius as 'the conspirators', who were already discussing ways of carrying out the murder and debating the best location for the deed: while Domitian was at his bath, perhaps, or at dinner. So this first conspiratorial group had been actively working towards the assassination for longer than the week during which Stephanus carried his dagger. Since Stephanus was a denizen of the palace, Suetonius' term 'conspirators' is presumably intended to refer to Parthenius and his people, who were also palace men – a sign of the 'official' version.

There were also others involved, however. The presence of Nerva in the palace at the time, and clearly expecting the murder – for he nearly collapsed on hearing the rumour that it had failed – is the sign of that. Dio has an explanation: it is said that Domitian had harboured suspicions about a group of men and written their names on a tablet, intending to have them killed. The tablet had been stolen from under his pillow by one of the boys, who had handed it to Domitia Longina, the emperor's wife, who had in turn warned the potential victims of their danger. These men had then formed their own plot, and had recruited Nerva as their front man.

This story is a nonsense, quite beyond belief. The holes and implausibilities in it are glaring. How did anyone know it was a list of men to be killed? Was it headed 'Those I intend to have executed'? Domitian would scarcely write *that* down, indeed he would scarcely need to make a list in the first place. How did he not miss the tablet from under his pillow? Did he have so many things under it that he did not notice one was missing? And one naming a set of plotters, at that. It had to have been missing for some days before the plot was formed, and for some weeks before it was successful, and yet Domitian never noticed it had gone. He always reacted quickly and decisively to such threats – as Stephanus' distracting message clearly recognised. Why should the boy who is supposed to have taken it do so in the first place? And why would he let Domitia find it? And so on.[4]

The story is evidently derived from the items in the original account referring to the dagger Domitian kept under his pillow, and to the presence of the boy in the bedroom. It seems to have been an invention designed to provide a pretext for the involvement of the men behind Nerva in the assassination, on the argument that it was kill-or-be-killed; it also helped to spread the blame to Domitia Longina. Nerva himself is also said to have been marked for execution, a fate he only avoided by Domitian's understanding – from an astrologer's prediction – that Nerva was scheduled to die soon anyway, from natural causes. This in turn is clearly an invention, to be dated after Nerva's own death.

And yet, despite its unbelievability, the fact of the existence of this story is in reality a pointer to this second conspiratorial group. If it was only a few palace servants who had been suspected of plotting, it would not have been thought necessary to invent such a story concerning a group of senators, a story which indirectly emphasised that other people besides the servants were involved – for these others can only have been senators. If Domitian had suspected palace servants of plotting to kill him there would have been no delay for consideration by the emperor in dealing with the matter swiftly and fairly privately. Few would have mourned the execution, however sudden and private, of a group of freedmen and slaves in the palace. Nor would it have been thought reasonable that Domitia Longina should intervene – these were only slaves and freedmen, after all. This section of the story is a clear sign that this second group was composed of senators, men who could talk directly and persuasively to Nerva, one of the most eminent of senators. And, since Nerva was the candidate in waiting, actually in the palace on the night of the murder, he was one of the conspirators.

Dio, whose account was written at a safe distance in time from these events – well over a century later, unlike Suetonius, who was a late contemporary – provides the next step on the way to unravelling the plot: Nerva was not the first man to be offered the chance of replacing and succeeding Domitian. 'Various men' had been approached before him. Dio explains that they had all refused, because, he says, they thought it was a device by Domitian to test their loyalty. This may be so, but none of them went so far as to report the approaches to Domitian himself, or so it seems, and if that was what they thought, by not reporting they were falling into Domitian's trap.

Nerva, however, accepted the offer. Neither the men who persuaded him nor those who preceded him in refusing are named by either Suetonius or Dio, but by implication there were a considerable number involved. More than one man had refused to be their candidate, indeed Dio's words imply that several men had been approached. And several more – presumably men who did not consider themselves likely to be accepted as emperor – had been doing the canvassing. One would think that ten or a dozen men was the absolute minimum number for those involved, and perhaps even double that. It is perhaps possible, by widening the search and considering the distribution of power at Rome, and by contemplating the office-holders of the time, to work out who these men were.[5] They clearly form two separate groups: the plotters and the candidates, though since the refusers did not inform on the plotters, they became accomplices before the fact. I will consider the plotters first, and those with the potential to be emperor later. This will need a considerable diversion.

All of the plotters must be men of power, which is to say, senators, magistrates, army chiefs. It is therefore necessary to investigate the disposition of the most prominent men of power in the empire in September of 96. The Senate, the army, the Praetorian Guard, the officials in Rome: these are the elements which determined the distribution of power, together with the people actually in the palace. The emperors had always to bear in mind the most prominent members of such groups: the senatorial leaders, the military commanders, the main palace officials. For within such groups there were particular individuals who were the leaders of opinion, at least for the moment: these included the consuls in office, the ex-consuls, the generals, the commanders of the armed forces in the city, as well as the heads of the various bureaucratic departments. In so far as it is possible, therefore, the participation or disposition of these prominent men of power must be determined.

On 1 September 96, seventeen days before the assassination, two new suffect consuls took office. One, M. Calpurnius [---]icus, is quite unknown, even to the extent of our ignorance of his full cognomen.[6] His political connections and disposition are unknown, and, since he apparently took no part in these events, they are not important here. The other consul, on the other hand, was a most notable man, with very interesting political and familial connections. Ti. Catius Caesius Fronto was the son or adopted son of the poet Silius Italicus.[7] Fronto's earlier political career is not known, though he will have filled the various offices in succession in the normal way over the previous two decades. In the ten years following his consulship, however, he took a prominent part in the work of the Senate, speaking, so far as Pliny's letters reveal, on behalf of several magistrates who were accused of extortion by the provincials whom they had misgoverned.[8] Juvenal also comments on his powerful speaking voice.[9] It is thought that one of Fronto's earlier posts might well have been as legate to the proconsular governor of Bithynia-Pontus, for he defended two of the former governors who were accused of extortion by the provincials there,[10] though this is not a particularly convincing argument.

The contrast between Fronto's invisibility before 96 and his prominence afterwards is most marked, particularly since his family was also prominent. Fronto's full name was Ti. Catius Caesius Fronto, various parts of which were used in different contexts; Silius Italicus' own full name was Ti. Catius Asconius Silius Italicus. The exact relationship was probably adopted son, or perhaps nephew, both suggested in different places by Syme, and hesitantly endorsed by Salomies,[11] though certainty is not possible. The relationship, whatever it was, did give Fronto some of the prestige of Italicus, and it may be assumed that Fronto shared the old man's political prejudices. The relationship also meant that Fronto was the brother of L. Silius Decianus, Italicus' own son, presumably, who had been consul just two years before. He is thought to have governed Crete-and-Cyrenaica after his term as praetor, and he became *curator aquarum* early in Trajan's reign.[12] Both Decianus and Italicus are to be identified as prominent followers of the Stoic philosophical persuasion, and followers of the Republican hero Cato Minor and the Neronian martyr Thrasea Paetus. We may thus assume that Fronto also held these opinions.

Fronto, in other words, was a prominent senator, from a prominent political family, a man who became especially visible in the years after 96, a lawyer particularly concerned, so far as we can see, to promote the rights of senators and their powers. The consistency with which he defended the extortion cases in Trajan's reign cannot be accidental. His sentiments and those of his family were surely well known before his consulship, and they included the wish to revive the strong influence of the Senate in government, even, in some men of similar opinions, to remove the imperial system altogether and revert to the Republican system, which they thought was rule by the Senate and the annual magistrates. This was, after all, the typical sentiment of the great majority of senators, reflecting the loss of power which they felt they had suffered at the emperor's hands. In extreme cases, this belief led to the group sometimes being denominated the 'Stoic opposition' and their senatorial supporters.[13] This loss of power was not something which they could blame wholly on Domitian, but, since he was the current emperor, and one who was particularly autocratic in his administration, he was the object of their almost instinctive hostility. In this sentiment Fronto apparently shared – and yet Domitian had agreed to his appointment as consul.[14]

The mutual opposition of emperor and some senators can be seen to exist, certainly, but it can also be over-emphasised, for on the whole the Senate worked well with the emperor. These two interpretations are not, of course, mutually exclusive: much of the work they did was routine administration, which would not provoke any disagreement. Both could see that the administration of the empire had to go ahead with as little interruption as possible, for, to put it at its lowest, all would thereby benefit. Senators who were selected as legionary commanders or provincial governors, and those whose progress up the magistrates' ladder had taken place at what they would regard as a normal speed, were in any case not likely to complain. Domitian retaliated decisively against his enemies, senatorial or not, once they were identified, and was alert to conspiracies, and so these enemies are likely to have remained fairly quiet, unless provoked or especially fearful. But senators were politicians, living in a society of oral communication. They talked incessantly, and without too much discretion. Individual sentiments and preferences would clearly be well known; animosities also.

So Domitian's selection of Fronto as suffect consul for the last four months of 96 (and his brother Decianus two years earlier) is of a piece with his general policy, which would seem to have been to appease as many senatorial interest groups and factions as possible. The consuls who had previously held office during 96 are a good illustration of the variety. The *consulares ordinarii* of 96, taking office on 1 January, and so holding the most prestigious type of consulship, were C. Manlius Valens and C. Antistius Vetus. They were a strange pair, both as a pair and as individuals. Valens was in his ninetieth year, and died either while holding office or soon after;[15] he had been in and out of offices for half a century, praetor probably in Claudius' reign, legionary commander before 52, and again in 69, but not apparently in office since. His selection has been seen as a gesture of contempt by Domitian for the Senate, though there is no ancient evidence for this.[16] His origin and family are quite unknown. His colleague, Antistius Vetus, by contrast, was a descendant of a family closely associated with power for two centuries, always by the side of a Caesarian, and the members of which had held a total of seven consulships in that time, many of them as ordinary consuls.[17] Antistius Vetus may have been from a noble family, but his own record shows no achievements at all, except his consulship.

The successors of these two men as suffect consuls, holding office from May to August 96, were another contrasting pair: Q. Fabius Postuminus and T. Prifernius, whose cognomen was probably Paetus.[18] Fabius was a successful military man, having commanded *legio* XV *Apollinaris* for, presumably, the usual three-year term. The legion had been stationed at Carnuntum since the end of the civil war in 70, and was currently involved in another war which had been organised by Domitian; Fabius' period of command is not known, but the station was always a crucial one, directly facing a group of barbarian states across the Danube with whom the empire had been at war more than once in Domitian's reign, and who, in fact, commenced a new war during Fabius' consulship. Fabius' family is unknown: he might be a *novus homo*, he might be of Italian extraction; he is unlikely to be a scion of the great Fabian family of the Republic. Essentially it seems he was promoted for his ability, and he went on to govern Moesia and Asia, and to hold the office of *praefectus urbi* in Rome under Trajan, a notable and able man, who had earned his consulship by loyalty and ability.

Fabius' colleague T. Prifernius Paetus was from Reate in the Sabine country, which was also the town of origin of the Flavian family. He was part of a complex of inheritances and adoptions in the Sabine area and beyond which developed into a consular family active for the next half century.[19] Prifernius himself had no known achievements other than his origin, his wealth and his consulship; he is not known to have gone on to any other achievements after his consulship. Perhaps these were also the only distinctions of Fronto's colleague in the third pair of consuls for the year, M. Calpurnius, whose full cognomen is unknown. Wealth was, by Domitian's time, the only basic requirement for a senatorial career, though intelligence and ability helped if one wanted serious employment. Origin was progressively less important, as provincials became more numerous in the membership. Individual achievement, particularly in army command, but also, as with Fronto and many others, in legal matters, could help, as could consular ancestors, which may have been the real qualification of Antistius Vetus. The membership of a provincial aristocratic network was another useful mark of favour. Two or three of these elements combined in one man could virtually guarantee him a consulship.

The construction of a consular list was one of the emperor's major tasks, though technically the consuls were still elected. Clearly emperors had to be careful, and total incompetence and blatant enemies could be blocked. But many senators saw a term as consul to be a right, and so devising the annual list was as delicate a political art as the construction of a modern Cabinet, with as many interests and factions to be included (or appeased) as possible, and the purpose was the same: to reward loyalty, to use ability, to deflect animosity, and to bring the possibly disaffected and any other critical groups within the constraints of the process of decision-making. If a politician takes part in a decision, he or she becomes in part responsible for it, and cannot – or should not, at least – publicly criticise it. The fact that the Roman Empire was an autocracy did not prevent these same constraints from operating, any more than they did in the old Soviet Union, or as they do in modern Europe and the United States.

Fronto fitted into the consular list for 96 as an Italian, as the son of a famous ex-consul and poet, as the brother of a consular, perhaps as the representative of a Transpadane aristocratic network, and as a noted senator, orator and lawyer, a formidable list of qualifications. His antipathy towards Domitian was clearly no bar to promotion in the face of these qualifications. Its origin was partly the dislike of some of

the senators for the institution of the emperor and was fully known; his elder brother
L. Silius Decianus had been praised for following 'the opinions of the great Thrasea
and Cato of consummate virtue' in a poem published in Martial's very first book,[20]
and when Decianus became consul himself, Martial looked forward to a third of the
family reaching that rank – Fronto was clearly expected to reach the consulship soon,
as he did.[21] So for Domitian to give Fronto his due in the scramble for office was a sensible political move, which would, so it would be hoped, reduce his antipathetic lean-
ings; any delay in his promotion would curdle his feelings even further and make him
an even more dangerous enemy. Even-handed treatment of such men was intelligently pacificatory, one might even say it was a sensible policy of appeasement, a
policy which is often sensible.[22]

It is necessary to take into account these details of Fronto's adopted parentage, his
connections and his experience in estimating the position he took in the crisis of September 96. Even if we do not know the earlier stages of his *cursus* – and nothing of his
career before his consulship is known, though a progression through the normal
career may be presumed – other facts do emerge, in particular with regard to his
father's life. Ti. Catius Asconius Silius Italicus[23] was independently wealthy and
became a famous poet, and by 96 he had long ago retired to live in Campania. He had
been born in Tiberius' reign, and had reached the consulship in that ominous year,
68. He was in fact ordinary consul that year, which makes him the choice of Nero, and
he was subsequently closely connected with another unfortunate emperor, Vitellius,
being one of the two men present as witnesses to his decisive conversation with
Vespasian's brother Sabinus, a conversation which persuaded Vitellius that all was up
with his imperial ambitions. Silius Italicus went on to govern Asia for a year during
Vespasian's reign, but then retreated to Campania, where he bought a villa formerly
belonging to Cicero and paid for the restoration of the tomb of the poet Virgil, an
interesting combination of devotions. There is nothing in his life to indicate any affec-
tion for the Flavian dynasty: the very opposite, in fact, as his outspoken admiration for
Cicero and his connections with Nero and Vitellius showed. Yet admiration for
republicans and association with two of the most hedonistic emperors is a strange
combination.

When his adoptive father was serving as consul, Fronto was in his early teens or
younger, if he reached the consulship in 96. He was thus a slightly younger contemporary of Domitian, and about the same age as Trajan, essentially a man of their generation. His experience in Rome in the civil war was presumably as deeply unpleasant as
that of Domitian had been; both of them will have suffered from the insecurity which
being the son of a prominent political figure produced at that time. Silius Italicus'
apparent support for Vitellius was perhaps not enough to render him a danger to
Vespasian, who was also a man who owed his consulate and his military command to
Nero, and who clearly gauged well the temper of the post-civil war times; he could
afford to be tolerant, and the allocation of provinces in regular order to consulars was
one of the measures which were an indication of the restoration of normality. But note
that Italicus never governed an imperial province, only Asia, a senatorial one – at least
as far as we know. Domitian was less tolerant than his father, and by 96 he faced a

more serious internal threat, but he did make Italicus' two sons consuls in 94 and 96; the fact that the decision to appoint them was the emperor's was perhaps not wholly a source of pleasure to the family.

Fronto and his father had another connection liable to lead him astray – at least from Domitian's point of view. Silius Italicus was from Patavium, probably adopted into the Silius family, his original name having been Ti. Catius Asconius.[24] The city of Patavium, in the territory of the Veneti, had been remarkably fecund in intellectual matters during the previous century and more. It was the home of Livy the historian, which is glory enough, but at least two poets of the imperial period came from there, Silius Italicus being the greater of them.[25] More to the point here, it was also the home city of P. Clodius Thrasea Paetus, an opponent of Nero to the death, executed in 66[26] – which gives extra point to Martial's comment that Decianus followed Paetus' opinions. Patavium was notable, so Strabo had remarked a century before, for its large population of *equites*,[27] implying a considerable spread of wealth in the community, and it is from the ranks of these men that some moved into the higher ranks of Roman society and took their political place in the city; in the Flavian period at least three other men who reached the consulship came from the city, and there are three others from the city who had not yet reached as high as the consul but who held lower offices, and one of them became consul later.[28] Further, the various Patavine families maintained friendly contact with each other when in Rome. One of Silius Italicus' names indicates an ancestor among the locally important Asconius family, who were not otherwise senatorial, and the heavy emphasis he places on the Patavine hero Pedianus in his long poem about the Hannibalic war is a link with his old contemporary, the other Patavine poet Q. Asconius Pedianus.[29]

These are all elements which must be taken into account in the estimate to be made of Fronto and his political attitudes and actions. His father's reputation among Pliny's circle was that of a *delator*, an informer, in Nero's time, and his later absence from the Senate was condoned, at least by Trajan;[30] in all probability, Domitian was pleased enough to have him stay in Campania, where his poetic fame protected him, but where his political voice, such as it was, was muffled. He had acquiesced to the rule of three such varied emperors as Nero, Vitellius and Vespasian – but he had also stayed at Rome under Galba and Otho. This may have dimmed his political lustre, particularly among the stricter Republicans. Italicus and Fronto were both lawyers, both rich, and both were Patavine patriots; presumably Decianus was of the same inclination. Fronto had advanced through the usual magistrates' ranks under Domitian, but his political and cultural background put him as much on the senatorial side of the political divide in Domitian's reign as his father had been in Vespasian's. At the same time his later behaviour after Domitian's death shows that he, like his father, did not abhor the imperial system as such. It seems, therefore, that the family were not so much pro-republican as anti-Flavian, and that their dislike was largely reserved for Domitian personally. Being beholden to the emperor for advancement to their just deserts – the consulship – cannot have improved their regard for him.

This then was the man who became consul on 1 September 96, a man being appeased for his enmity by a political advancement which he will have come to regard as his right; any gratitude to the emperor will thus have been absent. It is customary to regard the consul's office as increasingly ceremonial, even honorary, in nature, but it still had some residual powers. In the context of the events of September 96, it is particularly relevant to note that the consuls were responsible for summoning the senators to meetings of the Senate, and there they acted, among their other duties, as presidents of these meetings;[31] it is this function which made Fronto of particular importance in the crisis.

This function was in fact exercised immediately after the death of the emperor. The Senate was called into session next morning,[32] to accept the new emperor and to confer on him the requisite powers. The timing is very tight: Domitian died about noon of the previous day, and the resulting confusion in the palace would obviously delay the next moves. But in order to get the summons out to the senators, spread as they were through the city, and perhaps in the nearby countryside, a task which would clearly take some time, Fronto will have had to be contacted at once. If he had not been originally involved in the plot, it would take some time to convince him of the murder, and he would demand proof – a sight of the body, no doubt – which would delay matters even more. The cumulative delays would certainly add up to several hours, yet the Senate met next morning. I conclude that Fronto was a part of the original conspiracy, and so was able to send out the summonses in time.

Of course, it took more than a hereditary antipathy towards the Flavian dynasty, a reputed connection with Republican martyrs and a sympathy for the weakened position of the Senate, to make a consul act against the emperor. The fate of men who did so without success was clear: Antonius Saturninus was dead because he raised a military rebellion; the man who was the false-Nero who invaded Asia Minor was presumably dead for having set himself up as a competitor; Sallustius Lucullus was dead for presuming to name a new weapon after himself (rather than, one assumes, the emperor); even C. Vettulenus Civica Cerealis was dead, though all he seems to have done was exhibit a certain hesitancy in a dynastic crisis.[33] Domitian had been more strict, and was less amused by the antics of the opposition, than, say, his father had been. He had instead demanded subjection, combined with obedience, and even enthusiastic loyalty. He had not executed a consul while he was actually in office, but his own cousin T. Flavius Clemens had been executed immediately he ended his consulship – his *ordinary* consulship – only a year before.[34] The reputation that Domitian had among later historians, of striking fear into the hearts of the senators, was firmly grounded in deeds such as these, or, as the senators would see it, his misdeeds.

The current consul, Fronto, would thus seem to be identifiable as one member of the conspiracy; Nerva himself was clearly another, though only recruited after the plot had been under way for some time. It is not possible to pin down any other senator who was involved with any certainty, but a further conjecture may be made; this involves another considerable diversion.[35]

The consular lists for the next few years are strange. The 'normal' list contained six names, as in 96, or perhaps seven if the emperor held office for a short time. But from 97 to 100 this pattern was highly disturbed. There are unusual iterations, including three men receiving third consulships, and for many others, seconds, and there are unusually large numbers of suffect consuls. The last time such iterations occurred was in the period just after the civil war of 68–70, when several men were rewarded for their support of Vespasian in the fighting. The same would seem to be happening in the years from 97.[36] Some of these men are likely to have been pre-assassination imperial candidates in themselves, and they will be looked at later in the chapter, but others were not so eminent. That is to say, these lists may well include men who were involved (with Fronto and Nerva) in the original conspiracy, and whose reward was a, or another, consulship.

The list for 97 had probably been drawn up in part before Domitian's death. It seems that the lists were produced, on the few examples which can be dated, in September or October of the previous year.[37] Domitian was generally efficient in such matters, as in other areas of administration, and advance warning for the candidates was clearly necessary.[38]

The 97 list is, however, unusual in that it contained twelve names, double the usual number.[39] It seems likely therefore that the original list was expanded in the wake of Nerva's accession. It is most unlikely, for example, that Domitian would have awarded third consulships to the two men who headed the list, Nerva himself and L. Verginius Rufus, so it is a reasonable assumption that they were added as *ordinarii* after the September coup. Of the rest, six of the men would fit nicely as Domitian's original list, though a second consulship for Arrius Antoninus looks like Nerva's doing. If these three were added to Domitian's six, it would be sensible to expand the total to twelve, giving six pairs of consuls holding office for two months each. No one would thus be disappointed, and some extra men would receive promotion: a good political move.

The list of 98 was thus the first which Nerva constructed himself. It is headed, again, by the emperor, holding his fourth consulship but the appearance of Trajan as *ordinarius* for the second time must have been a late adjustment, since his adoption by Nerva was not announced until October. By that time the list would most likely have been prepared and published; this is all the more likely since it is clearly a very strange list. The rest of the men will be those being rewarded by Nerva. It would be impolitic and even dangerous to alter the list after publication; an insecure regime like that of Nerva needed to gather support, not alienate men gratuitously, which alteration would have done, as well as seeming indecisive.

The list contains the names of five men who were successive monthly suffects for Nerva, while Trajan held office as *ordinarius* for six months beside them. Then there follow three pairs of new consuls in office for two months each.[40] The list thus falls into two halves. The second part is the normal type, composed of the usual group of worthy men, all reaching the consulate for the first time, and these will be considered later. The first half, however, bears the marks of adjustment. Nerva and Trajan took office on 1 January as *ordinarii*, but Nerva resigned on the 13th, hence the suffects. This cannot have been the original plan, which will have been for three pairs to hold office for two months each. The addition of Trajan as *ordinarius* after his adoption, and after the original list had been drawn up, produced the anomaly of two *ordinarii* plus five suffects – seven consuls in six months. Originally the five imperial suffects included one who was intended to be Nerva's colleague as *ordinarius*. The obvious nominee is Sex. Julius Frontinus, who was to be *ordinarius* with Trajan only two years later. For a man who was not a member of the imperial family to hold two consulships within three years was virtually unprecedented, and betokens some major obligation on the part of the emperor; being compliant enough to surrender an ordinary consulship to the emperor might create such an obligation.

In 98 Frontinus was in office by 20 February, and so probably for the whole of that month.[41] His predecessor, filling the gap between Nerva's resignation and Frontinus' assumption of the office, was Cn. Domitius Tullus,[42] and Frontinus was followed by three other men; these five, with Nerva, I suggest, were the original list, each intended to hold the office for two months until the end of June, when the other six took over. The irruption of Trajan into affairs in October dislodged Frontinus as *ordinarius*, and forced a rapid readjustment with the return of Frontinus as a suffect.

These imperial suffects were thus a group of men who were especially close supporters of Nerva as emperor, and then of his settlement with Trajan, and so of Trajan himself. I would suggest that they may well have been, or have included, the men who had been involved in some way in the conspiracy, and whom Nerva was rewarding. Frontinus had prospered under Vespasian as praetor and consul (in about 73) and governed Britannia in 73–76, where he completed the conquest of the Silures of South Wales, a war which had lasted for thirty years. Under Domitian he had assisted the emperor in the German war of 82–83 and served as governor of Asia; in 97 he was *curator aquarum*, appointed to that office by Nerva; he was also, of course, the author of a book of stratagems for Domitian's military education, and a manual on the Roman aqueducts.[43] Cn. Domitius Tullus' career began under Nero as quaestor; he was adlected to the patriciate by Vespasian and served as consul in 74, and governed Africa in about 85.[44] His career almost exactly paralleled that of Frontinus, and both men came from Narbonensis.

The third suffect was very different. L. Julius Ursus may also be from Narbonensis, or possibly Spain. He was originally an *eques* who had a brilliant administrative career as *praefectus annonae*, Prefect of Egypt, and finally Prefect of the Praetorian Guard; he was then installed as suffect consul in 84 without going through any of the normal senatorial offices. It was a career of quite astonishing brilliance, only in part aided by a distant relationship by marriage to the Flavian family, for his career began before Vespasian's imperial elevation.[45] His adopted son (adopted early in Trajan's reign), L. Julius Ursus Servianus, was consul himself in 90; he married the daughter of P. Aelius Hadrianus Afer, and was thus related to Trajan; the future Emperor Hadrian was Servianus' brother-in-law.[46] The fourth of these suffects, T. Vestricius Spurinna, was from northern Italy, and had been consul in about 72; under Domitian he had governed Germania Inferior, and for exploits during that governorship he appears, at Nerva's instigation, to have been awarded triumphal honours by the Senate in 97.[47]

These four men had a long list of achievements in common: they were all consuls ten or twenty years before, high in favour with Domitian or even related to him, governors of high-status provinces, demonstrating either military distinction or administrative competence, or both. (In all these respects, they far outshone both Nerva and

Trajan.) They were all of a similar age, and three of them seem to have come from Narbonensis. And now they all formed a group who were suffects of one emperor and shared the *fasces* with his successor. They were also a set of men with clear affinities with Nerva himself, and provided the new emperor, who had 'never seen a province or an army' [48] with the vicarious experience he surely needed – and as such they were a strong contrast to the men on the previous year's list.

The fifth man of this group, C. Pomponius Pius, is quite different. Nothing is known of him personally, except for the fact of his consulship in 98, [49] and that he was the son of a consul of the same name. And yet he was in the illustrious company of four double-consulars and shared the *fasces* with the emperor; he is further distinguished by being suffect with Trajan for two months (May and June) where the others, double-consulars all, held office for one month only. Pomponius must have earned his place in this group in some way – if he was not simply one of the original list. On the surface he is on the list by right of inheritance and it may be significant that his father had been consul in 65, the year of the conspiracy of Piso, when Nerva was active as an informer. The father and the son are unremarkable, except for the timing of their consulships.

It may be that Pomponius in 97 had earned his reward by his participation in the plot to remove Domitian, and that the other imperial suffects of that year had done the same. These men are a suitable group to have been part of the plot which removed the increasingly threatening Domitian by Nerva, another man whose achievements almost exactly mirrored theirs, and whom they must have felt they could control. It might be objected that the distinguished group were so closely associated with Domitian, and the Flavians generally, that action against him was signal betrayal. But of this group, omitting Pius and Nerva for the moment, none owed their initial advancement to Domitian, and none had been particularly favoured in the last decade of his reign. Ursus had been consul in 84, Frontinus and Tullus had governed Asia and Africa respectively about 85, Spurinna's governorship of Germania Inferior was in the mid-80s. [50] Since then, Domitian's reign had, from the point of view of a senator, deteriorated. The disillusionment of these men may be assumed. Nerva was of this group in many ways, though he had retained Domitian's favour for longer, having a second (ordinary) consulship with the emperor in 90. His viewpoint was Roman, not provincial; courtier, not military man; and from there Domitian's reign looked to be successful and competent. But even Nerva will have come to realise in the early 90s that Domitian was losing support. His different perspective was no doubt one reason why he was only approached to participate in the plot fairly late, and is a good reason why he accepted, when other men of a wider experience refused.

The atmosphere in the Senate was clearly gloomy and resentful by 96. [51] The political climate was right for a coup, but that is not enough to make one happen. Even if it is not accepted that the men singled out above were among the plotters, it is clear from their participation in the new government, both under Nerva and under Trajan, that they welcomed it, and acted to support it. Within the Senate there were very few who were unhappy with the change – though that is not the case with the army. On the other hand, the number of plotters was fairly small, and there were plenty of senators who were perfectly content with the situation as it was under Domitian. More was needed to get the fearful and disaffected senatorial minority to act against the emperor. Support from elsewhere was required.[52]

The palace servants felt they were under threat, perhaps more so in individual cases than the senators. Stephanus' mistress Domitilla had been exiled, after her husband T. Flavius Clemens had been executed, and Stephanus himself had been accused of theft: all good reasons for him to hate and fear Domitian, and for him to be prepared to do something about it. Parthenius, however, was clearly the central figure, for he was a man of some authority with constant access to the emperor; the poet Martial had asked him to see that Domitian saw his poems.[53] The position was one obviously liable to corrupting influences, and was very unpopular amongst the senators, and even further afield.[54] Not long before his own death Domitian had ordered the execution of his secretary Epaphroditus, ostensibly on the grounds that he had helped Nero commit suicide, but surely, after all the time that had passed, for some more immediate cause.[55] In fact, a distinct problem has been discerned with the generality of the servants in the palace: another freedman, Abascantus, had been dismissed, and Domitian was in fact in the process of replacing his freedmen department heads by equestrian officers.[56] Parthenius had opportunities for personal enrichment which – whether or not he took those opportunities – rendered him vulnerable. He may well have feared accusation and/or exposure followed by demotion or dismissal, or, seeing Epaphroditus' fate, death. He was obviously not the only one, for he was able to persuade several others to join him in his plot, and the plot was well-enough known for Stephanus to offer his services for the deed.

There were therefore two distinct groups who were involved in compassing the death of Domitian. First, a group of imperial servants in the palace who feared for their jobs, their liberty or their lives. They were not numerous, and since Parthenius saw to the locking of the doors from the emperor's rooms to his servants' quarters, most of the other servants were loyal. But the plotters did have access to the emperor's person, and to his private quarters, and they had the nerve to carry out their plan. The second group were the senators, whose priorities overlapped with those of the servants; some feared for their lives, but others, such as Fronto, had ideological drives, feeling that the Senate's position in the state had been reduced too far. Others had a more practical concern, feeling that Domitian's character was unsuitable: that his autocratic tendencies not only threatened the lives of individual senators and the prestige of the Senate, but that they were a positive danger to the state itself. Only thus can a number of the most experienced senators have been enlisted on the side of the plotters. (Even if it is not accepted that these men – Fronto, Antoninus, Spurinna and so on – actually took part in the plot, several men of their rank knew of it, because they were the sort of men who were approached by the plotters to be the next emperor. The fact that none of them warned Domitian is a clear sign that they sympathised with the plotters' aims.) Beyond these two active and/or sympathetic groups were the majority of senators, whose general dislike of Domitian was evident in their welcome for the news of his death, and whose attitude assured the plotters that their action would be approved after the fact.[57]

At some point the senatorial and imperial servants' groups of plotters joined forces. This is where the involvement of Fronto, consul and known to be anti-Domitian, seems essential again. His assumption of the consulship on 1 September was known well in advance, for the consul list had been published in the previous year. The senator and the *cubicularius* would certainly meet before September, and more than once. Who broached the idea of assassination we cannot tell, but, according to Suetonius, the palace group was trying to formulate a plan when Stephanus joined it. Working back from 18 September, the date of the murder, we have a week in which Stephanus carried the dagger inside his bandage, and some days before that, at least, in which he and the other servants worked out the details. This takes us back to very near the time when Fronto took office. It would thus seem likely that Fronto (or whoever else was the senatorial plotters' front man) and Parthenius formed an alliance. At a guess Parthenius approached Fronto; the senator's political opinions were well known, but the problems of Parthenius' group of servants and freedmen were hardly likely to be known to Fronto.

So far as can be seen at this distance, these are the two groups who were the active conspirators, but other people and groups had also to be recruited, or at least neutralised in advance. One person whose participation in the killing has been questioned is Domitia Longina, Domitian's wife. In Dio's account, she is said to have found the tablet with the name of Domitian's next victims, and to have warned them, and Suetonius claims that she connived at the assassination.[58] The tablet story itself is, as argued above, quite unbelievable, but not so the possible involvement of Domitia. She would not be the first wife to wish her husband dead, and to help in his removal. She and her husband had been on the verge of divorce before, though that was many years in the past by 96.[59] She was still being referred to as Domitian's wife many years later, which might imply that she was willing to be thought proud of the relationship.[60] All of this is fairly superficial, and Domitia was never accused of more than advance knowledge of the plot, and even then only by rumour. Even advance knowledge seems unlikely. Domitia Longina as a participant can be ignored.

There were, however, other sources of power in Rome and its empire besides the palace and the Senate: the military, of various groups in and out of the city; notable provincials, fairly innocuous still though rising in importance through the connection of those senators who originated from outside Italy and who were steadily increasing in number; and the people of Rome, rowdy and exuberant but very dependent on the emperor's goodwill and a good administration. They had never indicated anything in the way of antipathy towards Domitian, but they were not notably enthusiastic towards him either. Of these the only group with any real power immediately to hand was the military, and that meant the commanders and officers of the units in and near the city.

In the city there were several high officials who had significant powers, both by reason of their command of armed men and by their personal and official prestige. The Prefect of the City (*praefectus urbi*) was responsible for order in the capital, commanding the Urban Cohorts, amounting to 4,000 men. He was of consular rank, one of the key officials standing as a link between city, Senate and emperor. For a man of his position it is remarkable that we do not know who held the office in 96.[61] It might have been T. Aurelius Fulvus, but the precise dates of his tenure are not known.[62] Hazardous though an argument like this is, it is surely significant that the prefect took no part in the events of 96, so far as can be seen – like Sherlock Holmes' dog that did not bark in the night. The Urban Cohorts had taken part in the coup of 41 after the murder of Caligula, and had been involved in events in 69 more than once, but not, it seems, in 96, even though the prefect's post had been enhanced in power under Domitian.[63] This would imply either that they were overmatched, or that their commander was able to accept events as they developed, or even that he was part of the plot.

The name of the Prefect of the Vigiles (*praefectus vigilum*) is also unknown. He had an armed force of seven cohorts, a total of about 3,500 men, but they were scattered in barracks throughout the city, were difficult to concentrate, and were more of a civil police force than a military unit. Similarly the Prefect of the Corn Supply (*praefectus annonae*) had some forces under his control and some jurisdiction, but again his men were scattered, from Rome along the Tiber as far as Ostia, though his headquarters were geographically close to the palace. None of these three officials are recorded as having acted at all in the crisis of 96.[64] The conclusion must be drawn that these prefects did not act because they had been taken by surprise by the events of 18–19 September, or that they had been squared beforehand, or that they approved of what was done.

In the immediate term, to seize power in Rome required either the co-operation of the emperor or his death; Domitian would scarcely co-operate in the loss of his power, so his death had to be accomplished. Domitian lived in his palace in the city or at one of his villas: in the Alban Hills, near Circeo, or near Orbetello.[65] Wherever he went, he was guarded by the soldiers of the Praetorian Guard, the other organised military force in Rome. This force was the most concentrated, and militarily the most effective, of all the armed groups in the city, consisting as it did of nine cohorts, 3,500 men in total, stationed in the Castra Praetoria on the Viminal Hill, frowning down on the city. Detachments attended the emperor wherever he went – the *cornicularius* Clodianus, who took part in the assassination, was one of these men. They could be used for other tasks as well, for ceremonial display, to guard other members of the royal family, as special troops in both peace and war, as special messengers, or to carry out special tasks, even to control rioting in the city if this overwhelmed the Urban Cohorts and the Vigiles.

The Praetorians were thus the most important of the armed forces in Rome for the conspirators. These troops were loyal to Domitian, but they could be persuaded otherwise if their commanders, the two Praetorian Prefects, were to be enlisted in the conspiracy. The troops knew full well their political value and power; they had been the instruments of the elevation of Claudius in 41 and of Otho in 69. Vespasian had controlled them by installing his own relatives as their prefects, though Domitian, running rather short of suitable relatives, had to use a different method. He chose men of proven loyalty, and appointed two prefects to hold office simultaneously, on the old Roman principle of dual magistracies, where one was supposed to act as a restraint on the other. The Praetorians could thus be decisive in any prolonged struggle for power in the city; only if they were absent or undecided were the Urban Cohorts or the forces of the Prefects of the Corn Supply or the Vigiles of any real account.

The crucial element in the reaction of the Guards was the attitude of the two prefects. This time we have some clearer information on the holders, though rather less than we would like, and significantly this is because they were involved directly in the events of September 96. The two men in office in 96 had risen to their posts by slightly different routes. T. Petronius Secundus had been Prefect of Egypt in 92 and 93,[66] which suggests a normal rise through the ranks in a typical equestrian career. Though we have no record of him as Prefect of the Corn Supply, he is likely to have held that post before Egypt. His Praetorian colleague, Norbanus,[67] on the other hand, had come to prominence in 89, when, as governor of Raetia, he had acted decisively against Saturninus' revolt in neighbouring Germania. He had been singled out for praise by Martial,[68] who hoped for his patronage, which in turn implies that Norbanus was a man worth cultivating. The poem is dated to 94, when Norbanus had returned to Rome after, it seems, five or six years in Raetia. His route to the Praetorian command was, therefore, an unusual one by this time, and was marked by a spectacular display of loyalty to Domitian in the Saturninus crisis.[69]

These two men owed their careers to Domitian's promotion, but their differing career-routes suggest that they would show differing reactions to the crisis. In the sources, only Petronius is said, by Dio and Eutropius, to have participated in the conspiracy;[70] Norbanus is mentioned by Dio as having some advance knowledge of the plot, but never accused of active participation. Even Petronius is not accused of directly wielding the sword; his role is less participatory than accepting. The anger of the Praetorian Guard later eventually forced Nerva to have Petronius killed, expressly because of his involvement in Domitian's death.[71] Norbanus vanishes completely from all sources, and the fact that no mention is made of him at the time of Petronius' killing implies either that he was already dead, or that he was not involved in the plot, or, of course, both of these. If Norbanus remained loyal to Domitian, as his conduct in 89 suggests would be his reaction, Petronius may have had to eliminate him. This would increase the anger of the troops. If he did nothing, he could have taken the opportunity to remove himself. But Dio explicitly says that they knew of the plot to assassinate Domitian in advance, though he reports it as 'it is said that'. These men certainly did nothing to prevent the killing, and that is clearly effective participation by omission. Their calculations were no doubt that if the assassination failed they could protect themselves by punishing the attemptors; if it succeeded they would welcome them. The absence of a reaction by the Guards to Domitian's death can thus be explained by the involvement, to whatever extent, of their commanders in the plot. The delay in the soldiers' quest for vengeance may be further explained by the later revelation of this advance knowledge on the part of their commander(s), and by the demagoguery of their later commander, Casperius Aelianus.

The later killing of Petronius is thus good evidence that he at least knew something in advance. In a wider context, it would be most remiss of any group of conspirators to fail to ascertain the Guard commanders' views, and indeed, to fail to attempt to recruit their support. This would certainly be a task both delicate and dangerous, yet it was essential. The conspirators did have something to offer. It was not necessary for the Guard commanders to participate personally, only that they do nothing. That is, they had to be neutralised. Yet one junior officer, the *cornicularius* Clodianus, is said to have joined in the second attack on the wounded emperor. As a soldier on duty in the palace, Clodianus must have been an officer of the Guard. It may be that he had been installed in the palace, and perhaps in the plot, by the Guard commanders (either or both) to report events to them. The accusation that he feared punishment for crimes he had committed may or may not be true. If he really was a criminal, it is very odd that he was on duty in the palace. The primary plotters would no doubt welcome such evidence of Guard involvement, and Clodianus is certainly reported to have helped finish Domitian off. He at least participated, even if his commanders did not.[72]

If neither the consuls nor the Praetorian Prefects took a direct and personally active part in the killing of the emperor and yet were clearly prepared in advance for the deed, this demonstrates the nature of the conspiracy. For the role of these men was to capitalise on the deed once it had been accomplished, and, most important of all, to have ready a willing replacement for Domitian. This had to be a man who was acceptable to the senators who were in Rome on the day and to the Praetorians in the Castra Praetoria, and who could be presented to the city, the military and the provinces as an acceptable ruler. Here, of course, was the problem, and the conspirators canvassed several men before persuading M. Cocceius Nerva that it was his duty and his destiny.[73]

Who the alternative, earlier and thus the preferred choices were is unknown, but it is perhaps permissible to point out some possibilities. Domitian's designated heirs, his child cousins, Vespasianus and Domitianus, boys in their early teens, were apparently not taken seriously, and the fate of them and that of their brothers and sisters is not known.[74] A senator of mature years and experience, and one who was actually in Rome in that September, was clearly essential. Nerva's qualifications, as defined rather minimally by Dio, were his nobility of birth, his amiable nature and the fact that he was under threat of death.[75] His more formal qualifications, which will have impressed the senators rather more, were his long experience of government and administration at Rome – since Nero's reign if not before – having held two ordinary consulships, and being a member of the emperor's *consilium*.[76]

The candidates who were in the minds of the plotters were therefore men with that sort of experience, and there were enough men with two consulships under their belts to provide a fair field of possibilities, but their experiences were somewhat different and this may be the explanation for Nerva being well down the list; it may also be a reason for their refusal.

It is possible to list several men who were Nerva's consular equals, though these are not discussed in any particular order. A. Bucius Lappius Maximus was the victor over the rebellious Saturninus in 89; he had been consul twice, in 86 and 95, had governed Pontus-Bithynia, Germania Inferior (*c.*87–89) and Syria (90–94), and was Italian born.[77] T. Aurelius Fulvus had been consul for the second time in 85, and previously governor of Hispania Citerior under Vespasian; he may have been Prefect of the City in 96; he had a son who had been an ordinary consul in 89;[78] he was from Narbonensis, which may well have counted against him a little in Rome. Other possibilities are two of the men who became consuls next year along with Nerva. One was

L. Verginius Rufus, consul in 63 and 69 and former governor of Germania Superior; he was a man who had been the first choice of the Rhine legions to succeed Nero as emperor in 68, but had then refused; he was now very old, but Nerva was old as well, and he accepted the post; if Verginius was asked again in 96, he set a record by refusing the purple twice.[79] The second man was Cn. Arrius Antoninus, who had also been consul in 69 and governor of Asia since; he had fewer qualifications than the others, and he may have come from Narbonensis, like Aurelius Fulvus; what puts him on the list is his reported commiseration with Nerva on the latter's accession, which suggests that Antoninus had seriously considered what it would be like to be emperor.[80]

The qualifications of these men are better in many respects than those which Nerva could muster. All of them had experience in governing provinces; three of them had commanded armies – Lappius Maximus, Aurelius Fulvus and Verginius Rufus; Nerva, notoriously, had done neither. These wider experiences may in fact be reasons for these men's (presumed) refusals: a doubt as to the reaction of the armies to the elimination of Domitian, who was popular with the troops and their commanders. That is, a greater knowledge of the empire was inhibitory of ambition. Nerva, on the other hand, did not automatically think of such an objection: his world was Rome and central Italy, government and the administration of the state, so he could accept. Ignorance lent him audacity.

The mingled progeny of Antoninus and Aurelius emerged as emperors later (the emperors Antoninus Pius, Marcus Aurelius, Lucius Verus and Commodus). These two are not necessarily men who had been approached by the conspirators, but they *were* men who had the same sort of qualifications as Nerva; since Nerva was not their first choice, one or two of them were surely canvassed, if only for their opinions. Their refusals were no doubt due in part at least, as Antoninus said, to dislike of the job, but maybe also to a distrust in the possible success of the plot. It is worth emphasising again, however, that none of those who had been approached said anything to warn Domitian of his danger. They were thus both compromised and neutralised, and they must have realised that they now had an interest in the success of the plot. If it failed, and any of the plotters were questioned, the fact that such men knew of it in advance was bound to come out.

All this does not necessarily imply an enormously long process of plotting and preparation. Indeed, the fact that the conspiracy succeeded suggests the very opposite, for Domitian was alert to plots, and a long process of preparation and discussion was bound to be noticed or revealed. An embarrassing number of men were clearly either involved or alerted in advance. The more who knew, the more likely it was that the emperor would find out. The arrival in the plot of Stephanus, a man who was actually prepared to carry out the assassination, may well have been the necessary moment of decision; the assumption of the consular office by Fronto may well have been the trigger for the start of the plot. At a guess, one would put the length of time involved at not more than a month.

The assassination thus came after a fairly brief period of conspiracy, but at the end of a process of plot and preparation which involved at least one consul, at least one Praetorian Prefect, several senators and at least seven members of the imperial household. The timing of the killing depended in part on the agreement of all these men to participate, on the recruitment of the willing Stephanus, and on Fronto being consul, but it was also necessarily determined by the activities of the victim himself. Here it is the military affairs of the northern frontier have which to be considered. This requires another lengthy digression.

One of Domitian's major concerns during his reign had been the frontier along the Rhine and Danube rivers. This concern had produced six separate wars during his reign, with the result that, by the year of his death, Roman attention had become centred on the lands beyond the middle Danube, opposite the province of Pannonia, in what is now Bohemia, Moravia and the Hungarian Plain. Domitian had fought two wars there already, in 89 and 92–93, conducted under his own personal supervision. It was a case of Roman aggression, an invasion of the trans-frontier lands of the tribes of the Marcomanni and the Quadi, in Bohemia and Moravia to the north, and those of the Sarmatian Iazyges in the Hungarian plain to the east, and in both cases he had been unsuccessful. In the second war, a legion, XXI *Rapax*, had been destroyed, and when, after an absence from Rome of eight months, Domitian had returned to the city, he had celebrated only an ovation, not a triumph, for his claimed successes. For a man who had already accepted twenty-two acclamations as Imperator, a mere ovation was markedly restrained, and it suggested a less than complete success in the war he had just fought: the three tribes – collectively described by the Romans as the 'Suebi and Sarmatae' – lived to fight again.[81]

One of Domitian's more attractive character traits was persistence and determination; another was thoroughness and a capacity for patient preparation. Peace, to such a ruler, after such a war, was not the end of the matter but a time in which to organise, the more certainly to win the next war. Therefore the years following the second war, 93–96, saw major preparations in Pannonia for another attack.

During that time a great concentration of Roman forces was achieved in and around Pannonia, supplies were gathered, and a commander was selected and installed. This was the new governor of Pannonia, Cn. Pinarius Aemilius Cicatricula Pompeius Longinus, whose career is fairly well known.[82] As was only to be expected in a sensitive frontier province at such a time he was primarily a soldier; he had probably been a military tribune at the time of the civil war in 69, and he reached legionary command in the mid-80s. His quality was clearly well appreciated, for he was given command of *legio* X *Fretensis* in combination with the propraetorian governorship of Judaea.[83] This was only a dozen years after the suppression of the great Jewish revolt: a more ticklish combination of place and offices can scarcely be imagined, demanding sensitivity, diplomacy and military decisiveness.

Pompeius Longinus carried out his joint responsibilities with success: he was one of the consuls of 90, the year when a large number of men reached that office, some at least as a reward in all probability for their conduct during the 'false-Nero' crisis in the east in 88 and in the revolt of Saturninus in the west in January 89.[84] After the customary break, his next appointment was to Moesia Superior as governor in 93, whence he was transferred to be governor of the neighbouring province of Pannonia.[85] He thus had direct and immediate experience of the northern frontier before his appointment to Pannonia. Since the emperor had planned the new war from soon after his return from the last one in 93, Pompeius Longinus' appointment to Moesia Superior and his subsequent transfer to Pannonia were clearly part of that plan. He was being worked hard, with only two short breaks in employment in the past ten years: clearly one of the great military men of the time.

In Pannonia in 96, Pompeius Longinus had under his control a force of no less than five legions, together with an equivalent force of auxiliary regiments. The exact stations of all of the legions are not certain, but XIII *Gemina* and XV *Apollinaris* were definitely based in the fortresses of Vindobona and Carnuntum, right on the river and facing the Quadi: XIV *Gemina*, was probably at Musellae, a little south of the river; the two legions originally raised from marines, I and II *Adiutrix*, were also stationed back from the actual frontier, in south-east Pannonia. There were also two more legions in the province which Pompeius Longinus had recently governed, Moesia Superior, where the new governor was probably L. Julius Marinus.[86] He had under his command IV *Flavia* at Singidunum and VII *Claudia* at Viminacium, both on the river and facing north into the Hungarian plain, the home of the Iazyges. In Moesia Inferior further to the east there were two more legions, V *Macedonica* at Oescus, and I *Italica* at Novae, conveniently close together, though not really close enough to be useful in a Pannonian war.[87] They were, however, neatly stationed to overawe Dacia, a land which had to be carefully watched.

In Pannonia the legions which had been held back from the frontier were moved forward, to Ad Flexum, Brigetio and Aquincum, all stations on or close to the river itself. As well as the legions, large numbers of auxiliary regiments were similarly concentrated into the frontier area. Those listed in a military diploma from Moesia Superior dated to June 96 included some units which had earlier been in Pannonia, perhaps moved out to allow accommodation for the heavy legionary concentration along the river. It is calculated that Moesia Superior held three *alae* and twenty *cohortes* of auxiliaries as well as its two legions – a force of at least 25,000 men in the one province.[88] Pannonia's five legions were supported by a proportionate number of *auxilia* – at least six *alae* and forty *cohortes* perhaps, unless more of those in Moesia were to be transferred. Certainly Pannonia and Moesia Superior in 96 saw one of the densest concentrations of military manpower in Europe for many years, a force of at least 70,000 soldiers.

The peoples who were to be attacked were those who had avoided conquest in 92–93, the Suebi and the Sarmatae. According to Tacitus in the *Germania*, which he was probably writing at the time that this third Pannonian, or Suebic-Sarmatian, war was launched (for the book was published in 98), the term 'Suebi' was a general one covering a large number of German tribes in the lands from the Danube to the Baltic.[89] Domitian was obviously not aiming to fight so many tribes, so far off; it was the closer Suebic tribes that were in his sights, those who lived close to the Danube, namely the Marcomanni and the Quadi in Bohemia and Moravia.

The time since the unsuccessful war of 92–93 had been used not only to make the substantial military preparations in Pannonia and Moesia, but also to prepare the ground diplomatically, with the aim of isolating the enemy tribes. Since they had links of kinship with the other Suebi, this was clearly a delicate task.

This is where the whole northern policy of Domitian has to be considered. In 83 and 89 he had fought wars with the Chatti, a German tribe on the middle Rhine. The Chatti were comprehensively defeated, and their territory was in part incorporated in the empire, the newly transferred lands being bounded by a fortified line.[90] This effectively broke the tribes of Germany into two parts. To the south of the Chatti, in the land later called Bavaria, the Hermunduri were firm Roman friends.[91] Eastwards of the Hungarian Plain, in the mountains of Carpathia, the Dacians had constructed a substantial state, ruled at this time by Decebalus. Twice in the 80s Romans and Dacians had fought wars, fairly inconclusively until a Roman invading army had defeated the Dacians at Tapae in 88. Decebalus' kingdom survived, clearly chastened,[92] and the two legions close by in Moesia Inferior were a standing warning against further hostility.

So to the west of the Marcomanni, Rome dominated southern Germany. To the east of the Quadi there were the Iazyges, a Sarmatian tribe, in the Hungarian Plain, then the Dacian kingdom, then more Sarmatae. Roman diplomacy succeeded in persuading Decebalus to make an alliance against the Sarmatae, with whom both he and they were at odds; in one of the Romano-Sarmatian wars, a Roman force under a centurion was allowed to march through Dacia to attack the Iazyges.[93] Then to the north of the Marcomanni and Quadi were the other Suebic tribes, the Lugii of modern Silesia and the Semnones of northern Bohemia. These were also contacted diplomatically and persuaded to make an alliance with Rome. The Semnones in particular had a strong influence as the senior Suebic tribe, and they had a notable religious influence on the others; their king Masyus, and an influential priestess, Ganna, were received at Rome by the emperor, and returned home with rich presents.[94] The Lugii were provided with both weapons and troops.[95]

The result of all this diplomatic activity was that the Marcomanni, the Quadi and the Iazyges were encircled and isolated by a series of Roman allies to their north, east and west, with the Romans holding the Danube line to the south. The Iazyges perforce allied themselves with the threatened Quadi and Marcomanni.[96] This system of alliances, no less than the military preparations, had clearly taken some time to accomplish. The transfer of Pompeius Longinus from Moesia Superior to Pannonia in the summer of 96 was the sign that all was ready for the war to begin.[97]

This war, and the heavy concentration of Roman troops in Pannonia and Moesia needed to carry it out, is relevant to the assassination of the emperor in September. Normally this sort of concentration of troops under one commander was something to be avoided under all circumstances and at all costs.[98] Saturninus had rebelled in 89 with the support of only two legions. Only a great emergency which threatened even worse consequences could have induced Domitian to concentrate five legions under the command of a single general so close to Italy. For Pannonia was next door to Italy and was connected to it by the Ljubljana gap, the route through the Julian Alps used by Vespasian's forces in their invasion of Italy in 69. A force of five legions plus auxiliaries under one commander could easily produce an army of 30,000 men for an invasion of Italy, where there was nowhere near that number of troops to face them, and yet still leave a large enough force in Pannonia to guard the frontier, particularly since a similarly large force in Moesia Inferior was available as a further deterrent to a barbarian invasion. It follows that Domitian had no fear of rebellion by this army, nor by its commander.

Having achieved this enormous concentration of force it had to be used at once, in the late summer and autumn of 96. The commander could not afford to wait, since the enemy had clearly received enough warning already, by the very gathering of the forces. The accumulation of supplies which had to accompany the formation of Pompeius Longinus' army also forbade delay, for a six-month wait would inevitably use up much of the stockpile. Domitian's notorious concern for financial matters would fret at the waste involved in any delay. (Not to mention the ridicule he would be subjected to if, having gathered this army, he did not use it: one of the main causes of Caligula's downfall had been his aborted expedition against Britain; no emperor could afford another fiasco on that scale.) So the invasion of the lands of the Quadi and Marcomanni was launched soon after Pompeius Longinus' transfer to Pannonia, in time to capture harvested supplies from the enemy. The resulting preoccupation of this large army, loyal to Domitian, was an important element in the crisis of state in September.[99]

Of the elements of power in the Roman Empire in September of 96, most of the members of the Senate were hostile or indifferent to Domitian, the military units in Rome were neutralised or unable to intervene, the army was fully occupied in the Suebic-Sarmatian war, and the palace servants had within them a cell of men willing to kill. The alliance of the consul and the palace group, and the neutralisation of the Praetorian Guard commanders, provided the chance to kill the emperor. This was, however, a purely temporary alliance, and could not be expected to last long. The army's involvement in the new campaign on the Danube prevented its intervention in Italy, at least in the short term. But there is one more item to take into account.

Domitian had gone to the frontier in the past for the Chattan war, for his two Dacian wars, for the two earlier wars on the middle Danube, and he had dashed off in person to deal with Saturninus' revolt. The quantity of preparation put into the new campaign was such that it is highly probable that Domitian wanted to be involved at some point, though Pompeius Longinus was obviously able to start the invasion without Domitian being present, for it had already begun before the emperor was killed. The conspirators may not have known of the emperor's plans, which may not have been announced in advance, just in case he did not go, but they did know of his preferences, and they will have known of the planned war, and so they had to assume that he might go.[100] Once the plot existed they had to carry it through before Domitian left on campaign; if they did not, the plot's existence would inevitably become known, and they would be damned anyway. So, having plotted, they had to make their attempt, and the war on the Danube warned them that their victim might vanish from Rome suddenly.

The war could not wait for the emperor's presence. It had to be launched before the cold weather, which closes in on the middle Danube by November, if not earlier; a campaign for three or four months (August or September to early November) would lay a good foundation for next spring, enabling the Roman forces to seize the locally available supplies which had been stored after the harvest – an autumn harvest, not a summer one as in the Mediterranean – and to attain positions from which to exploit next year. So it can be assumed that the trans-Danube invasion had begun earlier than the beginning of September. Domitian might wish to go north, but he knew he could not get away from Rome until late in that month, and so would not reach the Danube before, say, the beginning of October. The conspirators knew this, as did anyone who lived in Rome, and the date of the assassination is highly suggestive of their knowledge.

For September in Rome was a crowded and busy month, full of public events, and it was also one of considerable personal significance for Domitian. It was the month, first of all, of the *ludi Romani*, the Great Games, the oldest and largest and longest of the games in the city. It was politically unthinkable for Domitian to leave the city before the end of the games, which lasted until 19 September. (It would be different, of course, if he was already away; emperors were not necessary for the games, but to leave in their midst would be insulting.) Attendance was one of the necessary public appearances which no emperor could avoid, certainly if he was in or near the city. Those emperors who tried to dodge this duty were vociferously criticised,[101] and Domitian had always been assiduous in his attention to, and attendance at, these popular events. He had established four gladiatorial schools close to the great monstrous Flavian amphitheatre (the Colosseum) to provide trained victims for these and other games – one of these men was present at the emperor's death, ironically;[102] he had established an Odeon for musical and poetry concerts, one of his own favourite pastimes;[103] he had had built a new stadium for races and animal hunts;[104] his new palace was planned so as to overlook the Circus Maximus; and he was, in 96, in the process of having the damaged Circus Maximus itself repaired.[105] He will no doubt have contributed to the cost of the Games, and will have certainly wished to have this known and to receive the crowd's appreciation. The Great Games was a central event in any emperor's political calendar. Domitian would inevitably attend.

There was another reason for his presence in Rome at this month, one perhaps less publicly pressing, but, given his predilections, almost as important to the emperor personally. The Ides of September (13 September) was a date with an astonishing collection of anniversaries. It was, first, the occasion of a public feast to commemorate the founding of the oldest temple in Rome, that of Jupiter Optimus Maximus on the Capitol, a building which Domitian had had restored and decorated at great expense; the feast involved the attendance of magistrates, senators, the vestals and the images of the god himself and of Juno and Minerva.[106] In addition, or perhaps as part of the same feast, there was one for Minerva, and Minerva was the goddess who had Domitian's own chosen devotion; he had a small shrine to her in his private apartment in the palace.[107] The feast was an essential part of the games, but the inclusion of the extra element in honour of Minerva gave Domitian a further incentive to be in the city. As well, that same day, 13 September, was also the anniversary of the death of Titus, and the next day was his own *dies imperii*, the date of his formal accession to the throne.[108] As a collection of public and private reasons for being in the city on 13 and 14 September, these are hard to beat.

26

On the 14th there was also a parade of Roman *equites*, whose horses were provided by the state, riding in their tribes and centuries. The parade could well include several thousand horsemen; it started from a temple of Mars outside the city walls, wound its way through the streets to the Forum, along the Sacred Way and then past the temple of Castor and Pollux, and under the arch of Augustus. The parade, a Republican event revived by Augustus, commemorated the alleged assistance rendered by Castor and Pollux to the Roman army at the victory at Lake Regillus, after which they were said to have watered their horses in the Forum.[109] For an emperor whose armies were in the process of launching a new war against an enemy which had destroyed a Roman legion, and whose own accession anniverary was on that date, attendance at such an auspicious procession was surely essential.

All these reasons for Domitian being in Rome, however, would end with the last day of the *ludi Romani*, 19 September. The conspirators could assume that Domitian would remain in the city, living in the palace, until that date, but they could have no confidence that he would be present at any time afterwards. We do not know if he intended to stay in the city, go to one of his villas, or go north to the frontier; neither did the conspirators, in all likelihood, though one would expect the palace servants to have advance warnings of any move. At the same time, the relaxed social atmosphere of the *ludi Romani* would be an ideal time in which the conspirators could move about, mingle, contact each other, and discuss and finalise their plans. It was a time of festival, a time for dressing up, for betting, for drinking, when men and women mingled in the audiences, and boys and girls flirted. And senators and soldiers and imperial freedmen could mix and meet as well. Ideal plotting time.

It was during the latter part of this fortnight, the time of the *ludi Romani*, and the celebrations on 13 and 14 September, that Stephanus the steward wore the bandages over his feigned arm injury in order to be able to carry a hidden knife into the emperor's presence. If the 'week' he is said to have done so is accurate, he was prepared from 11 September to carry out the assassination. It was during that time of public celebration that the 'various men' were singled out as future replacements for Domitian by the senatorial plotters, and in which most of them refused the dubious honour; it was in that period that Nerva was persuaded that he was the one. And, in the palace, Parthenius organised the actual assassination, and lined up a group of supporters and assistants, both for himself and to assist Stephanus.

The approach of the end of the period of the Great Games thus forced the conspirators to act. By 18 September they could not be certain that the emperor would be in the palace for more than another day, and if he left, they could not be sure where he would go. If he went to the army, it was almost certain that their conspiracy would fail, either because it would be revealed or because some of the plotters would pull out, or both. And if the emperor returned to Rome victorious, the lack of support for him might well change to active popularity. So, having gathered their groups together, and emplaced a killer, they had to act.

27

3

NERVA

Nerva's accession as emperor was a surprise. He was old: in his sixties in a time when most men died before they reached fifty. His main supporters and those who may have been preferred to him by the plotters were of his age, or even older. He had a very narrow and limited experience of the empire, its government and its problems, and he had little or no experience of the army, which soon emerged as his major problem. He had no children, at least no sons – indeed there is no sign that he ever married – though whether this had any bearing on his selection and promotion is not known.[1] What he did have, and what presumably commended him to the plotters, and then to the Senate, was a status as a noble, a double consular – both as *ordinarius* – and an old award as *triumphator* with a public statue, and of course, an intimate involvement in court politics since the reign of Nero.

M. Cocceius Nerva's descent can be traced back to the origins of the Principate. Two, or perhaps three, brothers[2] from Narnia, Gaius, Marcus and Lucius Cocceius, were active in the 30s, first on the side of Marcus Antonius, then neutral, then with Octavian.[3] The eldest of the three, C. Cocceius Balbus, was consul in 39, and the second, M. Cocceius Nerva, in 36; Marcus was governor of Asia in about 36, when it was in Antony's sphere.

This ability to move with the times and the rulers was apparently heritable. The middle brother, Marcus, was the ancestor of the emperor a century and a quarter later (the others had no descendants of senatorial rank that we know of). All of the brothers had, of course, grown up in the continually worsening crises of the 50s and 40s BC, witnessing civil war and dictatorship; survival was difficult for men of consular eminence; the Cocceii did well to participate and survive.

Marcus' son, or grandson, and namesake was consul in AD 21 or 22. By that time his family was even more closely allied with the ruling family. His son, M. Cocceius Nerva, consul in about 40, had married Sergia Plautilla in Tiberius' reign. The marriage took place about twenty years before his consulship, and it was a marriage which linked two well-established families. He was the son and great-grandson of consuls; she was the daughter of a consul; and the two fathers were successive *curatores aquarum*, both appointed by Tiberius; more significantly, Nerva's father, a noted legal expert, was a close friend of that emperor, close enough to join him on his island retreat at Capri for several years.[4] This connection spread to the bride's brother, C.

Octavius Laenas,[5] who was married to Rubellia, the daughter of Rubellius Blandus and Julia, Tiberius' granddaughter. This brought the whole family close to the throne, which, given Tiberius' friendship with Nerva, was only to be expected.

The husband of Sergia Plautilla was consul in the reign of Caligula, and furthermore, towards the end of the reign, when the emperor's troubles increased, and the conspirators were gathering. By that time he had two children, the future emperor, born in 35 or so, and his sister Cocceia. She married L. Salvius Otho Titianus, who was consul in 52 in the reign of Claudius.[6]

By this time the Cocceian family connection with the royal family, never very strong, had faded. Under Nero, however, any imperial proximity of any sort became perilous. Rubellius Plautus, Rubellia's brother, was politely invited to exile himself, but then was killed by a centurion sent by Nero.[7] Three years later Plautus' widow, her father, and his mother-in-law were also effectively driven to suicide by Nero.[8] The emperor's fears seemed justified in that year, 65, when the ramifications of the Piso conspiracy emerged: and just at that point Nerva himself went to the emperor with some highly useful information.[9]

What the information was is not known, but it was sufficiently useful for Nero to be grateful. It is quite possible that the distant connection with Tiberius had put Nerva in danger, in which case there was no doubt some connection between Nerva's informing and the danger he apprehended for himself. He was rewarded with extraordinary honours by the emperor – decorations as an *triumphator* and a public statue[10] – but danger stalked him still, though now from a different direction. His sister Cocceia's marriage to L. Salvius Otho Titianus brought the family close to Nero in a paradoxical way, since Titianus' brother, M. Salvius Otho, had been married to the delectable Poppaea, who became the emperor's second wife – and one more of his victims. Titianus had been consul under Claudius, and the marriage presumably took place in the 40s, so its original purpose had been to make allies of two prominent families. But Cocceia's brother-in-law, M. Salvius Otho – the discarded husband of Poppaea – after languishing for years in honourable exile as governor of Lusitania, joined the rebellion of Galba, the long-term governor of the neighbouring province of Hispania Citerior. Then in January 69 Otho emerged as emperor himself, after arranging for Galba's murder by some dissident Praetorians.

Otho as emperor was, to any experienced politician in Rome, a losing cause from the start. His long absence from Rome left him wholly out of touch with the capital, and he had never held any office other than governor of Lusitania, where he had been sent by Nero to get him away from his former wife. Nerva was by this time of praetorian rank. His connections with Tiberius, Nero and Otho – three of the most disliked emperors – were not going to be conducive to safety in dangerous times. Yet he managed to keep his distance from Otho, while also keeping his life; further, he survived the rule of Otho's conqueror Vitellius, and then emerged under Vespasian as one of the few men honoured by that emperor with an ordinary consulship, as early as the year 71.[11] This is a remarkable record by any measure. The implication of that consulship in particular is that Nerva had been active in Rome on Vespasian's behalf during the civil wars, and from early on in the crisis. No evidence of that activity has survived: silent intrigue was obviously one of his accomplishments.

Nerva had clearly inherited the family's adept political manoeuvrability. Close to Tiberius, Caligula and Nero, related to Tiberius and Otho, yet he had survived. Two of his relatives illustrate other possible responses to the danger of being prominent. His cousin Octavius is nowhere recorded; he was the son of Laenas and Rubellia, and his son emerges in Hadrian's reign as consul in 131;[12] the father, a great-great-grand-son of Tiberius, evidently chose to keep himself out of sight.[13] By contrast, Nerva's nephew, the son of Otho Titianus, called L. Salvius Otho Cocceianus, reached the consulship in 82, early in Domitian's reign, perhaps in his thirties, for he was of patri-cian rank, and so could omit some of the earlier stages,[14] yet he will have held his ear-lier offices under Vespasian and Titus. So he was clearly in good odour with the Flavian dynasty. Yet he fell foul of Domitian for commemorating his other uncle, the brief emperor Otho, and was executed.[15] Flying too close to any emperor brought a danger of being burnt.

Nerva avoided both Octavius Laenas' hidden obscurity and Salvius Otho's too-prominent notoriety, and prospered. Not only was he consul under Vespasian, but he was awarded a second ordinary consulship by Domitian in 90, the year after the latter had crushed the dangerous rebellion of Antonius Saturninus in Germany in 89.[16] What he had done to merit this honour is not known – any more than what had been his service to Nero in similar circumstances.[17] Maybe the consulship was no more than a reminder to the Senate that both Domitian and his father had survived civil wars, or maybe Nerva had been especially supportive, perhaps by being the first and most con-stant adviser to show up in the crisis. But Otho Cocceianus was executed about this same time, and a number of other consular senators went the same way in the follow-ing years.[18] Politics at the top in Rome was a nervous business, where a single false step meant death. Nerva clearly stepped with care and success through this hideous politi-cal minefield. His family connections and his political alignment had been with virtu-ally every emperor from Tiberius to Domitian, in which each emperor's death was the time for a *coup d'état*, whether open or disguised, yet he lived. Not only that, but he was counted as an *amicus* – a trusted counsellor of Domitian[19] – to the very end, a trait which was evidently misplaced.

The appearance as emperor of this man, who had helped save the ghastly Emperor Nero and had now connived at the murder of the unpleasant but efficient Domitian, his apparent friend, must have stunk in at least some senatorial nostrils. His accession can only be characterised as an appalling betrayal of a man who had trusted him, who had regularly consulted him, and who had rewarded him for his loyalty and advice. This personal history was well known to all in the Senate. Beyond that personal ele-ment, also, the unmilitary Nerva was a most unsuitable figure as a ruler for an empire such as Rome's, which was military to its core.

In person, the new emperor was about sixty years old[20] and in poor health, with few relatives to assist him in a political environment where relations might or might not be trustworthy, but where anyone else had to be assumed to be untrustworthy. His career of intrigue, discussion and consultation did not suggest any decisiveness or originality, and he was far too old and unwell to develop such qualities now. Also, his personal achievements were scarcely startling: he had, as Syme noted, 'never seen a province or an army'; indeed it seems unlikely that he had ever travelled more than a hundred or so miles from Rome itself.[21]

He was accepted as emperor at a meeting of the Senate on the morning of 19 September,[22] when he was awarded the usual offices. There was no hint of a move by any of the armed forces in the city to avenge Domitian. The Praetorian Prefects – if Norbanus survived – successfully held their men in check; the Prefect of the City did nothing, for his Urban Cohorts could scarcely act in defiance of the apparent will of the Praetorian Guard; the Vigiles were equally helpless. But these acceptances, apparently joyful by the Senate, and passive by the troops, were only the first step; the real decision would be made by the armies in the provinces and on the frontiers, though their reactions would take some time to become manifest, partly because the most important army was on active service, and partly because of the sheer time involved in spreading the news.

The news of the death of the emperor, particularly of his assassination, was sensational by any standards, and it spread as fast as any news in the ancient world. Within Italy it would move at the speed of a galloping horse, and to the Mediterranean coastal provinces it would go at the speed of sailing ships. The sailing season was now almost over, but it was not yet the winter close season; ships could still sail until early in November, and urgent messages, of which nothing was more urgent than this news, would go even in winter. From Ostia a ship might reach Alexandria in ten days with a favourable wind, or perhaps in three weeks under more normal conditions. Corinth could be reached in five days at best, though ten was more likely. Tarraco in Spain was only four days to a week away, Carthage no more than two or three days.[23] The great coastal cities of the western Mediterranean would thus all know the news within a week, and those round the eastern basin by early October, almost certainly. It would take only a little longer to reach the main inland places, most of which were fairly close to the coasts.

Overland, the messenger would need access to relays of animals to make his best speed. In 69 the news of the revolt of Vitellius at Colonia Agrippinensis had reached Rome in nine days, and that was in January, when the Alpine passes were blocked;[24] a week would be ample for the news of the murder of Domitian in Rome to reach the Danube in September, when the Alpine passes were easier. A day or two more would be quite sufficient for it to reach Moguntiacum on the Rhine in Germania Superior and Colonia Agrippinensis in Germania Inferior, and in the other direction, Viminacium in Moesia Superior. Thus the news will have reached the commanders of a dozen legions, half the Roman army (three in Germania Superior and two in Inferior, five on campaign in Pannonia, two in Moesia Superior) probably before the end of September. Two more legions further along the Danube in Moesia Inferior will have got to know by the end of September. The British legions would have to wait a little longer, but they will surely have heard the news in the first days of October.

It was on the Rhine and Danube that the real decisions now lay. There were major armies also in Britannia (three legions) and the east (six legions divided between the three commands of Cappadocia, Syria and Judaea), but they were too far off to affect the immediate issue, as were the two Egyptian legions and the single legions in north-west Spain and Africa: only if the crisis went on for any length of time would the intervention of these more distant, isolated and relatively small armies become important – as had happened in 69, when the western legions had divided in their allegiances and Vespasian's expeditionary force from the east had eventually been decisive. The sheer numbers of the northern legions, combined with their proximity to Italy and Rome, made their reactions the crucial ones.

These reactions had to take place in the context of their present activities, but they were also influenced by memories of the recent past, and conditioned in part by their attitudes towards the dead Domitian and the living Nerva. The German armies on the Rhine had made the running at first in 69, offering the throne first to L. Verginius Rufus, and then successfully to A. Vitellius. The Pannonian armies, on the other hand, had been neutral until they had joined with the eastern army of Vespasian in gaining the final victory for him later in the year. The legions in the British army had participated only distantly by sending vexillations to the Rhine army, and the province as a whole had remained paralysed by the indecision of the governor and the legionary legates for most of the former crisis. Even the single legion in Africa had been involved when the governor there had apparently claimed power for himself. The reasons for these varied responses had often been no more than gubernatorial pique and military rivalry, annoyance that one army had put forward its own candidate, who was thereby automatically unacceptable to others.[25] The confusion of the western armies was strongly contrasted with the unity displayed by those in the east, a unity brought about by intelligent diplomacy. Clearly this confusion could happen again, which would ensure a progressive collapse of the state once more. The problem was how to avoid such an outcome, and it clearly exercised many men in the next year or so. The fact that a civil war did *not* happen in 96 does not mean that the danger of one did not exist, nor that such a danger was not apprehended. In fact, the information we have on reactions strongly suggests that the crisis came dangerously close to conflict.

We do have a rather problematic account of the reaction of one group of soldiers to the news. It is a story related by Philostratos in his *Lives of the Sophists*, written a good century or more after the events. It is difficult to know how much to accept of the story, particularly since some details are clearly wrong, and others are mis-applied. Yet the general scenario is believable, and the overall atmosphere in the military camp in which it is set seems all too likely.

Philostratos is describing the journeys of the orator Dio of Prusa, called Dio Chrysostom, who had been exiled by Domitian in the aftermath of the execution of Dio's patron at Rome, T. Flavius Clemens. The story Philostratos relates is set in Moesia, which Dio will have visited on his way to the Dacians, about whom he was composing a monograph. In the summer of 97 he passed through Olbia on his way westwards, and so Moesia, probably Moesia Superior, could have been reached in the autumn.[26]

The news of Domitian's murder will have reached Moesia by the end of September.

Travelling along the army's communication network, it would move out from the governor to the legions and then on to the auxiliaries, by which time it will have been well into October. Civilians no doubt heard about it from the soldiers. When the news arrived at the camp of auxiliaries Dio was visiting at the time, it seems to have been winter, or near to it; this is relevant to the story told about Dio there. The news should, of course, have delighted him, since it was his enemy who was dead, the man who had sent him into exile, and a man whom he could claim as his friend was the new ruler; however, it is the reaction of the soldiers that Philostratos describes which is important here.

The soldiers – the private soldiers, not the officers – were instantly angry, and began working themselves up to some sort of mutiny against the new government, or against their officers. The officers will have had a somewhat clearer notion of the situation at Rome, of the peril they would be in if the mutiny eventuated, and of the need to consult with their fellow soldiers in other units before taking any precipitate action. For a small unit a mutiny could only lead to disaster; and anyone else involved in a mutiny, innocent or implicated, was liable to suffer as well. Dio is said to have jumped on to an altar, naked, and got the attention of the soldiers – such a display in winter in the northern Balkans would certainly do that. He began by quoting Homer in Greek: 'Then wily Odysseus stripped his rags'. This is unlikely to have meant anything to the ordinary soldiers of an auxiliary regiment, whose common language will have been Latin, but it may have amused the officers, and it certainly appealed to Philostratos and his aristocratic and philhellenic audience. Dio is then supposed to have gone on to denounce Domitian. If he really did this, he must have been a notably persuasive orator, since the mutiny was supposed to be an angry outburst caused by the arrival of the news of that emperor's murder. Nevertheless he is said to have persuaded the troops first to listen, then to calm down, and finally to abandon the projected mutiny.[27]

The problems with this account are many. Philostratos wrote the story over a century after the event, and he is scarcely the most reliable of authors. There is a regrettable lack of specific detail in the story – which fort was it? what auxiliary unit? where were the officers at the time? what language was being used? (The army used Latin, Dio was quoted in Greek.) And so on. The conclusion must be that the story may well be fiction.[28] On the other hand, its overall atmosphere does carry a good deal of conviction. The immediately unsettling effect on the soldiers of the news of the murder of the emperor rings true, and is paralleled by that of the Praetorians in Rome, whom Suetonius describes as being 'deeply unsettled' by it.[29] The rapid second thoughts the soldiers had over their potential mutiny also seems likely. If Dio really did behave as Philostratos claims, it is no wonder the troops were distracted, and perhaps his main service was to give them time to reflect. At the same time, if he really did denounce Domitian, it is unlikely he did so to such an audience, though one can easily believe that his opinions were well known – the officers might have been more susceptible to such a denunciation. It may be also that the soldiers were angry at the murder of the emperor, rather than the killing of Domitian personally, which would help Dio's case. Dio must have been an exotic figure in that army camp, and could easily get attention;

his apparent familiarity with the wider world, including imperial politics, would lend him authority. Philostratos may well have run a number of stories together for his account, adding a considerable dash of his own imagination to sauce it, and as an event the whole episode is perhaps unlikely. But it does give a small insight into the tensions of the time and into the problems which the army commanders and governors had to face all along the northern frontier.

One factor making for an acceptance of the new situation rather than sliding into an insurrection was clearly the involvement of the huge Pannonian army in active warfare beyond the Danube. The commander there, Pompeius Longinus, had little choice but to accept the coup in Rome, at least in the short term. His forces were in the process of fighting Domitian's war, but disengaging from the enemy to avenge the dead emperor was scarcely an option, since it would only stimulate his present enemies. We do not know what fighting actually took place, but the invasion of the trans-Danube lands had been well signalled in advance by the assembly of the mighty army and its supplies, and it is reasonable to assume that the Iazyges, the Quadi and the Marcomanni had mustered their own forces to resist. The invasion had thus stirred up the enemy, but victory had not yet been won, and the evidence, thin though it is, suggests that the fighting did not end until 99. Turning the Roman forces around in the midst of the fighting, and after only a month or so, would simply leave the army all the more vulnerable to attack as they withdrew, and would then open up Pannonia, and probably Noricum and Moesia Superior, to invasion by the active enemies, bent on revenge. The prospect of such an invasion, which could well be envisaged by the commander and officers of an auxiliary unit, may have been more persuasive than Dio's antics and words in dissuading a mutiny at the camp he was visiting in Moesia Superior.

Pompeius Longinus and his fellow commanders had to consider a much wider context than the immediate war. They knew that any events on the northern frontier reverberated along the whole length of that frontier to the North Sea and to the Black Sea. In 69 the civil war had brought barbarian invasions across the Danube and a revolt on the Rhine. In 89 the brief uprising of Antonius Saturninus at Moguntiacum had produced a sympathetic rising by the Chatti and a conflict, the 'First Pannonian War', with the Marcomanni and the Quadi. The invasion of the empire by the Dacians in 84 was no doubt in part the result of Domitian's preoccupation on the Rhine the year before. Nothing happened anywhere along the northern frontier without its effects on the rest of the line having to be considered.

In the context of the new war, for which the contemporary name seems to have been the 'Suebic-Sarmatian' war, Pompeius Longinus, a man with years of experience on the frontier (and with experience in that other area of intricate military–political–social–religious affairs, Judaea), had to bear in mind the delicate diplomatic balance which Domitian had achieved along the northern frontier, in Dacia, in southern Germany, among the Semnones and Lugii, in order to isolate the enemy nations. That balance would not necessarily last very long, and any victories won by the Iazyges, Quadi, and Marcomanni would put appalling pressure on it. Decebalus and the Dacians would be very tempted to break their peace with Rome – a peace which had been negotiated with Domitian only seven years before, and which Decebalus might well consider to have been abrogated by the emperor's death. In northern Germany, north of the territory of the Chatti, which Domitian had annexed, the Bructeri had maintained a local supremacy for some time, but, as later events demonstated, this supremacy was precarious. An attack by them across the Rhine was an obvious option for a tribal leadership which might be feeling the political ground shifting beneath it; one king had been foisted on the tribe about ten years before, and the tribe was destroyed in warfare soon after Domitian's death; premonitory signs of this were surely evident, and in fact it may have been the murder of Domitian – in whose name the Roman-appointed king had been emplaced – which was the trigger for the ene-mies to close in.[30] The news of the death of the emperor who had reduced the Chatti, a tribe which had been in much the same situation as the Bructeri, might seem a wel-come opportunity to make a raid into the empire as a way of bolstering internal authority. A Roman withdrawal from a war in central Europe, for which enormous preparations had been made, on top of the death by assassination of the emperor in Rome, in his very palace, and by Romans, would be even more enticing, and if that withdrawn army then marched on Rome, no German, Sarmatian or Dacian would doubt that the empire was about to fall and that it was their duty and pleasure to help the process along. Harking back again to the events of 69, there had been invasions across the Danube and Rhine, and a major revolt by the Batavi of the Rhine delta; it had taken major Roman efforts to repel and suppress these.

The decision that Pompeius Longinus made when he received the news of Domitian's death was thus important not merely for Nerva and his backers in Rome, but for the whole northern frontier of the empire. No doubt the war faltered for a time while the news from Rome was digested, the generals' and officers' grip on the army was enforced and the implications were absorbed. One must expect that the news of Domitian's death was accompanied by, or soon followed by, reassuring messages to the general and the army from Nerva, from senators, and perhaps even from the Prae-torian Prefect or Prefects, both official and private, all urging acceptance of the situa-tion. A coin proclaiming the 'Agreement of the Armies' (*concordia exercitum*) was one of the first issued in Nerva's name: as much a hope as an actuality.[31] Pompeius' deci-sion – and since the Pannonian army did nothing, at least for the moment, this is what it must be assumed to have been – was clearly to accept Nerva as emperor, at least for the moment, and to get on with the war. But one of the factors in the army's accep-tance of the situation was surely the knowledge of Nerva's quality, his age and the state of his health. Like Domitian, the generals must have known that Nerva would not last long. The army could accept Nerva because of that.

Pompeius Longinus had command of the largest Roman army, and so his decision on Nerva's accession was the most important in the first instance, although the com-manders of other armies elsewhere in the empire were also entitled to be consulted. Pompeius Longinus' legionary commanders in particular, but his officers and men more generally, had to be taken into account, and their opinions would count; but once his and their decision was made, the equivalent decisions by the governors in the neighbouring Moesian and German provinces were effectively pre-empted. For if the armies there were to declare against Nerva, the frontier considerations which had to have weighed most strongly with Pompeius Longinus were replaced by new factors. If civil war broke out in the empire, and that is what a *pronunciamento* by any army would amount to, it would also mean that Longinus' army could well find itself stranded in barbarian country without support. The German and/or Moesian armies, if they decided to intervene, would need to do so by marching on Italy, and to do that they would need to march across the rear of the Pannonian army. This was not a prospect which was at all pleasing to that army or to its commander.

It is odd, and perhaps suggestive, that in this crisis we know the names of only one or two of the four governors involved – L. Julius Marinus in Moesia Inferior is one. The names of neither the governor of Germania Superior, nor that of Moesia Superior, are known. However, new governors for both German provinces were appointed during 96. For Germania Inferior the new man was L. Licinius Sura, a Spaniard who had been consul in 93, and perhaps took up his new post before Domitian's death – installation during the summer would be likely.[32] The other new governor was M. Ulpius Traianus in Germania Superior, clearly selected for his loyalty to Nerva, or rather for his acceptance of Nerva's elevation, for he had earlier been conspicuously loyal to Domitian, though there is no trace of his holding any post since his consulship in 91.[33] The governor he replaced is not known, however, and Trajan did not take up his post until late in 96. The appointment of Trajan would help bolster the official version of the assassination as the work of a disloyal, treacherous group of servants in the palace. Both he and Nerva were old associates of Domitian, Nerva as a longstanding counsellor, Trajan as a spectacularly loyal army commander who had marched his army all the way from Spain to Germany to oppose Saturninus, and had received an ordinary consulship in 91 as a reward.

The appointment of Trajan as governor in Germania was thus a deliberate political move by Nerva to help ensure the loyalty of the northern armies, and his sending off of Trajan from Rome to take up his appointment in Germany was made into a piece of political theatre designed to emphasise the junction of army and emperor.[34] Sura in Germania Inferior and the unknown governor in Moesia Superior may thus be presumed to have shown their loyalty to the new regime in good time, however reluctant their individual decisions: acquiescent, perhaps, rather than actively welcoming, like that of Pompeius Longinus.

The failure of the northern armies to intervene against Nerva was all very well for the moment, and this will have become known in Rome during the first half of October, no doubt to everyone's relief – the despatch of Trajan northwards will have been the decisive public gesture which showed the army's decision. But another decision was bound to be required soon. Nerva's age was known, his ill health soon common knowledge.[35] A decision on the succession would soon be required. To those in Rome, at least, it was clear, very quickly, perhaps from the moment of his accession, that a successor would be needed in months rather than years. Trajan's presence in Rome in September and October will have allowed him to make this point to the army commanders in the north as soon as he arrived in his province.

There were, of course, those who wished to anticipate the choice of a new emperor.

After all, if one emperor could die by violence, so could his successor – and everyone remembered the assassination of Galba in 69, killed in fact because he chose unwisely in the matter of his successor, by spurning Otho, who had expected to be chosen. Otho's reaction had been to plot with some of the Praetorian Guard. Galba's chosen successor, L. Calpurnius Piso Licinianus, had therefore been killed at the same time as Galba himself. A nice political complication thus arose in 96: a chosen successor was needed to bolster the regime, but a bad choice might provoke its overthrow, either by disappointed suitors, or by the chosen one himself, impatient for the fruits of power. And if the choice was delayed, the danger of a coup by another ambitious man was just as real and present.

Nerva was not a decisive man, able to make a quick, accurate decision, but he surely knew what the political situation was: and his political experience, after all, over a period of four decades, had honed an ability to sense accurately just what was in the political wind, and then to move to take advantage of it. He, like his senatorial contemporaries, remembered 69, all the more vividly for having been involved. His survival to die a natural death, and the choices he made, though they were slow in coming, show that he did indeed retain his political ability to the end of his life; it was, however, a very near thing.

All this, in outline if not in the detail, was obvious to those in Rome who were politically aware, and that included most of the senators. They met on the morning of 19 September, probably unexpectedly, and probably with many of them still unaware of the crisis. The announcement of Domitian's death, when it was made by the presiding consul, who no doubt provided adequate proofs, was greeted with delight. The senators indulged in an enjoyable round of post-mortem denunciations and vengefully ordered the removal of images of the dead man from their house, apparently sending out for ladders to do so on the spot. A senatorial decree was agreed that inscriptions naming Domitian should be effaced, and that statues of him should be overthrown and the precious metal in them recovered. Votive shields and adulatory arches of the dead man were ordered to be removed or dismantled. There could be no doubt of the Senate's collective feelings.[36]

The new emperor was presented to his former colleagues and a decree was passed awarding him the imperial powers. In reply he made the standard declaration made often before by new emperors: that he would not execute any senators.[37] He also ordered the release of anyone detained for trial on a charge of *maiestas*.[38] This was reasonable, since he himself was the greatest offender, having compassed the death of the man the others were accused merely of defaming or threatening. These gestures of respect for the Senate were no doubt fully expected, but they were also hypocritical. Every earlier undertaking not to execute senators by an emperor had been broken, and sooner rather than later. And if an emperor really carried out that promise he would not last very long as emperor: it was, as his own elevation showed, out of the Senate that the threats against an emperor came. Nerva may have assumed that a new era had dawned, and that the competition of Senate and emperor would henceforce become a harmonious combination. In the immediate term, however, the Senate would be the major source of opposition to him, as it was to every emperor, and Nerva's long experience must have warned him of that. The competition, rising to hostility, between Senate and emperor was inherent in their situations, and conflict would sooner or later see blood spilt, one way or another. If Nerva did not execute senatorial plotters, then, like Domitian, he would probably end up by himself being killed by them. On the other hand, he could scarcely begin his reign by standing in the Senate and refusing to agree not to execute senators.

It may have been this prospect – of opposition rather than the hoped for co-opera-tion – which prompted the old senator Arrius Antoninus to make a speech contrasting the two. He claimed that the Senate, the people and the provinces were to be congrat-ulated on the new emperor's appointment. To the emperor, however, he extended his commiserations, remarking that the burden he took up was heavy, that he would suffer both inconvenience and danger, that he would be criticised whatever he did, and that his friends would fasten on him demanding favours.[39] It is a revealing glimpse of the life of an emperor, and a comment on what Domitian had had to put up with. Fifteen years of that would try anyone's patience, for the most importunate 'friends' were, of course, the senators. It was an oblique warning that Nerva's promise to the Senate was unlikely to be kept, unless the senators themselves moderated their behav-iour and demands.

The Senate meeting and the award of imperial powers over, the new emperor was supposed to attend a meeting of the people's assembly, the *comitia*, at which their approval – or, presumably, their disapproval – of his accession, would be signified. But the *comitia* meeting may well not have taken place; instead there was an *adlocutio*, an announcement only, of the accession. Presumably this actually took place, though the only record of it is on a coin. The *comitia*'s existence was only vestigial by this time.

This is one of a whole series of coins produced very early in the new reign, announc-ing or publicising a whole group of new or renewed policies. The coins represented, in part, an inheritance from Domitian, for whom a new set of coins had recently been produced. For most of his reign Domitian's coinage had been fairly dull, but in the last issues in 95/96 it would seem that a new mint-master had been appointed, and had produced a new, interesting and imaginative set of coins.[40]

Most of the silver and gold coins were much the same as the types produced previ-ously. They usually showed Minerva in her various poses – she was Domitian's own favoured deity – or Germania sitting in despair, commemorating his victories, or just an altar. There was also, however, a new group of coin types showing temples containing the figures of various gods: Serapis the Egyptian god, Cybele from Asia Minor, Minerva (again, and of course), and Jupiter – two deities from the Greek east, two from the Latin west. But on the bronze coins there suddenly appears a whole series of previously unused types. One shows an equestrian statue, presumably an image of the giant statue of Domitian himself on horseback which had been erected in the Forum to mark his victo-ries over Germans and Dacians. Another coin shows a triumphal arch, again no doubt one of those of Domitian, though this type had appeared before. Along with these is the type showing a helmet and shield; these three all connect with Domitian as a warrior, and with the anticipated victory in the new war on the Danube. Then there are three types invoking single deities: the owl of Minerva, the eagle of Jupiter and Fortuna, the goddess whom everyone invoked. There is also a coin showing a view of a round temple, with a king on a throne inside the building, and with soldiers on guard on either side: this might be seen as a sign of Domitian's megalomania, or of his royalist and hereditary pretensions, or it may be an indication of his nervousness, an indication that he knew of his personal and political isolation. It is also, of course, a statement of the true political condition of the Roman empire, but this was not an interpretation which the Senate would wish to accept. The last of these types, all issued in the last year of Domitian's life, is even more suggestive. It shows a three-storey building, the ground floor heavy and solid, the middle storey low and wide, and the top storey tall, columned and architraved, clearly looming. This appears to have commemorated the completion of Domitian's addition to the imperial palace, and it shows a view of the palace as it would be seen from the Circus Maximus, which was, of course, the view most likely to be familiar to ordinary Romans. History's irony ensured that it was no sooner completed and commemorated than its author was killed within it.

These new types are not all entirely unprecedented – most of them can be paralleled one way or another in earlier reigns, but their appearance together as a set all at the same time implies, at the very least, a shake-up in the administration of the Roman mint. Nothing so imaginative had been produced for years, and the same imagination is evident in the coins issued in Nerva's name. It would, of course, take some time for the mint to be able to produce new coins for the new regime. Those already prepared for issue in Domitian's name had to be melted down, new dies had to be engraved, the new emperor's profile had to be drawn and engraved, the types and legends had to be chosen – Nerva himself will have been involved here – and the dies drawn and engraved. In the meantime it seems that some of Domitian's coins prepared for later release actually slipped out into circulation, for a few exist announcing him as 'TRIB POT XVI' ('holder of the tribunician power for the sixteenth time'), which he would not have reached until after his death.[41] The preparations for the new coins could clearly be done speedily enough, however, for a large number of Nerva's early issues show him with two consulships, which means that they were produced between 19 September and the end of December, when he entered on his third.[42] The matter was clearly urgent, and the mint no doubt had to work at great speed, but the work was done well. Nerva's head is a noble Roman one, with a splendidly hooked nose; not at all the head of an old and sick man close to death.

One of these coins is the one mentioned above, commemorating Nerva's accession. It is likely to have been one of the very first to be issued. It shows Nerva standing on a platform, from which two other men behind him are speaking to a group of men standing lower down, on the ground. These auditors are dressed in togas, as citizens. The whole scene is taking place before a temple. It is entitled 'adlocutio Aug' – 'the address of the Augustus'. This is a representation of the scene of the announcement to the people of Rome that they had a new emperor. This announcement was all that remained of popular participation in the political process, except for riots in or out of the circus. The scene's appearance on a bronze coin is the equivalent of the announcement itself, so that non-attenders might participate vicariously. The coin, indeed, might even be the *adlocutio* itself. There may not even have been a public event.[43]

This activity at Rome, in the Senate and in the Forum was all, in effect, contingent upon events in the north. The real decision on the emperor's tenure of office was made by the northern armies, and their acceptance of the new regime was not known until early in October. Meanwhile, as all unsteady governments do, Nerva began to implement a number of measures, designed above all to enhance both his apparent legitimacy and his popularity. One of his earliest acts was to cancel the sentences of exile and the confiscations of property which had been handed out by Domitian.[44] At once these relaxations of government control led to a hunt by the victims for revenge against those whom they blamed for their treatment by Domitian. Informers, or those who were believed to be such, were hauled out and faced with accusation and condemnation. The process, of course, instantly called up a new set of informers, who retailed information which was designed to discredit the earlier informers. And those who were accused then accused their accusers. There was clearly plenty of material lying around for use. But this was personally dangerous for Nerva. He had, or so it seems, been some sort of informer at the time of the Piso conspiracy in Nero's time, and his reward of an ordinary consulship from Domitian in the aftermath of the rebellion of Antonius Saturninus in 89 has the whiff of the same sort of behaviour. The confusion and unpleasantness of recrimination was hardly the atmosphere that upright senators expected when the man they considered responsible for their ills had been removed. So the situation was not allowed to last very long: while he was still consul Caesius Fronto was heard to comment adversely on the chaotic situation. It was a direct reversal, he pointed out, of the tight grip Domitian had maintained. The comparison was taken note of. Nerva then clamped down in some way, though exactly how is not known – presumably by simply refusing to act on accusations, and letting this be known.[45]

The new emperor had to make a number of official appointments, either choosing new men, or confirming the old. He did not dare touch the army commands, at least until October, when Trajan went to Germania Superior, but he certainly could deal with those nearer to his person, in the city. Of these the crucial ones were the Praetorian Prefect and the Urban Prefect. The latter, the less important of the two, was a post occupied in Domitian's last years by T. Aurelius Fulvus, twice consul, a political survivor whose career had begun, like Nerva's, in Nero's reign, and again like Nerva, he had prospered under both Vespasian and Domitian: a safe pair of hands. The occupant of the office under Nerva is nowhere recorded, unless Fulvus was retained, as seems likely.[46]

The Guard was a different matter. It seems that Nerva quickly shed the two Praetorian Prefects inherited from Domitian, Norbanus (if he survived) and Petronius Secundus. They had been disloyal to one emperor, and so their loyalty to the new one could not be assumed. In their place he reappointed a former prefect of the Guard, Casperius Aelianus, apparently without a colleague.[47] This process may well not have been a wholly voluntary act on Nerva's part. Aelianus later used his power to turn against his predecessor, Petronius Secundus, and it may be that the troops had shown their displeasure at the policies of Petronius and Norbanus, and that the appointment of Aelianus, an appointee of Domitian in his first term as prefect, was a sop to them.

Certainly it was shown later that Nerva had little influence over either the new prefect or the soldiers themselves, so the appointment of Aelianus was perhaps an attempt to defuse a dangerous hostility: to appease the troops, in other words. The soldiers had agitated for Domitian to be deified.[48] It was all the more necessary, therefore, to demonstrate the widest possible senatorial support, through the new consular list for 97, for one thing, though even this might not deter the Praetorians from action.

It was also necessary to finalise and publish that consular list for the coming year. It has been argued in Chapter 2 that this list was in its original form already prepared by Domitian before his death, and that Nerva expanded it after his accession, inserting himself and L. Verginius Rufus as *ordinarii*. If Domitian's list retained the pattern of his last few years, it will have contained six names, as well as his own and Rufus'; it is likely therefore that Nerva added four more names. Two of these are likely to be the two men who received second consulships, M. Annius Verus and, as will be argued later, M. Cornelius Nigrinus Curiatius Maternus. It does not seem to be possible to determine who the other two were, even by guessing. These men merit a detailed investigation, for they are a group whose membership of this list marks them out as conspicuous supporters of Nerva and his new regime. If any man on Domitian's list had been outspoken in his dissent from Nerva's accession, it is quite sure that he would not have been retained as consul, certainly not in the very first list produced by a nervous and insecure government. The lesson of Fronto, a Domitianic opponent, and his participation in the plot to emplace a new emperor, will have been taken.

The new consular list for the next year will have been drawn up or confirmed quickly, therefore, and publicised as soon as possible after the accession, no doubt during October. The *ordinarii* were to be Nerva himself, of course, as consul for the third time – and it was his third time as an *ordinarius* as well – and his colleague was to be L. Verginius Rufus, again for the third time.[49] This pairing was a signal that there was no competition between these two ancient survivors of Nero's reign, for Rufus had been the German army's first choice for emperor back in 68, and it may have been a subtle compliment to that army; it would do no harm if the officers and men thought so, anyway. Given the other names on the list, though, it seems most likely that Nerva was actually rewarding friends and colleagues. It is also a reasonable guess that Rufus had been one of the senators approached by the conspirators before they fixed on Nerva.

In order to emphasise, or to collect, the widest possible range of support, and to adjust the original list after Nerva and Rufus were added, each consul in 97 was to have only two months in office. This provided a total of ten places for the suffect consuls. In March a second consulship was to go to Cn. Arrius Antoninus, the man who gave Nerva advice. He was another survivor of the events of 69, when he had first been consul while Vitellius controlled the city, but, perhaps more important for Nerva, he was the senior figure in a potent aristocratic network which centred on Gallia Narbonensis and extended into Spain, whose members included T. Aurelius Fulvus, P. Julius Lupus and M. Annius Verus.[50] Antoninus had been an early, even a decisive supporter of Vespasian in 69, so his rapid adhesion to Nerva in 96 nicely complemented, or cancelled, the Neronian and Othonian connections of the new emperor himself. It is likely that he had also been one of those solicited as successor to Domitian by the conspirators.

Antoninus' colleague as consul in March and April was another whose name called up memories of the events of the past: C. Calpurnius Piso.[51] The name is not complete on the stone, the remains reading only '[...]ius Piso'. Presuming 'Calpurnius' is correctly restored – and the 'Piso' is distinctive of that family – the exact identification is still difficult. F. Zevi restored the *praenomen* as Gaius, and this may be a man descended from L. Calpurnius Piso 'the Pontifex', consul in 15 BC, by a little-known branch of the family, which included the C. Piso who was the 'decorative and feeble' conspirator against Nero in 65.[52] If all this is correct it contains some curious connections. Nerva's first honours were given him by Nero for information provided at the time of that conspiracy; and now here was Nerva honouring the son (or perhaps the grandson) of the principal conspirator and victim. The evidence is all very tenuous and involves too much conjecture for comfort; if it is even generally correct, however, it is a sign of Nerva casting his net very wide indeed in his search for aristocratic support, or perhaps attempting to heal old wounds among senators in the knowledge that a purely senatorial candidate for the imperium would not necessarily meet with wider approval.

The rest of the list is less a reminiscence of past politics and more a timely reward for past administrative and military services, and most of these would fit easily into a typical Domitianic list, consisting as it does of men who could have expected to become consuls in 97 in the ordinary course of politics and their careers. Several of the consuls were connected. M. Annius Verus[53] from the city of Uccubi in Baetica in the south of Spain, who had been made a patrician by Vespasian when young, was related by marriage to Arrius Antoninus. His career is not attested between his adlection to the patriciate and his consulship but he had, no doubt, held several more junior posts. He was still young, and went on to hold second and third consulships under Hadrian (121 and 126), and the post of *praefectus urbi* early in that emperor's reign, but with no other apparent distinctions.

Another related pair were L. Neratius Priscus, Verus' colleague in May and June, and L. Domitius Apollinaris, in office in the following two months. Priscus [54] was from Saepinum in the Samnite country, the son of a man who was consul only a decade before. His elder brother Marcellus had been consul two years before in 95. Marcellus was married first to Corellia Hispulla, daughter of Q. Corellius Rufus, one of Nerva's old colleagues; their son Corellius Pansa was consul *ordinarius* in 122. Marcellus' second marriage was to Domitia Vettilla, daughter of Apollinaris. The Neratii had been, like Apollinaris, fully involved with Domitian's government, but they also had some connections with the opposition. Their grandfather, M. Vettius Marcellus, had been married to Helvidia Priscilla, a sister of Helvidius Priscus, who was a leader of the group who were troublesome to both Nero and Vespasian – hence the younger Neratius' cognomen. Further, Helvidius Priscus' father-in-law was none other than P. Clodius Paetus Thrasea. Both men had died by imperial order, Thrasea Paetus by suicide by order of Nero, Helvidius Priscus executed by order of Vespasian. Thrasea Paetus' home city was Patavium, which also provided a link of sorts with

Caesius Fronto and Silius Italicus. Such connections were surely present in the minds of the new regime, which sought support particularly among the senators. Apollinaris, father-in-law of Neratius Marcellus, also brought in another connection. He was married to Valeria Vettilla, the daughter of P. Valerius Patruinus, consul in 82 and the able and loyal Flavian governor of Syria in the crisis of 88. He had probably governed Cappadocia and Galatia before Syria, a total of almost six years in the east. Domitius Apollinaris himself had governed Lycia and Pamphilia until two years before.[55] The inclusion of these two in Nerva's first list is another sign of him including potential opponents, notably a group who might have been antagonistic to the Flavian emperors.

Another of these consuls with experience in the east was Apollinaris' colleague, Sex. Hermetidius Campanus,[56] governor of Judaea about 92–93, and so in post there at the same time that Apollinaris was in Lycia. By contrast Q. Glitius Atilius Agricola,[57] in office in September and October, had experience in the west. He was from Augusta Taurinorum in Transpadana, had had a comprehensive legal, military and administrative career in Italy, Spain, Syria and Gaul, and, like Apollinaris and Campanus, he had recently held a post as governor of Gallia Belgica that normally led on to the consulship without delay; he was in Belgica until 97, and perhaps he had boosted his prospects by early loyalty to the new regime; he became an important player in the succession crisis during his time as consul.

The two other known, or presumed, consuls of the year are as remarkable as all the rest. One was P. Cornelius Tacitus, the historian, whose career has been the subject of a good deal of investigation. He was from Narbonensis and had experience as legionary commander and provincial governor; he also had connections with Thrasea Paetus.[58]

The colleague of Agricola in September and October is probably M. Cornelius Nigrinus Curiatius Maternus.[59] It was for a long time thought to be L. Licinius Sura, who must now be reallocated to (very likely) a consulship in 93, but who will figure later in this story. Nigrinus is, as Sura was, a most interesting consul to be found just at this point. For a start, and most significantly, this was his second term as consul, even though he was the first of his family to reach that rank, and he only held the office late in the year: under normal circumstances one would expect an iterating consul to hold office much earlier, especially in such a large college.[60] These are circumstances which will be discussed in more detail later.

Nigrinus came from Spain, from Liria in Tarraconensis, where his career is recorded on an incomplete but restorable inscription. He began by serving as military tribune with *legio* XIV *Gemina*, probably shortly after it finally left Britain for its new station at Moguntiacum in 70. He was one of the large group of men adlected to the patrician order by Vespasian in 73/74, as was Trajan's father, after which he served as reviser of the census at Rome and then as commander of *legio* VIII *Augusta*, again in Germania Superior. At some point he was adopted by Curiatius Maternus, a poet and senator who was an early mentor of Tacitus[61] – here is another interconnection in this consular list. Nigrinus was employed almost continuously for the ten years after his legionary command: as governor of Aquitania, 79–82, consul for the first time in 83, governor of Moesia in 85 where he oversaw the division of this large province into two new provinces, Superior and Inferior, after which he served as governor of the new province of Moesia Inferior during the difficult early wars with the Dacians. He then had a break, and went to Syria as governor in 94 or 95; he was in that post when Domitian was assassinated, and was still there in the early part of the next year, in which, as I shall argue in Chapter 6, he was to serve his second consulship.[62]

This consular list, therefore, was probably a compilation of the selections of both Domitian and Nerva, and is to be seen as a reflection of the support Nerva expected in the first month or so of his principate. He had support from a pair of senatorial family networks that included relations of those who had suffered for their philosophic–political stance under both the Julio-Claudian and the Flavian regimes; important governors – Agricola and Nigrinus – who were actually in their provinces when named for the list, were clearly expected both to provide support and to influence their gubernatorial neighbours; a balance between senatorial stay-at-homes such as Calpurius and Antoninus, and busy repeat-governors (Nigrinus) was attempted, as was a mixture of Italian and European provincial senators. There was experience in many of the provinces of the empire among the names on the list. There was also, inevitably, a strong representation of men who had done well under Domitian. That is, it was made clear that no purge was contemplated, a message reinforced by the earlier suppression of the varied accusations which were flying about and the complete failure to replace any provincial governors. It is noticeable, however, that none of the men involved in the Suebic-Sarmatian war were included in the list (though there are still two unknowns). The excuse might well be that they could not be spared, but by omitting them, it was also possible to hold out the inducement of the reward of a consulship in exchange for both victory and loyalty.

This list will have appeared within a month of Nerva's accession. By that time the new regime will have felt that it was over the initial period of danger. Rome was quiet. The Senate was supportive, perhaps even excessively so. The Guard was in safe hands. No trouble was apprehended from the provinces, not that such trouble would worry the regime if all else was well. Above all, the absence of any adverse reaction from the armies in the north – and after a month they had had plenty of time to react – showed that the emperor was firmly enthroned. It was then time to rule, and to deal with the issue of the succession.

4

REACTIONS

The initial reaction of the Senate to the death of Domitian was, according to Suetonius, writing two decades or so later, joyful.[1] This was followed by a number of measures designed to efface the public memory of the dead emperor: ordering the removal of his votive shields, his statues, his very name in inscriptions, demolishing his triumphal arches and so on.[2]

This episode of cheerful destruction was followed by the infinitely less pleasant process of revenge: informers were denounced, detainees released; then more revelations and a new crop of informers until the consul Fronto complained.[3] This was stopped before the end of December, when he left office; it all lasted perhaps only a few weeks. The episode cost many informers their lives, though only a few names are known – the 'philosopher' Seras and three others[4] – but only the names are recorded, not what they did, who they denounced, or anything else. Exactly how many is 'many' remains unknown. The very vagueness of the term suggests that by Dio's time the precise number was uncertain: perhaps it was never known; perhaps it was never more than a rumour.

The sequel not long after shows clearly enough that the practice of informing had not ended, for it is clear that the emperor had advance information of the Crassus plot.[5] Indeed the practice could not end, if the government of the empire was to continue, for the alternative – an investigatory police force – did not exist. In particular the practice could not be stopped in the city of Rome, for it was there that most plots against the government originated. The unpleasant connotations of 'informing' clearly derive from those informed against: from the plotters, that is, and those connotations proceed from the assumption that plotting against the government is quite acceptable, even legitimate, while support for the government is somehow traitorous. The continuation of both the practice and the attitude indicates clearly enough that the government of Nerva was not safe from plotters, any more than that of Domitian had been.

The reactions of the non-senatorial population of Rome are unknown.[6] Indeed the non-participation of the Roman *plebs* is something quite remarkable in this whole period. The nullification of the *comitia* – and therefore of any official record of its meetings which ancient historians could consult – is one aspect. It has been suggested that meetings did take place, in the form of the more informal *contiones*,[7] but these would not be recorded in any official way. There are scarcely any indications of any meetings at all – though there is a regular notation that 'the Senate and People' have decided something or other;[8] yet this is clearly no more than a standard legal phrase, and cannot be taken to imply popular participation in the absence of other evidence: indeed most such enactments were probably imperial, rather than senatorial, initatives.

Yet the government was clearly very conscious of the need to ensure popular quiescence, perhaps all the more so since there was no official channel for popular participation in affairs. The civic mob was a frightening thing, and the need to defeat a civic riot even more daunting. Nothing would destroy an emperor's popular acceptance more quickly than the need to deploy the Praetorian Guard to put down a riot. The Guard was therefore used only very sparingly in such a role. The memory of the events in 69, when the Guard was so used,[9] usually made it unnecessary to use more than a detachment of the Guard in riot suppression. But to use it at all would imply that the government had somehow lost control of the city, and that its policies had gone seriously wrong. The memory was something that would destroy popular support for years. It was the task of the government to pursue policies that ensured no riot happened in the first place. It had to be aware of popular opinion almost as much as any modern poll-consulting party or government.

The lack of reaction both to the murder of Domitian and to the whole period of Nerva's rule therefore implies that the policies of the new regime were more or less successful in maintaining popular support, or at least acquiescence. Suetonius remarks that the murder of the emperor was greeted with indifference, which is a contrast with the Senate's joy and the troops' uneasiness.[10] The reaction of the soldiers was not an immediate threat, and the Senate's joy meant active support in the city. The people could not, however, be ignored. Indifference was a long way short of active support; they had to be persuaded to be supportive, if possible, or at least continue to be indifferent.

The indifference said by Suetonius to have been the popular reaction means it is even more difficult than usual to make a modern estimate of reactions, either to Domitian's murder, or to Nerva's rule. The evidence is patchy, anecdotal and very difficult either to collect or to interpret. The reactions of Dio Chrysostom's soldiers, for instance, cannot necessarily be taken as 'typical' of the reactions of soldiers generally. Suetonius' 'indifference' can all too easily be taken for the empire-wide reaction, whereas he was talking only of the city of Rome. Neither is therefore satisfactory. So in the usual way, in the absence of direct evidence, it is necessary to make an estimate by indirect means.

The early policies of the government in pursuit of both military and *plebs* support is indicated above all in the coins that were issued.[11] For Nerva's reign they can be closely dated. The first set are marked 'Cos II', and thus come from the period just after his accession. The next group are marked 'Cos II Desig III', and so come from the period before he entered on his third consulship in January. There are thus two dated issues in the three-and-a-half month period between his accession and 1 January. The date of the change from one to the other is not known, since we do not know the date of the announcement of the new consular list for the next year was made, after which Nerva was officially 'designated'. It has been argued in the last chapter that this took place fairly early in the new reign, and I would suggest that it was certainly published by the end of October. The first issue of coins therefore came from the first six weeks or so of the reign, between 19 September and the end of October, and give a good indication of the early measures of the regime which were designed to gather support.[12]

These early coins appeal to virtually every slogan and aspiration which any Roman could imagine. There were vague hopes, such as '*pax*' and '*iustitia*', there were assurances, such as '*salus publica*', there were anticipations, such as '*victoria*',[13] and appeals to the popular goddess '*Fortuna*'. Rather more specific to this particular regime were '*libertas publica*', which was what the Senate had celebrated when the death of Domitian was cheered; an unusual statement was that Nerva promised '*aequitas*'.

There were also coins whose legends seem to have been directed at specific groups. The *libertas* coins, in both silver and bronze, had perhaps different connotations for rich and poor. *Libertas* to the Senate meant the chance to rule, beside, or in some hopeful breasts, instead of, the emperor. To the *plebs* it may have meant something rather more basic, and certainly freedom *from* the Senate might be one reaction. But the coins inscribed *Annona August*, were directed specifically at the *plebs* – the citizens who received the corn dole in the city. It was to them also that the coin commemorating *adlocut Aug* was directed, and it is significant that this was produced only in the first set of coins, and was not repeated in later issues. The coins which proclaimed *concordia exercituum* – 'the Agreement of the Armies' – were in part no more than hope, at least at the beginning of the reign, since in the first weeks no one in Rome can have known what the reaction of the armies was, and part gratitude, once the agreement of the armies to the accession of Nerva seemed to have been achieved.

Like the *concordia exercituum* coins, most of the slogans were repeated throughout the reign, being continuing aspirations. The *adlocutio* coins were issued only at the start, in the first of Nerva's coin issues, for they commemorated a specific event. The *iustitia* coins in silver were repeated all through the reign, but the bronze versions appear only in the very first issue, as though the slogan was directed specifically at those who were using the more valuable coins. Only one other coin was issued in the first two issues alone, and so not repeated after January 97. This was a coin, only in bronze, which reminded the readers of the gift by the emperor to the citizens of 75 *denarii* as an accession present.[14] This was the *congiarium*. A similar present had been given to the armies, the donative. Much of this had in fact gone to the Praetorians, and in all cases the officers acquired a great deal more than the soldiers. But both *congiarium* and donative were bribes in all but name. The fact that the *congiarium* was commemorated on the coinage does suggest, to come back to the point at which this coin discussion began, that the Roman *plebs* exerted a good deal of pressure, even when not baying for blood, on the government.

The evidence for Roman reactions outside the Senate is thus only indirect; it is even more tenuous for reactions outside the city. Only two individuals have their reactions documented. That of Dio of Prusa on his military research journey in Moesia has already been noted.[15] The other is that of Plutarch in Greece. But, once more, it has to be deduced. He seems to have celebrated the new reign by attending the City Dionysia at Athens next spring,[16] and then beginning the work for which he is now best remembered, his *Parallel Lives* of famous Greeks and Romans, an original concept in which he built on his earlier biographer's work on the lives of the Roman emperors down to Vitellius. Neither Dio nor Plutarch could seriously affect events, even though they had contacts at the very peak of Roman society – Dio knew Nerva as a friend and was perhaps related to the Flavians in a distant way,[17] Plutarch was a friend of L. Mestrius Florus, consul in the early 70s, the man who procured Roman citizenship for him,[18] and he dedicated his main works to Q. Sosius Senecio. Both Dio and Plutarch had been moderately prominent in Flavian times, and so had to be very careful during the difficult time when Nerva tried to rule the empire. Dio, even though his sentence of exile was cancelled, and even though he was a friend of the new emperor, made no haste to return to Rome. Plutarch seems to have decided not to go to Rome again, and spent the rest of his life at home, researching and writing. But both men reflected on the situation of their times: Plutarch turned to history while Dio wrote about kingship for the modern Alexander, Trajan, with no detectable effect;[19] both began new spurts of activity after the death of Domitian, as, of course, did Tacitus; his malign influence extended even into scholars' studies.

The Dionysia at Athens was celebrated with particular magnificence in the winter of 96, the year Plutarch attended, and this, it seems, was due to the news from Rome, that Domitian was dead; so here is a reaction from a Greek city, mirroring that of the Senate at Rome. Since the Dionysia was a celebration organised by the city, which had the usual oligarchic ruling council, the pleasure has presumably the same source. Yet this is something of a surprise. Domitian had been good to Athens, and he had served a year as *archon* of the city; his father seems also to have regulated the philosophical schools of the city, an action which had helped revive them after a period of decline. These schools were a source of wealth for the city,[20] which should therefore have shown some gratitude. The fact that Athens celebrated the death of its benefactor is another indication that Domitian's unpopularity had extended a long way.

One other individual reaction, of a paradoxical sort, is recorded by both Dio Cassius and Philostratos. It is a story of Apollonios of Tyana, the wandering sophist who later inspired, for a time, a devotion very similar to that given to Christ. He is said to have known of the murder of Domitian at the time it took place, even though he was at Ephesos in Asia Minor at the time.[21] Vividly described, the vision is best seen as one of the many stories invented either by Apollonios or by his followers. But it is another sign that the story of Domitian's evil and unpopularity were wholly accepted in later days. That is, the Senate's justification for his murder became the orthodox version. And that, of course, was dangerous for emperors who overstepped the mark. It is thus richly ironic that one of Apollonios' followers was the Emperor Caracalla, and that Philostratos' life of the sage was composed at, or for the delectation of, the court of the later Severan emperors, all of whom, including Caracalla, were murdered.

There is one other source which may give some idea of popular reaction to the coup at Rome. The Senate had ordered the erasure of the dead emperor's name from public inscriptions as part of the attempt to damn his memory. As the word of this condemnation spread through the empire there was supposed to be a great chipping away of Domitian's name from public monuments. Where this was done another name was sometimes inserted, but mostly there was left simply a blank on the stone. In either case it was obvious to anyone seeing the erasure or the change that another's name had been there once, and, at least for the next century, the only obvious victim of much erasure was Domitian. The result was that Domitian was commemorated even more emphatically by the absence of his name than by its presence. As ever, the attempt to change the past was futile, even self-defeating.

Investigation of this erasure process, however, provides some surprising statistics, made possible by the collection of inscriptions published by A. Martin.[22] Martin's purpose was to study the titulature adopted by Domitian, but his collection of materials can serve this purpose also. It turns out that the Senate's order was obeyed only partially and patchily; indeed, since it appears that less than half of the examples of Domitian's name show erasure it may be better stated that the Senate's order was widely, and in some cases, wholly ignored. Of Martin's list 130 inscriptions show erasure, but well over 200 were left untouched.

The reasons for this are only conjectural, but they would include not hearing of the order, though this is perhaps unlikely since the majority of inscriptions were in cities; the attitude of the provincial governor was relevant, but the main reason for non-compliance must be unwillingness to obey. Most of the inscriptions obviously come from cities which had their own councils, who would be the men to decide on obedience, on employing the stonecutter, and on financing the measure. That they did not erase the dead emperor's name means that they had no wish to do so, perhaps because they had fonder memories of Domitian than the Senate at Rome, or, more prosaically, because they did not wish to go to the expense of the work. Studying these erasures is thus a very crude measure to estimate reactions to the killing, to be sure, but the incidence of erasure does give some indication of feelings about the dead man and about the local reactions to the news of his death.

The first problem in dealing with this evidence is its uneven distribution through the empire. Two areas, Italy and Asia-with-Cappadocia-Galatia, account for over half the total number, and Rome itself alone accounts for 15 per cent. By contrast the rest of the European provinces from Britannia to Chersonesus Taurica count fewer inscriptions than Italy alone, and a third of those are from Hispania. Little can be concluded, perhaps, from the single inscriptions from seven provinces: Corsica, Dalmatia, Chersonesus Taurica, Noricum, and each of the three Gallic provinces; there are none recorded from Sardinia and Germania Inferior.

Nevertheless it does perhaps say something that most provinces where evidence exists are apparently indecisive, in that there are very few with a clear strong majority of erasures over non-erasures, or vice versa. Taking the areas with substantial numbers first: out of seventy inscriptions in Asia, forty-four showed the emperor's name erased, twenty-six were not erased – roughly two out of three erased. Next door in Cappadocia-Galatia the numbers were twelve and four – three-quarters erased. But in two neighbouring provinces the proportions were reversed: three and six in Pontus-Bithynia (one-third erased), three and five in Lycia-Pamphylia.

In Italy, where one might suppose the Senate's instruction would be heeded most of all, only one region (*regio* I – Latium and Campania) had a significant number of inscriptions: out of twenty in that region Domitian's name was erased from only one. In the other regions of Italy the reaction was almost as clear: only two erased out of ten. And in the city of Rome itself, out of fifty inscriptions, the emperor's name was erased from only nine. The pattern for the whole of Italy is quite consistent: no more than one-fifth of Domitian's inscriptions showed erasure.

In Italy and Asia the decision on whether to go ahead with erasure was presumably one for the city's councils in each locality. In Rome, one would have assumed that the Senate was ultimately responsible, but in some other areas it seems likely that it was the responsibility of the governor. Britannia, for example, was scarcely urbanised to any extent yet, but only one example of erasure is known, out of the total of four inscriptions. At the opposite end of the empire, Egypt shows much the same pattern: nine erasures out of thirty-four. Both provinces were governed in 96 by men whose loyalty to Domitian is highly probable. In Britannia the governor Metilius Nepos had been consul in 91,[23] the year in which at least one consul (Trajan) had been rewarded for an extreme display of loyalty in the crisis of the rebellion of Antonius Saturninus; it may be assumed that the other consuls of that year were also notably loyal. In Egypt the Prefect was M. Junius Rufus, who had been in office for two years by the time of Domitian's death.[24] The post of Prefect of Egypt went to proven loyalists – as indeed did that of governor of Britannia, who had three legions under his hand – since it was absolutely necessary to ensure that the corn supply was despatched regularly and on time to Italy. The failure of supplies in Rome was the single most likely cause of a regime's unpopularity in the city. Both governors, as it happened, easily adapted themselves to the new Nervan regime, but the record of erasures in their provinces, in so far as this can be taken as an indication of the governors' attitudes, suggests they did so without enthusiasm, seeing no need to condemn their former employer's memory.

Four other areas show evidence in double figures. In both Syria and Spain the numbers of erasures outnumber non-erasures. In Syria seven out of ten inscriptions show the name erased; in Spain the three provinces counted twenty-six inscriptions between them, with sixteen erased. But there the three provinces varied: in both Tarraconensis and Baetica erasures outnumber non-erasures (eight and seven respectively, against three and three); in Lusitania only one was erased, against two non-erasures. The reasonably strong anti-Domitianic sentiment in Baetica and Tarraconensis is particularly interesting in view of the Spanish origin of several of the men who promoted the Spaniard Trajan in the disguised coup next year – as is the similar sentiment in Asia, where the evidence suggests that the local elites were also involved in that coup. The figures from Syria, though relatively small, also are a reminder that the province was perhaps a source of trouble in the coming year.

In another area, north Africa, again divided into three provinces, the totals are small – fifteen inscriptions in all – and the local sentiment apparently undecided. Six out of fifteen of the inscriptions show erasure; nine non-erasure. In Greece, to which

Macedonia may be added, there were again fifteen inscriptions, of which only four show erasures. These figures may be contrasted with the anecdotal evidence: Plutarch and Athens were pleased, but Greece as a whole was apparently not particularly vengeful.

In provinces where the army may be considered to have had a strong influence, and where urban local government was poorly developed – along the Rhine–Danube frontier – the record is equally indecisive. In eight provinces along the frontier line from Belgica to Moesia Inferior, there are only nineteen relevant inscriptions: six show erasure, thirteen non-erasure. In the case of the provinces particularly involved in the Suebic-Sarmatian war, and in the coup which put Trajan into the succession next year, Germania Superior, Pannonia and Moesia Superior, four inscriptions show erasure, nine do not. (To these might be added one erasure from Noricum and two non-erasures from Raetia.) For provinces where the army was exceedingly prominent, where Domitian was well-regarded – he had expanded Germania Superior – this is a most ambiguous response to the Senate's instruction.

It will be seen that in most provinces the number of inscriptions is so small that few definite conclusions can be drawn, though in some of the more important areas – Italy, Asia, Egypt, Spain – there are surely enough to work with. The conclusion is that there were distinct variations in provincial reactions. In Italy in particular the failure of the local communities, including Rome, to follow the lead of the Senate in its condemnation of Domitian, is overwhelming. On the other hand, three of the richest provinces, Syria, Asia and Spain, do condemn, if not quite so decisively as Italy failed to.

The overall figures, for the whole empire, suggest two reflections: that Domitian's name was by no means so universally execrated as the Senate and the senatorially-based historians implied, and that the Senate's condemnation was widely ignored; and, second, that the ambivalence of the reaction was dangerous for the new regime installed in September 96. The failure to agree decisively with the Senate meant that there was a wide basis of popular support – even if it was only potential – for any process of reaction against the new regime on behalf of a rehabilitation of Domitian and a continuation of his policies if one should be mounted. This was a danger which must have been obvious to Nerva and his advisers.

There is, of course, yet a further conclusion which might be drawn: that most people were quite indifferent to the events in Rome, as Suetonius had said, and this may be the truest interpretation of the figures. But this was not something on which the new regime could rely, in the empire any more than in the city. It was therefore necessary to set to work to earn that support. The jury was out.

5

THE EMPEROR'S WORK

Bearing in mind the brevity of the new emperor's period of rule – only sixteen and a half months – the quantity of measures he enacted is considerable. He legislated on marriage law, on several areas of tax law, on games and public entertainments, and made an initial attempt to reverse what was seen as the impoverishment and depopulation of Italy – as well as continuing the imperial work of new building and maintenance. This is a lot of legislation. The question immediately arises, therefore, as to the origins of, and reasons for, these acts. Some of them are obviously reactions to Domitian's rule: removing abuses, rectifying wrongs. Others are simply measures which were already in train when Domitian died, and which Nerva's government saw through to completion. The rapidity with which some were enacted suggests that both of these motivations were present; the real problem is to decide which measures were Nerva's own – if any.

It is not always easy to distinguish these differing origins, particularly when some of them were more or less ascribed to Trajan after Nerva's death. But those reforms which are known to have been undertaken early in the reign must be reforms of abuses which were already known and disapproved of under Domitian. The reform may have been begun by Domitian, but if it was instituted under Nerva, Nerva clearly deserves the credit. If a measure was not a reform, yet was enacted early in the new reign, it is all the more likely that the preparatory work had been done by or under Domitian.

It is, however, not always easy to sort out motivations. Two examples may provide cautionary notices. Nerva enacted two measures of social policy. He is said to have forbidden the practice of castration, and he forbade uncle–niece marriages.[1] On investigation, however, it turns out that the first of these had already been enacted by Domitian.[2] Presumably, as with so many such laws, it had been ignored – and Domitian certainly continued to employ eunuchs – and it continued to be ignored, for the lack of any enforcement machinery conflicted with demand for the product. In the case of the prohibition of uncle–niece marriage, this may be a posthumous slap at Domitian, who was rumoured to have had an affair with his own niece, Julia, the daughter of his brother Titus, and had been said to have intended to marry her.[3] It may also have had other origins, of which we know nothing.

The evidence for Nerva's early measures comes from the coins above all. In addition to the claims and assurances expressed by vague terms such as *Fortuna* and *Iustitia*, one of the early coins promised '*Fisci Judaici Calumnia Sublata*', 'relief from abuses of the Jewish tax'.[4] This appeared in the first issues, and was repeated in the second and third, and so it was a measure which was proclaimed from September 96 for the next twelve months. It was a tax imposed on Jews by Vespasian after the revolt of 66–73 [5] at a rate of two *denarii* per Jew, the money to go to the rebuilding of the Temple of Jupiter Capitolinus which had been burned down during the civil war. It had clearly been sub-ject to abuse by tax collectors, as the reform indicates. (In addition, it may be pointed out that the Capitoline temple's rebuilding had been completed.) Nerva's measure was not a relief for the Jews, for the tax was not cancelled, but a relief for those who had been made to pay the tax wrongly – that is, those who were identified as Jews by tax collectors, but who were not. Dio Cassius comments that informers accusing people of 'adopting the Jewish way of life' were no longer to be tolerated,[6] and this may be connected with the problem of the tax. These would be non-Jews. Alternatively it may be that the vic-tims were Jews by origin who no longer practised their religion.[7] Either way it seems that some who should not pay were being compelled to, and Nerva was now extending his protection to a specific group of taxpayers whose complaints had been loud enough to reach the imperial ears. It has to be said that it seems unlikely that oppressed Jews would succeed in so impressing a Roman senator that he would make it one of his first actions, on unexpectedly becoming emperor, to put the abuses right. A group of Romans, on the other hand, would be much better placed to have that effect. That the reform was undertaken as soon as Nerva became emperor does show that it had been a problem in Domitian's reign, which Domitian had done nothing about, and that Nerva identified it as a cause worth dealing with; it was clearly identified by him as an abuse worth recti-fying. It may also be connected with the general reaction against informers which char-acterised the early weeks of Nerva's rule, and perhaps with a wish by Nerva to distance himself from the Flavian dynasty, one of whose major achievements had been the reconquest of Judaea.

A second tax that Nerva altered was the inheritance tax originally imposed on citi-zens by Augustus. The rate was 5 per cent, and it had always been particularly unpop-ular.[8] Nerva altered the conditions of the tax so that even more legatees were exempted from payment than had been the case before. Some groups had already had the tax remitted, and now inheritances from mothers or from fathers to children (as opposed to adult offspring) were also remitted.[9] It is clear that this tax was an ideal way for emperors to gain easy popularity by extending exemptions without seriously eroding the tax income: Augustus had done so almost as soon as he imposed it, and Trajan exempted some more people.[10]

On a more general point of taxation policy, Nerva transferred disputes between tax-payers and the *fiscus* from judgement by a procurator to one by a praetor. The implica-tion, of course, is that the procurators had favoured the *fiscus*, whereas a praetor's court was more likely to be just, or perhaps to be more responsive to popular opinion and pressure, and so favour the taxpayer. Trajan later made further changes to the system, for which he earned Pliny's praise. But Pliny carefully did not mention that the main change – the use of the praetor's court – was an innovation of Trajan's prede-cessor; a notice in the *Digest* reveals the truth.[11]

Nerva was generous with the cash reserves inherited from Domitian, whose financial stewardship is seen to have been cautious and prudent, despite the costs of much building in the city and of the frequent wars.[12] The reforms of the Jewish tax and the inheritance tax, and the less onerous and biased judgement system, will have reduced the expected income to the treasury – and Nerva reduced the tribute to be collected from the provinces as well – though the income reduction was perhaps not by very much in total and would not take effect for some time. He did not cancel the *aurum coronarium*, the 'gifts' of golden crowns from local communities, which was in effect an accession tax. The reductions in taxation were counteracted by these expected receipts, and, at least in the short term, by the senatorial decision to melt down Domitian's statues made of precious metals, and to turn the resulting metals over to the mint for coining. Nerva also cleared out some of the furnishings, both metal and furniture, from the palace and sold them.[13] Again the treasury would receive an immediate benefit, but it was a measure which could not be repeated.

As Dio says, this last measure may have been because Nerva ran short of cash, but it was a measure which he might well have undertaken anyway. Frugality appears to have been one of his character traits.[14] This could well have harmed him in popular estimation, which expected generosity, but, perhaps at the same time, he rescinded Domitian's banishment of pantomime actors.[15] And during 97 he issued a coin with the legend '*Neptuno Circenses Instituit*',[16] referring to a set of games which probably took place in the Circus Maximus. This was presumably a new celebration. Neptune was a god who had had no major celebration in the city until then; the *Neptunalia* was in late July,[17] in the midst of the Games of Caesar's Victory; boosting them may have been Nerva's personal contribution. This is the only sign of his interest in either Neptune or the sea, but Neptune had connections. As a sea-god Neptune connected the emperor with victory, with Julius Caesar, with supplications for safety at sea and with his professed concern – as shown on other coins – for the corn supply; Neptune was also a god of inland waters, and Nerva's government did work on repairing the Roman water supply. This collection of subjects dealt with by one single measure would appeal to any politician. The new games were thus a neat, economical gesture.

Adjustment to the games was perhaps another area in which Nerva could claim to have dealt with something which had been neglected by Domitian, and the return of the mimes was a clear concession to popular wishes. The mimes were regarded with great suspicion by Roman governments, presumably because of the scope they provided for satire at the government's expense; they were banished again by Trajan,[18] who had no need to court popular approval – and perhaps he had a thinner skin than Nerva. As a survivor of the reigns of Caligula and Nero, Nerva had surely seen it all before. In the same set of coins another issue commemorated the relief afforded to local Italian communities by cancelling their obligation to fund the imperial post.[19] This appears to have been a heavy burden,[20] and one which will have borne unequally on communities along the main arterial roads. By relieving them, Nerva could justify his boast that he would observe and promote *aequitas* and *iustitia*.

The cost of his various measures was high. The *congiarium* and the donative to the army will have drastically reduced the quantity of ready cash in the treasury – and this may well be another reason for the large number of new coin issues produced. Apart from these large one-off payments, there was also a continuing need for regular expenditure on everyday matters. This would include the building work which Domitian had begun but which had not yet been completed. The palace had, it seems, been finished within the last year or so of Domitian's reign – a coin depicts it[21] – and Nerva was able to open it to the public view, with the nonsensical new name of *aedes publicae* – the People's House.[22] No doubt this opening referred to a few rooms not previously available, for there were large areas of the palace which were already open to the public. The palace was, after all, above all else an administrative centre, and the offices in it had to be available to callers; the great audience halls and banqueting rooms were similarly accessible; other rooms, offices and servants' quarters, would scarcely be worth viewing; no doubt the emperor's private rooms were still inaccessible.

Several other buildings begun by Domitian were still in process of completion, and work on them was necessarily continued. Nerva only seems to have seen one completed during his reign: the Forum Transitorium, placed between, and connecting, the Forum Pacis of Vespasian and the Fora Augusti and Iulii. This new building thus carried a considerable symbolic load, and its alternative name, Forum Nervae, added to that symbolism.[23] It should have been called after Domitian, but this was not possible now.

Other Domitianic building commencements took more work and were only completed during Trajan's reign. It follows that work on them continued throughout Nerva's time. The Circus Maximus had been damaged by fires in 64 and again in Domitian's reign, and it was only completely restored and repaired under Trajan; it was in use in Domitian's and Nerva's reigns, so the repairs will have continued under the latter. Next door to his own new forum, which became Nerva's, Domitian had begun the reconstruction of the Forum Iulii, and of the Temple of Venus Genetrix, which it contained; both of these were finished only in 113. Rather more startling, the great Forum of Trajan was originally begun under Domitian. No doubt the work on the Forum Iulii was part of this new work, but it is clear that the whole plan was originally put into motion by Domitian; Nerva's reign no doubt also saw some progress on it. Another Trajanic building, the huge Baths of Trajan, had originally been begun by Titus, and some work appears to have been done there under Domitian; whether it continued for long is not clear; if it was still a-building in 96, it will also have continued under Nerva. Nerva himself did not reign for long enough to begin anything new, nor is it even known if he wished to do so. Perhaps he was content to have Domitian's work in the Forum Transitorium attributed to him.[24]

Some caution, however, is also necessary in all this. Much of the evidence for Domitianic work on these buildings is in the form of dated bricks used in the work; these were certainly manufactured in Domitian's reign, but they were not, of course, necessarily used then; they could well have been available for use years after being made, so as evidence they are clearly not definitive. They were, however, made in his reign, and so no doubt the intention was to use them then. It is clear, despite these ambiguities, that Domitian's building programme continued through to the end of his reign and beyond, through Nerva's and into Trajan's reign.

It is also clear that Nerva's reign saw considerable road-building work continuing in

Italy and the provinces, where the evidence consists of milestones bearing his name. These have been found in Spain, Germania Superior, Pannonia and Asia Minor, dated to Nerva's reign,[25] and there are several from early in Trajan's reign which may well commemorate work which was begun earlier.[26] In Italy all three emperors are named in connection with work on the Via Appia, connecting Rome and Campania.[27] There was also considerable work done on at least two of the aqueducts watering Rome, the Anio Novus and the Aqua Marcia.[28]

This all cost money, and after less than a year, the pinch was felt, or at least some alarm was voiced.[29] The new emperor, in accordance with his stated intention to rule along with the Senate, handed the problem over; this was a clever move, forcing senators to confront the real problems of imperial finance. A commission of five senators was set up to investigate and recommend retrenchments and economies.[30] Two of the members are known, and were eminent senators: Sex. Julius Frontinus and T. Vestricius Spurinna, both of them on the consular list for the next year.[31] L. Verginius Rufus refused nomination, having broken his thigh in a fall;[32] the other three members are not known. The involvement of Verginius Rufus provides a rough date: he had his fall at the end of his consulship, and he died during Tacitus' consulship (which he held in November and December), so the offer of membership was made and refused between March and October.[33] The commission was set up therefore sometime in mid-97, after Nerva had been emperor for between six and nine months.

The commission reported in the same year, before Nerva died (in January 98); how thorough it had been is difficult to say. The timing suggests it was no more than a public relations exercise. Its recommendations might be thought to corroborate that view. The abolition of 'many' sacrifices, horse-races and public spectacles was suggested, but none of these would seriously change the overall problem of the supposed shortage of cash.[34] The actual problem was perhaps no more than a publicity stunt, to pacify some restless senators, worried at apparent extravagance. One member of the commission, Julius Frontinus, was thus simultaneously suggesting economies, and, as the newly appointed *curator aquarum*, recommending increased spending on two of the Roman aqueducts. It may well have been during this time, while the commission was investigating, that an odd notice in the 'Chronographer of 354' applies, that Nerva handed out 62½ *denarii funeraticium plebi urbanae instituit*, which appears to have been a grant of assistance to Romans towards funeral expenses, including the provision of a memorial. It seems most unlikely that this was a handout of cash, as Syme[35] assumed; it was more likely a provision which had to be applied for, like a modern 'death grant'.

Some of these measures are unclear, both in meaning and effect, but the cost to the treasury of Nerva's various spending initiatives and obligations was surely very great, and the economy commission's recommendations were clearly mere palliatives. Yet Trajan could distribute a donative to the troops and a *congiarium* to the citizens in 99 without difficulty.[36] One might suspect that Nerva and the Senate were colluding to find an excuse to stop handing out cash, by producing the scare-story of the need for economies.

It was also quite possible to find cash to pay for repairs to the damage caused by yet another flood by the River Tiber.[37] New granaries – *horrea Nervae*[38] – were built or acquired for the better storage of grain for the public corn supply; since both Vespasian and Domitian had done the same,[39] this might be seen as a continuing programme of improving or replacing old storage facilities. Indeed one wonders if this was actually under imperial government control; the naming of storehouses after emperors may not in fact mean that they were responsible for having them built, only that that particular piece of building was completed in their reign. Nerva celebrated his care for this on coins issued in 96 and 97, marked *Annona Aug*, and on another later in 97 with the legend *Plebei Urbanae Frumento Constituto*,[40] though whether this can be interpreted as going so far as reforming the administration of the corn dole seems unlikely – the building of new storehouses would probably be sufficient excuse for such a coin issue.

The legend *Tutela Italiae* appears on one coin issued in the first half of 97. The picture shows Nerva seated on the curule chair of a Roman magistrate, extending his hand to a woman – Italia – with two children, a boy and and a girl, standing between them.[41] The uncertain legitimacy of this coin does not detract from its appropriateness. Describing Nerva as the 'protector' or 'guardian' of Italy or Italians, is, for once, not a mere slogan, but a reminder of several measures which were taken in his principate for the benefit of Italians specifically.

One of these measures is perhaps not aimed at Italy in particular, but it certainly applies there. A change was made to the law on legacies, so that cities were able to inherit more easily from individual citizens.[42] This practice had not been uncommon earlier, and the law was that immediate family members should receive a minimum of a quarter of the deceased's legacy.[43] The new measure was no doubt enacted in response to a public wish, though it does not seem very likely that the number of such legacies was seriously increased.[44] More directly affecting Italy, indeed directed particularly at it, was a new *lex agraria*, designed to promote the settlement of poor Romans on farms. A fund of 60 million *sesterces* was set up by which land was to be purchased and then distributed to needy Romans. This is the last law known to have been enacted by the *comitia*. The momentary revival of this moribund assembly may have been another publicity stunt; it was scarcely a revival of the institution. Another senatorial commission was put in charge of the operation, both to purchase the land and to distribute it.[45]

This fund might be seen as yet another extravagance, or perhaps as yet more evidence that Domitian had left a bulging treasury for his successor to spend. In fact, it is most unlikely that the money came out of the treasury as a lump sum – any more than would the funeral grant. This sort of operation would take several years to complete. The land had to be found, had to be bought, surveyed, and subdivided into plots. The candidates had to apply and be interviewed. To purchase all the land at once would simply drive the price up and so reduce the impact intended by reducing the available land for distribution. It must therefore be assumed that the operation was intended to take some years, with the round sum stated in the act to be drawn on from the treasury as required.

Alternatively, it may only be a notional figure. One interpretation is that the land to be allotted to settlers was in fact *ager publicus*, which was already available and unoccupied – in fact, it has also been read the other way, that because some *ager publicus* was unoccupied the scheme was set up.[46] Certain indications exist which count against these interpretations. First, the notices about the measure that we have speak of both 'purchase' and 'distribution' by the commission, and the only possible item which had to be purchased is the land. (The settlers may have been provided with tools and a hut to live in when they started out, but it seems unlikely that these would have cost 60 million *sesterces*.) If there really was unoccupied *ager publicus*, it is doubtful that it would have been of much agricultural use, since the good land was surely already in use. To provide the settlers with poor land would simply defeat the object of the scheme, which was partly to move people out of Rome, partly to remove them from the ranks of the poor, and partly to put them to useful work; putting them on poor land would keep them poor, and no doubt they would soon remigrate to the city. If any *ager publicus* was suitable and available it would surely be included in the land to be alloted; but it has to be assumed that most of the land would need to be purchased.

The amount of money allocated to the problem, 60 million *sesterces*, sounds a lot – which, of course, it was – but in terms of government resources, it was small. It has been calculated that a quarter of century earlier, Vespasian had an annual tax revenue of 1,200 million *sesterces*, and this had probably increased since.[47] The sum allocated for the land scheme was thus less than 5 per cent of the annual revenue, and if it was to be spent over a number of years, the burden on the treasury was probably no more than 1 per cent of annual revenue. The sum was also only roughly one-third more than the cost of the *congiarium* paid to all citizens on Nerva's accession.[48] The emperor was not being quite as generous over funding the land allocation as it seemed.

The price of land in Italy (and I am assuming that this scheme applied to Italy, not the provinces),[49] has been calculated at between 500 and 1,000 *sesterces* per *iugerum*,[50] though in some areas, such as Apulia, land was cheaper than in other parts of the peninsula. These figures, of course, are not based on extensive records. But, supposing a cost of 500 *sesterces* per *iugerum*, the lowest of the range the allotted funds would buy 120,000 *iugera* (which is something over 80,000 acres or 32,000 hectares), assuming that the whole sum was used to buy land. If the cost of land was 1,000 *sesterces*, these numbers must of course be halved. If even the larger area of land was all allocated to settlers, it would hardly affect the population of Rome at all seriously. Suppose each settler took an allotment of 10 *iugera* (only 6 or 7 acres), no more than 12,000 men would be moved. It seems unlikely that anyone could be persuaded to move from Rome on the promise of 6 or 7 acres of land: 2,000–3,000 settlers at the most, therefore, would be affected by this scheme. If Rome really had a population of 1 million, the scheme would move a maximum of 1.2 per cent of that population out of the city, and more likely less than a quarter of that.

It was, nevertheless, a gesture which will have helped some Romans to a better life. It was also a measure in the full tradition of the Roman state and Senate. Such land settlement schemes had been the very stuff of earlier Roman history, and had been the main method by which Republican Rome had fastened its grip on the Italian peninsula. (Narnia, from which Nerva's ancestors had come, was one of these colonies, founded four centuries earlier.) For Nerva to revive this practice and to put senators in charge of it was fully in keeping with his proclaimed policies of *Roma Renascens* and senatorial partnership. References to the revered *divus Augustus* on his coins, the greatest maker of such settlements in Roman history, were in a similar vein.

The success or otherwise of this resettlement scheme is not known, nor whether it continued beyond Nerva's death, though it certainly got started: one of Pliny's letters refers to Q. Corellius Rufus, another old senator (consul in Vespasian's reign) as one of the commissioners, who had chosen a minor intellectual and former governor of the Graian Alps province, the equestrian Ti. Claudius Pollio, as one of his assistants.[51] It might be supposed that, given that the scheme would take some years to run, its fund allocation might well fail to materialise later – or, of course, there may have been few or no volunteers to change the life of a poor man in Rome for that of a slightly less poor man in the countryside.

The original Roman policy during the Republic and to some degree in Augustus' time had been to use these land allocations to establish *coloniae*, islands of Roman citizens in conquered territory, where they would be landowners and so the local rulers. Nerva's reign saw at least one of these cities, Scolacium in Bruttium, revived by direct government action of some sort. The colony had been originally founded by C. Gracchus two centuries earlier, and renamed at that time Minervia. Now it was renamed again, as Colonia Minervia Nervia Aug. Scolacium, in commemoration of whatever assistance Nerva had provided.[52] It seems possible that this was one of the sources of land for the commissioners of the *lex agraria*, though there is no evidence for this. The other great social measure which was developed in Nerva's reign especially to assist Italy was the *alimenta*.[53] This was a set of schemes to subsidise families with children by providing them with cash handouts from funds developed out of mortgaged lands and the treasury. They were thus designed to encourage procreation on the perception that the population of Italy was declining. They were set up to be separate from the normal government funding, presumably because they would then have to compete with other needs – wars and donatives particularly – which would later be seen as more immediate, in a situation where the tax product to the treasury was largely inflexible. So the *alimenta* were provided by means of interest derived from land. This gave an indication to the administrators of the expected income each year – the rate seems to have been roughly 5 per cent. Each local scheme was funded on the basis of an anticipated number of children to be subsidised.

There were other and earlier examples of such charities, based on private bequests, such as the one set up by Pliny for the city of Comum,[54] and it has been argued that Domitian had already set up the government *alimenta* before he died.[55] The evidence for this is particularly tenuous, and the idea cannot be accepted. Nevertheless, the major schemes were certainly based on considerable experience with other, private and local schemes which had existed in the past.[56] They also fit in with the series of government measures designed to provide assistance for Italian communities who were widely thought to be going through bad times. Domitian's edict requiring wheat to be grown instead of vines,[57] and Nerva's own *lex agraria* were both part of this sequence.

The *alimenta* are not recorded in any inscription until three years into Trajan's reign,[58] and not on his coins until 103.[59] But a long inscription on bronze from the city of Veleia in Liguria shows that the scheme there – it was all locally based – was started by 98.[60] It seems therefore that the initial government suggestion, if that was what began the process, will have come a year or so before that local beginning. The scheme required local landowners to volunteer to become involved, and this clearly took some time to arrange; the whole scheme took nearly a decade to set up and get going at Veleia.[61] Another is known in some detail from Ligures Baebiani in Samnium, where it began in 101.[62] On the basis of these datings, and on the attribution recorded by a fourth-century author,[63] credit for originating the government scheme is generally now awarded to Nerva rather than to Trajan. In actual fact it seems more likely that he took up the basic idea and gave it a push in a direction which applied to the whole of Italy. Trajan took credit for it on his coin of 103, by which time it had clearly achieved sufficient momentum to be reckoned successful, and so was worth claiming credit for; Nerva would have done so if he had lived long enough.[64]

The scheme was not compulsory, and relied on local interest and enthusiasm. At Veleia there are traces of an earlier, private scheme which was perhaps overtaken by the larger government scheme: several of the men involved in the private scheme can be found involved in the latter.[65] (In fact, it may be that Veleia, because the government scheme came along just at the time when the private scheme was being organised, was one of the earliest communities to benefit.) It is also noticeable that of the seven private schemes known from Italian towns, only one of those towns has produced a record of being involved in the government scheme as well.[66] It may thus be that the government scheme was designed mainly for towns which had not acquired a private scheme already.

The towns which are known to have adopted *alimenta* are those where inscriptions have survived recording the fact. There were undoubtedly others, but Italy is a well-researched field epigraphically, and it is likely that most participating communities are known and that their geographical distribution, as shown by present knowledge, is accurate. They are heavily concentrated in central and southern inland Italy.[67] A total of fifty participating towns and cities can be listed.[68] Only two of the old Greek cities of the south, Neapolis and Locri, used the scheme, and only three places in the northern *regiones* IX and X (Industria, Acelum and Brixia) did so. The rest are overwhelmingly small towns in the hills of the spine of Italy, mostly well away from both Rome and the coast, and so dependent largely on their own resources. Only six were on the coast, and only three were within 20 kilometres of Rome. This distribution might be a result of the discovery of the inscriptions which record the participation of the towns in one way or another; it might be a product of fashion, of a general feeling amongst these towns at this time that being part of the *alimenta* scheme was the done thing. The Emperor Nerva encouraged Pliny and his peers to give generously to local communities,[69] and what an emperor suggested was very likely to become, for the moment at least, the thing to do. More reasonably, this distribution of participants may well be a reflection of a real crisis in these places and in this area. It will not do to underrate contemporary perceptions of the social and economic condition of central and southern Italy.[70] It is clear that the governments of Domitian, Nerva and Trajan were seriously concerned and searching for ways to provide policies that would correct the situation.

At the same time it has to be pointed out that both Domitian and Trajan recruited new legions, and this was always done in Italy. Domitian raised I *Minervia* in 83, and Trajan raised II *Traiana* and XXX *Ulpia*, probably in 104.[71] Even accepting that both were formed around cadres transferred from existing legions, and even if, as has been suggested, some of the recruits came from Spain,[72] the majority of the men were still recruited in Italy. If this is so, it simultaneously implies that the population problem was not so serious as contemporaries thought it, but that their perception would be that the problem was being aggravated by the recruitment. The replacements for casualties and discharges came generally not from Italy but from the provinces.[73] The demand on the Italian population was thus intermittent, not continuous, but these demands came approximately a generation apart.

The success or otherwise of these various measures is problematic. The central government participation in *alimenta* continued for over a century,[74] but disappeared during the economic and political disasters of the third century.[75] On the whole, since the purpose was to encourage the production and rearing of children, it is probable that they had some effect. It was certainly possible for Marcus Aurelius to raise two more new legions in Italy in the 160s,[76] and for Septimius Severus to recruit three more there a generation later.[77] So at both times there was no real shortage of young men. But government schemes which run against the social grain are in the end doomed to failure, and it seems clear that the basic problem in the reduction of population in the Italian towns was a voluntary restriction on procreation. The disappearance of the *alimenta* after the time of the Severi might be the result of the problems which the empire faced during the third century, as the chronology of inscriptions suggests (though the production of inscriptions faded away just at that time); but it may also be the result of the unwillingness of the population of Italy to co-operate, and the end of the *alimenta* would be due to the final realisation by the government that its policy was futile.

On a wider imperial scale, Nerva's reign was too short for him to have much of an effect on conditions in the provinces. The records of road building are perhaps not to be seen as the result of central government initiative, even though the costs must have been borne out of taxation, but more the continuing process of repair and reconstruction always necessary for buildings, and so organised locally. He is said to have reduced the tribute paid by the provinces,[78] but no figures are given; he accepted the *aurum coronarium*, the golden crowns given by communities at the accession of a new emperor, a conclusion arrived at because, since we are told that Trajan refused another instalment of this voluntary tax on his own accession early in 98[79] it was only because two such taxes in two years was too much to expect local communities to have to pay.

In other respects, however, Nerva's works and appointments show his Italian and Roman experience and background. This was manifested in the attention he paid to

Italy in the *alimenta* programme, and in the *lex agraria*; it also followed in part from his professed willingness to work with the Senate, which was overwhelmingly Roman and Italian in composition. His colleagues in the consulship were not exclusively Italian, but the majority of them were either from Italy, or from a relatively small group of western provinces, above all Baetica and Narbonensis. The number of senators from the eastern and African provinces was still small, but they had been appearing in the consular lists with some frequency in the past decade – five between 90 and 94[80] – and it was thoughtless of Nerva to ignore them in his own lists. By contrast the lists for 97 and 98 both included two men each from Narbonensis and Spain, and possibly more.[81]

Nerva, as emperor, had the power of veto over a whole range of posts in Rome and in the provinces. It is not altogether clear how active any emperor was in the selection of men to fill these posts. In many cases it almost looks as though they were filled by rote. In the case of consuls, however, the emperor clearly had a large say, as he also had in the cases of the more important government governorships. There was also a series of important posts in Rome. The command of the Praetorian Guard has already been noted, where Nerva appointed Casperius Aelianus to replace Norbanus and Petronius. It also seems likely, though proof does not exist, that he appointed a new Prefect of the City, in the person of T. Aurelius Fulvus.[82] These men had command of the main armed forces in the city; Norbanus, Petronius and Aurelius' predecessor had failed in their duty to protect one emperor; they were necessarily replaced. In one other Roman post, *curator aquarum*, Nerva is known to have appointed Sex. Julius Frontinus in the place of M'. Acilius Aviola, who had held the post for two decades. Frontinus' comments in his handbook on the water supply suggests the Aviola had not been as efficient as he should have been[83] – though this is what a new apointee would say.

Nerva had also, of course, appointed senators to such bodies as the economy commission and the agrarian settlement commission, though clearly he will have consulted the Senate on these. However it was done the choices were hardly well made, since of the four men we know, two were dead before the end of 97 – Verginius Rufus and Corellius Rufus. Other appointments cannot be precisely located in time. Some were certainly occupied by men from Domitian's reign right through to Trajan's.[84]

The occupants of the provincial governorships are a similar mixture of holdovers and a few identifiable new appointments. The reign is too brief and too confused to be certain of more than a few of Nerva's selections. It can be assumed that men who took up their posts in 96 had been appointed by or under Domitian, since they will have travelled to their posts during the year and so were appointed early on in the year. The single exception is Trajan, who was appointed in October 96 to Germania Superior;[85] from October 97 it is necessary to assume that appointments were made at least partly by Trajan, or under his distant influence and with his approval. This must also be the case, all the more so, for those who took up their appointments in 98. Since appointments were made fairly early in the year, to allow men to prepare and to travel to their posts, any man who can be seen to have taken up a governor's post during the first nine months of 97 was Nerva's choice. Except, of course, that in some cases, such as

Asia and Africa, the emperor had only a very limited choice, since those posts went by rotation to certain senators, and their entitlement could be predicted. Then there is the added problem, basic to the whole discussion, that the names and dates of most governors are either uncertain or totally unknown.[86]

In these circumstances it is not possible to draw any too-definite conclusions from the limited information we have, though there are some interesting pointers. The successor to Trajan in Germania Superior in late 97 was L. Julius Servianus, consul in 90 (and to be consul again in 102), a safe pair of hands in a delicate province; he will have been appointed with the active consent of Trajan himself, or even at his insistence.[87] The new governor of Asia is not known, though he will have been one of the men who had been consul in 83 or 84, according to the normal practice.[88] One of the consuls of that time, Marius Priscus, went to Africa as governor. His earlier career is not known, but he scarcely enhanced the reputation of the Senate by exploiting his position, and the uncertain authority of Senate and Princeps, in a notoriously rapacious manner. He was so greedy and violent that even the Senate was eventually constrained to find him guilty of oppression.[89] His behaviour was as good an argument for the principate as could be found in any province. Nor was that of the governor of Baetica, Caecilius Classicus, who seems to have been even worse, and who was also eventually condemned by the Senate, though he died before trial. His gains were confiscated.[90] The governor of another 'senatorial' province does not seem to have behaved in that way. Senecio Memmius Afer had governed Aquitania in 94–95 and went to Sicily in 97–98, then on to be consul in 99; he was a relative of Silius Italicus and Caesius Fronto. He seems to have had a spotless record, or at least he was not prosecuted.[91]

The only other governor who is known to have been appointed under Nerva – and here the emperor had more latitude – was Q. Sosius Senecio in Gallia Belgica. This was an important position, in particular since the administrative centre of Augusta Trevirorum housed the offices and treasury of the procurator for both German provinces as well as Belgica, an arrangement set up by Domitian no doubt to separate the legions, the governors and the cash.[92] Senecio went on to be consul in 99;[93] the fact that he was a neighbour of Trajan's province during the events of the autumn of 97 suggests that his promotion to the consulship was in part due to his behaviour in that crisis. He was scarcely, in that case, a Nervan loyalist.

In fact, none of these men deserves such a description. Nerva did not, of course, have time to develop a specific group of friends, a party, though his support in the Senate was extensive. It is noticeable, however, that, where particular attitudes can be discerned, as in the cases of Marius Priscus, Caecilius Classicus and Sosius Senecio, nothing indicates any gratitude on their part towards the old emperor. Indeed the behaviour of the first two was clearly damaging, and that of the third close to seditious.

It may be that one other gubernatorial appointment can be discovered. A fragment of a military diploma dating from 97 carries the name Fronto as governor of, probably, Moesia Inferior, or it may possibly be Thrace.[94] But exactly who this Fronto is, is not clear. It has been assumed to be Ti. Catius Caesius Fronto, the consul of late 96 and son of Silius Italicus, who had gone on to govern a province directly after leaving his consulship.[95] On the other hand, posting that particular man, a lawyer, a man with minimal military experience, and deeply involved in the death of Domitian, to a military province just at that time, when trouble from Dacia might be apprehended, and when there was resentment among the soldiers at Domitian's death, in which Caesius Fronto had been involved, cannot be described as an appointment which would be sensible, appropriate or diplomatic. Moesia Inferior was a province which needed a competent military man, particularly when a war was being fought in Pannonia. L. Julius Marinus is attested as governor in January 97,[96] so 'Fronto' took over in the summer of that year. This is a remarkably quick appointment, if it was Caesius Fronto. Earlier governors had waited several years to reach that province after holding the consulship – Sex. Octavius Fronto, consul in 86, was governor in 92;[97] when he took up the appointment is not known, though since the tenure was two or three years, he was probably appointed about 89 or 90, three or four years after his consulship; Marinus was consul in about 93, and reached Moesia perhaps in 95. One would have expected the governor who took over in summer 97 to have been consul at least two or three years earlier.

There is an available candidate. C. Caristanius Fronto, consul in 90, had had military experience as the commander of an auxiliary *ala* and as the legate of *legio* IX *Hispana* in Britannia under Julius Agricola in the early 80s, and administrative experience as governor of Pontus-Bithynia and Lycia-Pamphylia.[98] By 97 he was getting on in years – his earliest known post was in the civil war, so he was in his fifties or sixties – but he was safe, competent, a Flavian loyalist like Servianus and Trajan, a contemporary of Nerva himself – and he was a much more suitable man for Moesia Inferior than Caesius Fronto. The appointment of a man in his sixties might also reassure his northern neighbour Decebalus of the Dacians, who would surely be nervous by now, with a Roman army invading Bohemia and the emperor he had made a diplomatic agreement with dead, in part by his successor's contriving. However, the uncertainties of both the name and the province preclude a clear conclusion to the matter.

There is one other notice of Nerva's activity in the provinces that deserves mention. The imperial policy in Britannia, after the victorious but essentially indecisive result of the campaigns of C. Julius Agricola in 77–84, was to consolidate. The northern frontier had been gradually withdrawn from the edge of the Scottish Highlands to southern Scotland (and eventually to the Tyne–Solway line, the line of the later Hadrian's Wall), and in the 90s one legion was permanently withdrawn from the province.[99] By the 90s, also, there was a considerable number of soldiers in the remaining legions who were due for discharge at the end of their service. There had been heavy recruitment in and after the civil war of 69–70, to bring the army up to strength after the heavy casualties of those years, and these men were now completing their time. In Britannia the two former legionary centres of Lindum and Glevum, whence the legions had been removed, were selected for settlement, and they were constituted as *coloniae*.

Lindum Colonia was founded in Domitian's reign and was originally called after that emperor, though his name was dropped after his killing and *damnatio*.[100] Glevum Colonia was called (like Scolacium in Bruttium) Nervia, a name it kept,[101] but how much Nerva was actually responsible for Glevum's foundation is less than obvious.

The process of founding a *colonia* was not an easy or a quick matter. The fact that two *coloniae* were founded in close succession in a single province implies an overall imperial policy, even a plan, and it would seem reasonable to see Domitian's government as responsible for originating that policy – after all, the first of the *coloniae* was certainly constituted in his reign – and Nerva is thus best seen, once more, as the legatee and beneficiary of his predecessor. So his name attached to Glevum only dates the final act, not the policy nor the work which preceded the founding.

There were no doubt other projects in train during Nerva's short reign which only bore fruit under his successor, just as the building activity in Rome, or the organisation of the *alimenta* in Italy, took years of work to accomplish. The amount any single emperor could achieve, even in a lengthy reign such as that of Domitian or Trajan, was, in a huge state such as the Roman empire, very strictly limited. The two British *coloniae*, for example, are clearly in the line of imperial policy which had settled time-expired soldiers in new cities, though that policy was slowly changing. Scolacium, an old colony reinforced, shows one aspect of the new policy, while another was the practice of awarding colony status to existing urban settlements. Nerva's reign, in other words, showed no change in this area.

Another of these ongoing projects was the war which had begun during Domitian's last month or so. We know nothing in detail about the events of this war, except that, given its contemporary name of Suebic-Sarmatian war, and the accumulation of force in Pannonia and Moesia Superior, the war was in all probability being waged in the enemy's territory. Indeed if it had involved an invasion of the empire it is very probable that a mention would have been made of it. Such an event would be particularly useful as a stick to beat an opponent with in the fast-moving political developments at Rome. Nerva issued a gold coin claiming *Victoria Aug.* as one of his first group in the month or so after his accession,[102] but it was not repeated in the second issue later in the year in November–December. If the coin is not simply the articulation of a hope – or a lie – it commemorated some sort of military achievement, but the war was still unfinished. By November the army will have probably gone into winter quarters. Another *Victoria* coin was issued in the first group in 97,[103] no doubt as a reminder of the previous year's work. Again it was not repeated in the issues of September of that year, though another came out in the brief issues of early 98,[104] before Nerva's death. These issues would seem to be the normal unspecific slogans put out by emperors on a regular basis, without reference to any particular victory in the field. But then in October 97 a despatch arrived at Rome claiming victory, this time on the word of the commanding general rather than the hopes or claims of the emperor,[105] though it was not decisive, and looks very much like a political claim rather than a solid achievement. Trajan still had to remain on the Danube frontier well into 99 before he could afford to go to Rome.[106] Throughout his reign Nerva's army was fighting Domitian's war.

6

THE SUCCESSION PROBLEM

The second thought in many minds, particularly senatorial minds, as they celebrated the death of Domitian and the accession of Nerva – that being the first thought – was surely to wonder about who should or would or could succeed the new emperor. Old, in poor health and childless, Nerva was all too obviously an interim ruler. The normal expectation of life for a male at birth in the Roman empire was no more than thirty-five years, though if the child survived to the age of five it improved to fifty or so.[1] For men of senatorial and imperial rank it was more – again only if the child survived – due to a better and more substantial diet and better medical attention. But a man in his sixties, senator or not, was living out his last years, and could die at any time. And that was not counting the possibility of assassination.

Nerva was already the oldest man to accede to the throne, with the unhelpful exception of Galba – Pertinax, a century later, was the same age at his accession[2] – and the history of the previous century strongly suggested that he would be murdered. Only Augustus and Vespasian certainly died of 'natural causes': old age, in their cases. The exact causes of the deaths of Tiberius, Claudius and Titus are uncertain, but they may well have been murdered, and there were certainly rumours to that effect at the time. The rest all died violently one way or another. Caligula was assassinated by members of the Praetorian Guard, and Galba, again unhelpfully, given his analogous situation with that of Nerva, was lynched by the Guard. (Again, so was Pertinax.) Otho and Nero committed suicide, Nero being assisted by one of his freedmen; and now Domitian had been murdered in the palace by a group including a Praetorian Guard and several palace servants. No betting man would have taken odds on Nerva dying in bed.

There were those, no doubt, who took altogether too seriously Nerva's professed intention to work with the Senate. He certainly made efforts in that direction, as is shown by the co-option of senators on to the Economy Commission, the commission to organise the *alimenta*, and the Agrarian Commission. Those who thought that the Senate should be the ruling body of the whole empire, and that the imperial super-structure should fade away, or be abolished, may well have felt that Nerva's reign and practice could be made the first stage of a return to Republican methods. If they did so think, they ignored the bitter reality: that the army looked to the emperor as its commander and paymaster, not to the Senate, and that the army, even though the commanders were senators, simply would not take senatorial direction. An attempt to abolish the post of emperor, unless it could be accomplished slowly and carefully, by consultation and agreement, would only produce a civil war.

There was thus no real alternative to continuing the imperial system. An emperor – active, supervisory, competent – and preferably militarily able and sensitive, was a necessity. And, given Roman inheritance practices, the emperor could expect a close relative to succeed him. The problem was that Nerva was too old to be active, though he was reasonably competent and, helped by his senatorial friends, he could supervise the operation of the whole system well enough. But his life and experience had no military elements in it, and this was a crippling handicap. Further, to make him even more vulnerable, he had no close relatives – indeed relatives of any sort are extremely difficult to discover. He was, of course, connected through his mother with the old Claudian branch of the first dynasty, of which an Octavius Laenas was presumably a living representative. But the current Laenas makes absolutely no mark on the records, and is only assumed to exist only because another Octavius Laenas became consul in 131, under Hadrian,[3] and so an intervening generation seems needed. But there was never any suggestion of him succeeding Nerva; even Hadrian, ever suspicious, does not seem to have thought of him as a threat, and indeed made him consul when his time came. The only other known family branch of the Cocceii was by way of the emperor's sister, who had married the brother of the Emperor Otho; he had been killed off by Domitian, apparently without issue.

So Nerva would have to be succeeded by someone who was not one of his blood relatives. This could be achieved in two ways: either an heir could be adopted – thereby confirming the priority of the familial link – or otherwise designated by Nerva himself, presumably in consultation with his senatorial friends, or alternatively a plot could be organised to have Nerva himself killed; the killer would then presumably make himself emperor. Nerva had not exactly discouraged that second method by his own means of assuming power. His life was therefore under threat from the time he became emperor. And the responsibility for guarding that life lay with the Praetorian Guard, which, as gradually became clear, was collectively very unhappy at what had been done to Domitian – and the Guard had killed emperors before. The matter became even more difficult with the possibility that an adoptee might try to hurry along the moment of his inheritance, a temptation which would exist from the moment of his adoption.

The feeling that Nerva was not legitimately an emperor was not confined to elements in the Guard. There were plenty of men, in the army and in the Senate, to list only those who counted, who were unhappy at the sight of Nerva enjoying Domitian's position. They were especially men who had supported Domitian and who might reasonably assume that Nerva was the man responsible for his murder. The prevalence of this attitude may be one of the reasons for the stories which soon circulated putting the whole blame for the murder on the palace servants; anyone in the know in Rome would not be fooled by such a transparent excuse for very long.

Domitian's wife was still alive, as were the boys whom he had chosen as his heirs, Domitianus and Vespasianus. They were young, in their early teens, but Nero had been only seventeen when he inherited: youth was no bar, in other words, even if Nero was hardly a satisfactory precedent. Under Domitia Longina's guardianship they might well be acceptable to many. Domitia Longina was a political player in her own right, both as the widow of Domitian and as the daughter of the martyred general Cn. Domitius Corbulo, victim of Nero. No doubt the other rumour, that Domitia was involved in the killing of her husband, was in part aimed at this possibility. A Flavian restoration was thus not wholly out of the question.

Then there were other men who had blood or family connections with earlier emperors. So murderous had been the past century, however, that most imperial relatives were dead, or, if still alive, were keeping very quiet. All close relatives of all previous emperors were dead, but there were families with fairly distant, or indirect, imperial connections, which might be thought to provide a quasi-hereditary claim. For a sympathiser with the idea of senatorial participation in government, as Nerva had shown himself to be, these families might be considered to be the best from whom to choose a successor. There were several possibilities.

As an example, there was the family of the Cornelii Dolabellae, of high republican aristocratic extraction, a family which had held consulships for at least five generations. In addition a Dolabella had married Sulpicia Galbilla in the past, a lady related to the Emperor Galba and the whole long line of Sulpicii, who had been aristocratic for at least the last three centuries; and Servius Cornelius Dolabella Petronianus who was consul *ordinarius* with Domitian in 86 was the son of a woman who had been the former wife of the Emperor Vitellius. In certain circumstances such a 'relationship' was significant. On one reading of recent history Galba – the supplanter of Nero – and Vitellius – the avenger of Galba and the enemy of Vespasian and the Flavians – might be considered the legitimate line of succession, and so a connection with both would be thought to provide an imperial claim. But such a claim had to be pushed to be heard, not neglected; ambition was one of the qualities Roman senators admired, and its absence was a fault. It may be that the consul of 86 was dead by 96, though if not he was not politically active. His son was still too young; he only reached the quaestorship early in Trajan's reign, and so was still in his early teens in 96. It seems that neither showed any interest in obtaining the throne. The younger man accumulated priesthoods, which seems to have been a hobby, but it was scarcely a recommendation for imperial power.[4]

Of a similarly exalted ancestry, however, was C. Calpurnius Piso Crassus Frugi Licinianus. In the fashion of the time he wore his illustriousness not in displaying his abilities or in his personal worth but in his accumulation of names. He was descended from the *triumvir* M. Licinius Crassus (consul in 70 and 55 BC) in a family which was consular through and in six successive generations. He was also descended from L. Calpurnius Piso Frugi, consul in 133 BC. The link was the adoption of a Crassus by a Piso in Augustus' time.

Nerva's Crassus had been consul in 87, though not as *ordinarius*;[5] he was thus in his early forties – his consulship would come at the age of thirty-two – a generation younger than Nerva, and roughly the same age as the dead Domitian, and, as it happened, also of Trajan. Crassus may have had expectations of a second consulship from Nerva, but his name was not on the list for 97, which was available from not long after the assassination of Domitian, and it may have been this which provoked him to lay a claim to the succession. He could point to a history of closeness to imperial power, a history which had burnt the family badly. His cousin C. Calpurnius Piso, who was on the consular list for the next year,[6] had almost as much to complain about, for his grandfather had perished in the civil war of 69, murdered when governor of Africa, in the interests of, if not at the orders of, Vespasian; in the intervening generation, C. Piso's father, Calpurnius Piso Galerianus, is not recorded as consul. This branch of the family accommodated itself well enough to the Antonines, if not to the Flavians, with other members as consuls in 111, 172 and 175, though without a great deal of distinction elsewhere. This was the way of survival, but it was not the way chosen by Nerva's Crassus. This Crassus was a nephew of the Piso Licinianus who had been Galba's choice as his successor, a decision which lasted only so long as it took Otho to organise the assassination of both Galba and Piso by the Guard; another uncle had been murdered while governor of Africa in that deadly year. It was a sequence of events which could well fester in a son's mind, particularly when he found himself subject to such a jumped-up family as the Flavians. It cannot have helped that his cousin was on the new consular list for 97.

Then consider his likely attitude to the new emperor. Nerva was a man who had been especially favoured by all the Flavian emperors – consul *ordinarius* under Vespasian as early as 71, a member of Domitian's inner circle, consul *ordinarius* again in 90 after the defeat of yet another conspiracy. And now he was emperor, having betrayed, in a peculiarly distasteful reversal, his friend Domitian. Here was quite enough to make Crassus feel hurt, angry and vengeful. Nerva was, to his view, in the place where his father or himself should have been, and had got there by a series of betrayals.

Crassus seems to have felt he had a right to the empire by sheer descent. But his exalted descent did not necessarily mean that he was intelligent. To such a man, even Nerva was of fairly undistinguished ancestry – and was therefore unfit to rule. He began to plot against Nerva, beginning apparently early on in the new principate; the precise timing is not clear, but it was in the first few months of the reign. The publication of the new consular list might have been seen as a provocation by him, just as the killing of Domitian had been an inspiration, but it is likely that his ambition was kindled as soon as Domitian was dead.

The problem was that this was exactly what he was expected to do. His discontent was no doubt vocal and obvious, and he will have been known to have been disgruntled even under Domitian. A government which had been installed by a *coup d'état* was going to be particularly vigilant in case of repeat attempts inspired by its own success. Crassus certainly made some of the right moves: he made 'vast promises' to the soldiers, no doubt meaning in this case the Praetorians – the body which had murdered his uncle; but Crassus would scarcely have approached Casperius Aelianus, Nerva's appointment as Guard commander, and if he did not he could not count on the Guard, and Aelianus would clearly hear of his approaches. He also approached and got the help of some friendly senators. But since these were the expected moves they were easily detected, and one would have thought that experienced Praetorian officers and senators would see rapidly enough that he had no chance of success, and would ensure that Nerva was kept fully informed. Certainly Nerva knew all about the plot. He brought the plotters to his box at the games, probably the Plebeian Games in November 96, to scotch the whole thing. He handed over swords to Crassus and his fellows to inspect, no doubt with some equally pointed remarks, and thereby revealed to them that the plot was blown. In effect he dared them to kill him there and then, in public. They backed down, as they had to in such a place, no doubt realising that the emperor would scarcely do such a thing without loyal guards nearby to prevent their success, or immediately avenge it. Nerva then exiled Crassus and his wife to Tarentum. It does not sound as if Crassus was very bright, and his support melted away at the first challenge.[7]

Senators were not wanting to urge Nerva to have Crassus executed, despite the emperor's recent publicly taken oath on the subject.[8] So much for the solidarity of senators, one of whose members these men were asking to be executed; so much for the expectations of these senators with respect to Nerva's oath; and so much for the elimination of the *delatores*, who had clearly been present and active. Nerva sensibly refused an execution: martyrs were not wanted in this administration, at least not so early. The fiasco necessarily reduced the authority of the whole Senate, which was a benefit to the emperor, and it defused any further opposition from that source, at least for the moment. Nerva displayed good political sense in merely exiling Crassus. Crassus, however, did not thereby learn the lesson: he was to be exiled by Trajan, also for conspiracy, and finally he was to be executed by the more impatient and unsteady Hadrian.

The defeat of the Crassus conspiracy was not difficult, because it all happened in Rome soon after Nerva's accession to power, where and at a time when the government and its supporters were sensitive, vigilant and strong. The city, for the moment at least, was therefore secure enough for the regime: no other plot could be hatched for some time. The government had established itself. The work it was doing, in devising consular lists, in legislating and so on, was also a good indication that it was in control.

Yet Nerva was still essentially a weak emperor, dependent on the support of the Senate and the Guard, and a man regarded with suspicion and dislike by those who mourned for, or merely remembered and regretted, the stronger and more capable Domitian. And these included the army, to speak for the moment collectively. At no time in his reign could it be said that Nerva established any real authority over the army and the provinces. After a *coup d'état* the new government needed to enforce its authority by some sackings and new appointments, but Nerva had confirmed in office all those already in post when Domitian was killed, and replacements were only sent out as and when a man's term of office expired. This was sensible, in a way, for it provided a clear continuity in the administration, but it might also be interpreted as a weakness. The result was that every army, every legion and most provinces were controlled by men appointed by his predecessor, none of whom had been consulted over the coup, and most of whom disapproved of it. And of those who were appointed two at least – Marius Priscus in Africa and Caecilius Classicus in Baetica – were conspicuously corrupt; that they, like the emperor, were appointed by the Senate, only reflected badly on both.

Continuity is all very well as a policy for an established government, but for one which has seized power by fraud and violence it can only be assumed to indicate a clear knowledge of its own weakness. That is, Nerva confirmed the governors and commanders in their offices – to which the dead Domitian had appointed them – because he did not dare remove them. And they themselves would soon appreciate the strength of their situation.

The governors who could come to such an appreciation quickest were those who commanded the larger armies: these were the governors of Britannia, the two Germanies, Pannonia, the two Moesiae, Egypt, Syria and Cappadocia-Galatia. In the circumstances of Nerva's reign the crucial men were in fact the Pannonian and Syrian governors. These commanded the two largest armies, and in 97 in particular the Pannonian army was enormous, five legions plus auxiliaries, though it was handicapped by being engaged in the Suebic-Sarmatian war. The Syrian army was also particularly large – four legions – but its governor was handicapped in other ways: one of his legions was in Judaea under the immediate command of the governor there. No responsible Roman commander could possibly remove it; one of the other legions at least must be used to guard the Parthian frontier if the army marched west. To his north was the governor of Cappadocia-Galatia, with two legions. The Syrian governor could not move without the agreement and co-operation of his colleagues in Judaea and Cappadocia-Galatia, and perhaps in Egypt as well. On the other hand with their agreement he could field an army which, as Vespasian showed in 69, gave him instant control of the whole empire east of the Hellespont and Cyrenaica.

The other armies were too small or too distant to seriously affect the issue. The Spanish legion was in a remote corner of the peninsula, the British legions had a frontier to hold and a Channel to cross, the African legion was too isolated; the Egyptian forces were probably handicapped by the fact that the Egyptian governor was of equestrian rank, and could not (yet) aspire to the purple. The German legions, two or three in each province, might be interested in promoting a man to power; they had tried to do so before in 69 and 89, though with only momentary success in each case. And since 89 the German treasury had been located in yet another province, Belgica, so that yet another governor and a procurator had to be involved in the event of a coup. The Moesian armies might also be interested in promoting their men. But with the great army in and about Pannonia, both the German and Moesian armies were thoroughly outmatched.

The armies of Pannonia and Syria were thus the most important military weights in the scales of the succession, but only if their commanders chose to make them so, and the actual candidates for the succession were not, as it turned out, necessarily those commanders. If the commander of the largest army had been the automatic candidate, the man Nerva adopted would have been Pompeius Longinus, the Pannonian governor and commander of the army fighting in the Suebic-Sarmatian war. That it was not him but the governor of Germania Superior, M. Ulpius Traianus, who was chosen needs to be explained. And to do so it is necessary to cast the explanatory net much wider that just the armies, or just the Senate.

So far the Senate, the Praetorian Guard, the army or armies, and to a small degree the people of Rome have been noted as having had some say in the choice of emperor. Both Augustus and Vespasian had emerged as emperors from a crowd of competitors as a result of their control of the armies which had won civil wars. The rest (ignoring the three evanescent rulers of 69) had become emperors by right of succession, which had been confirmed by their nomination by their predecessors. Even Claudius, when his predecessor had been murdered, was made emperor because of his kinship with that predecessor. Nerva had, alone among the whole group, become emperor by means of a plot by a group of senators, the group of palace servants, and probably the Praetorian Guard commanders. He had little or no kinship connection with previous emperors. That is to say, none of these groups could foist an emperor on the empire by itself, unless it was the army by means of a civil war; even then an army's candidate would be a senator, because army commanders were senators, and he would need to work with, and be acceptable to, the Senate. It followed that the matter of the succession had to be sorted out by a consensus decision – or by a civil war. If a successor to Nerva was to emerge rather than be imposed it would have to be by means of a fairly lengthy process in which a whole variety of interest groups would be consulted, or rather placated.

It is to be taken for granted that all of those involved wished to avoid a new civil war. This is not to say that they would be successful. There was no intention in 68 on anyone's part of initiating a civil war, but one resulted nonetheless. The problem was that there was no machinery in the empire by which all the interest groups involved could be consulted in an open and formal, legal and constitutional way. If anywhere it should have taken place in the Senate, but no such debate seems to have happened at any time, except in secret, or at any rate private, conversations. And even if there had been an open discussion there is no guarantee that the result of such a discussion would have been accepted by everyone. This was the result of the lack of clarity in the ramshackle system which might be called the Roman constitution. The existence of the emperor devalued senatorial authority, while the continued existence of the Senate was a reminder that the emperor's was only a semi-legitimate power.

The men who could be said to be candidates for the imperial power were all senators: all the governors, all the army commanders and legionary commanders, all the magistrates and former magistrates were members of the Senate, as indeed was the emperor, and the next emperor would also be a senator. Not for more than another century would an emperor come from the great numbers of non-senators. All the prospective rulers were known to each other, at least distantly, and this personal aspect may well have been an element in the final choice. Indeed, it is difficult to discern any particular reason why Trajan should emerge as emperor, unless it was his character and personality which particularly impressed his contemporaries, especially his fellow army commanders; there were others just as suitable.

7

THE ARISTOCRATIC NETWORKS

Character and personality alone were never enough to recommend an imperial successor, still less mere ancestry. Trajan was a major player in the succession game because he was a member of more than one of the major interest groups in the empire, and in his person more than one of such groups intersected. These groups formed networks by means of interconnecting elements such as birthplace and province of origin, career and colleagues, and, above all, blood and marital relationships. These will be explored in this chapter, but first the man himself will be examined.

M. Ulpius Traianus, consul in 90, was the son of M. Ulpius Traianus, who had supported Vespasian from the beginning of his bid for the empire. The father had been praetor about 60, governor of Baetica in the mid-60s, and then gained command of *legio* X *Fretensis*, which was soon fighting in the Judaean war under Vespasian. There he was also a colleague of Titus, who commanded another legion in that war. He was rewarded with the consulate in (probably) 70, in Vespasian's first list, possibly held the governorship of Cappadocia-Galatia in the early 70s, was governor of Syria in 74/75–77/78, and governor of Asia in 79, much earlier than he could have expected, and had been adlected to the patriciate in 73/74;[1] he was not, however, employed after 79/80, though he seems to have lived on for some time.[2] (To be sure, Asia was normally the last appointment any senator had, and perhaps too much should not be read into this item.)

So, despite an ancestry of only one generation of nobility, Trajan (the son) had a flying start in the political stakes, having a highly distinguished and successful father, and in the particular circumstances of 96–97 the father's lack of employment by Domitian could be seen as a mark in the son's favour. In addition Trajan had substantial marital connections, which were formed well before his father's rise in the 70s. Trajan's mother was Marcia, of the family of Q. Marcius Barea Soranus, a distinguished consul and governor in the second quarter of the first century. Her sister had married Titus briefly in the 60s, and was the mother of Julia, whom Domitian is said to have loved.[3]

Trajan and Domitian were thus near contemporaries. On his father's side, Trajan's aunt had married into the Aelius family, which came from their home town of Italica in Baetica; her brother-in-law was a senator, and her son P. Aelius Hadrianus Afer reached the rank of praetor before he died in 85 at the age of thirty-nine; he was the father of the future Emperor Hadrian; Trajan acted as Hadrian's guardian after Afer's death.[4] Trajan's sister Ulpia Marciana married C. Salonius Matidius Patruinus, praetor in the mid-70s, but who had died by 78.[5] Her daughter Matidia married twice, first to an unknown man called Mindius, and second to L. Vibius Sabinus:[6] a daughter was born of each marriage and Vibia Sabinus married her distant cousin Hadrian about AD 100.[7]

Hadrian's sister Aelia Domitia Paulina[8] had meanwhile married L. Julius Servianus, who was consul in 90 (the same year as Nerva's second consulship) and twice later in Trajan's own lists. He was later the adopted son of L. Julius Ursus, consul in 84 and 98, who was probably the brother of P. Julius Lupus, consul also in 98. This was a remarkable family, originally equestrian in rank, descended from a man who was Prefect of Egypt in 70 – another of Vespasian's early appointments. Ursus had himself been Prefect of Egypt and the Prefect of the Praetorian Guard, before being appointed consul by Domitian without any of the preliminary magistracies.[9]

P. Julius Lupus was married to Arria Fadilla,[10] the daughter of Cn. Arrius Antoninus, consul in the terrible year of 69 and then for a second time in 97, one of Nerva's senatorial friends and colleagues. Antoninus may have been a candidate of the plotters in 96, and he certainly commiserated memorably with Nerva over his accession at the senatorial confirmation.[11] Arria Fadilla had been married earlier to T. Aurelius Fulvus, consul in 89 and the son of a double consular, who had held the office in 70 (again) and 85: another Flavian favourite.

Fulvus' son, revealing his ancestry in his names, was T. Aurelius Fulvus Boionius Arrius Antoninius, (the future Emperor Antoninus Pius).[12] He was married to Annia Galeria Faustina, the daughter of M. Annius Verus, consul in 97.[13] Verus had two sons, another Annius Verus who was married to Domitia Lucilla,[14] whose ancestors included Cn. Domitius Tullus, another man with a second consulship in 98, and who had held his first, with his brother, in 79.

The Ulpii were thus members of the high aristocracy of the empire, and were connected with a whole series of similar families. Their marital links were with a group of families – Aelii, Arrii, Aurelii, Julii Lupi, Annii, Domitii – who had become closely interlocked by mutual bonds. They were also geographically connected, in two sets. The Ulpii came from Italica in Baetica, an old Roman colony, and they could trace the family origins to Tuder in Umbria [15] (only a day's journey from Narnia, the home town of the Cocceii, as it happened). Italica also has epigraphic evidence of a family called Trahius – M. Trahius in the first century BC, and L. Blattius Traianus Pollio in Augustus' reign (having dropped the 'h') – which is the origin of Trajan's cognomen; this is clearly a family which, though rich (Pollio helped furnish the city theatre), did not venture out into the rough seas of Roman politics.[16] The Aelii were also from Italica, though they originated from Hadria on the Adriatic coast; Hadrian's mother, Domitia Paulina, was from Gades, on the Spanish Atlantic coast;[17] the Annii were from Ucubi in Baetica.[18] This was a distinct Spanish, even Baetican, group.

The second part of the network included the Aurelii who were from Nemausus in Gallia Narbonensis [19] as were the Domitii.[20] The origin of the Julii Lupi is not known, though one guess is 'provincial' and another is, a little more firmly '?Narbonensis'.[21] It was Trajan who provided one of the main links between these two groups, the Spanish and the Narbonensian, for he was married to Pompeia Plotina, whose family is not known but who apparently came from Nemausus, where Hadrian built her a commemorative basilica after her death.[22] The other families with which they were linked, the Salonii, Vibii, Marciani, were Italian, perhaps in many instances from northern Italy. The Arrii were perhaps from Narbonensis or north Italy.

Here we have a network of linked families, in distinct geographical sets, linked by matrimonial knots, and in particular raised by repeated favours provided by the emperors of the Flavian family. The whole group was also active, politically, militarily and administratively. They appear repeatedly as consular colleagues, in 70, 79, 97, and in the early years of Trajan's reign. They had held at least nine consulships between them, and had governed many provinces. This was a working group, not a set of aristocratic drones, like Crassus; if some were not employed in Domitian's reign, that was Domitian's choice, not theirs. Note also that these links were all relatively recent, most of them formed within the previous generation, and that the central element was Trajan's father, the first M. Ulpius Traianus, whose marriage to Marcia was the original block upon which the rest of the structure was built, and that the essential link was Trajan himself.

This was not, of course, the only such network which existed at the time. It is particularly well known because it was these family connections which produced the emperors of the next dynasty, from Trajan to Commodus. Even if it had not done that, however, its significance would have been substantial. It was by such means that the western provinces were being drawn into a full participation in the political life of the empire. It was done, as with all these families, by bringing the Italian-descended families settled in the republican period in the colonies in those provinces into the Senate. Baetica and Narbonensis were the areas where such settlement was densest in the west. By marriages and other links in their home cities, the colonial families could therefore also bring into the network the non-Italians – if they had the necessary wealth, of course – though this took a good deal longer and was never more than partial, even tentative. It goes without saying, though perhaps it does need to be repeated, that all these families were exceedingly rich.

The process of linking these families together would appear to have taken place in the context of Rome more than their home cities: that is, the individuals involved made their ways into Roman politics and only when they were well on to the career ladder did they link up with other families, by whatever means. It was only at Rome, by their election as magistrates, and appointments as army officers, and so by their consequential presence in the Senate, that these men took on an imperial significance. M. Ulpius Traianus the elder, for instance, seems to have made his Flavian connection in Judaea on military service, after his marriage with Marcia, of the Roman family. At the same time they all required a firm and secure base in the home province, and it is noticeable that Traianus' sister was married to another prominent man in their home town. The Aelius–Domitius marriage, similarly, was presumably organised in Spain, from where both families came, though it was not until the marriage of Hadrian with the daughter of Vibius Sabinus in 100 that the family reached the political heights.

The Aurelius–Arrius link was, however, clearly one formed in Rome. The junction of these two groups by such links as the marriage of Trajan and Plotina clearly magnified their influence; the sum was, in this case, greater than the parts.

Other networks were developing at this same time by similar means. Plautia, the daughter of the great aristocrat L. Aelius Lamia Plautius Aelianus, whose house was related in ways to Claudius and Vitellius, made three successive marriages, to L. Ceionius Commodus, C. Avidius Nigrinus and Sex. Vettulenus Civica Cerealis. These men were of families from Bononia, Faventia and the Sabine country, respectively. This is another example of the formation of an aristocratic network, one which was largely Italian, and which eventually joined the Spanish–Narbonensian network to form the later Antonine monarchy.[23] No doubt there were networks forming in Africa, but there were only very few senators from Africa as yet. In Asia Minor, however, a major network was in process of formation during Domitian's reign. This one was much more strongly based locally and had weaker connections with Italy than the Spanish–Narbonensian group. It is also less well known because it was not the producer of emperors. It was potent, nevertheless, and it had its effect in the imperial crisis of 96–98.

The settlement of Italians outside Italy had, of course, started earliest in the western provinces, particularly in Spain, and so it was the descendants of those men who had moved into the upper ranks fairly smoothly, with little or no resistance.[24] They could claim old citizenships, they had wealth and showed cultivation, and they widened the pool of Latin-speaking talent. Senators from Gaul appeared just as early, including at least one man who was probably of native Gallic origin.[25] By 96 a western provincial origin for a senator was not at all unusual, as the Spanish–Narbonensian network showed. One count suggests that 15 per cent of senators were from western provinces at the start of Domitian's reign, and that by 96 this had risen to 17 per cent. These men were no problem; after all, they were really not much less Italian than men from Cisalpine Gaul. Africans took longer, there being fewer of them, and they were descended from later settlers: there were only half a dozen by 96.[26] But it was men from the provinces east of the Adriatic who were slowest to explore the Roman way of ascent.

This was partly due to prejudice against easterners and partly the result of a lack of opportunity. The number of Italian settlers in the eastern provinces had been relatively few; they had reached their new homes generally later than those in the west, and they were well scattered. The earliest colony east of the Adriatic was Corinth (46 BC), and further east there were none until Augustus' time. The ravaged condition of the eastern lands after the civil wars which brought the death of the Republic also inhibited any wider ambitions for a time, and it took great initial wealth to break into the charmed circle of the Roman aristocracy. Nero's mania for Greece and Greek things had been some help, but more telling was the success of Vespasian, who had gathered support from all over the east, and whose core of military power was the legions of Syria, which by now were thoroughly permeated by eastern recruits, and in some cases were worshipping Roman gods in eastern guises.

So easterners began to arrive at Rome under Nero and reached the Senate in small numbers in Vespasian's reign, and rather more noticeably under Domitian.[27] Given the necessity for these men to climb through the obstacle-strewn *cursus* of the Roman system, their delayed arrival is not all that surprising. But it does seem that Domitian had detected a potential source of political support in them, for they certainly took on a substantially greater visibility during the later years of his reign.[28] It is especially noticeable that they tended to be favoured with governorships close to or in their homelands, which is an unusual divergence from the standard Roman practice.

Take, for example, the man who was promoted, probably in 96 and therefore by Domitian, to be the praetorian governor of the province of Lycia-Pamphylia. This man was L. Julius Marinus Caecilius Simplex.[29] He was the son of L. Julius Marinus, consul in 93, who perhaps originated from Berytos in Syria.[30] This city was the only Roman colony in the Levant, established by Augustus soon after his victory at Actium, and reinforced and expanded about 15 BC by Agrippa. The veterans of two legions formed its settlers, and its territory eventually stretched inland to include the valley of the Bekaa, including the site of the Baal of that valley, where the great temples of Baalbek arose. These colonial lands stretched from the Mediterranean coast to the interior desert, and so cut Syria in two, separating the eternally bubbling Judaea from the less hostile but more heavily garrisoned northern Syrian lands grouped around the great cities of Laodikeia, Apamea and Antioch.[31] Marinus was the first man to emerge on to the Roman political stage from this colony; after his consulship, he was made governor of Moesia Inferior in 95 or 96. (His cognomen has provoked suppositions that he was of Syrian race, since Marinus could be the Latinisation of a Syrian name,[32] but it is also a good Latin word; it is hardly a surprising cognomen for a man from a coastal city.)

Marinus had married Caecilia, the daughter of Cn. Caecilius Simplex,[33] who had been consul in 69, one of those who were caught up in the frantic events in Rome in that awful year. The son of Marinus and Caecilia collected his names from both families and went through the full rigour of the Roman governmental system: a road curator was his first post, then tribune of the *legio* IV *Scythica*, stationed at Kyrrhos in north Syria. His next post was as quaestor to the governor of Macedonia, then he was aedile and praetor in Rome. He learnt the work of a provincial governor in Cyprus and then in Pontus-Bithynia as legate to the governors of those provinces, in the latter case under his own father in 89. Back in Italy he was curator of another road, the Via Tiburtina, and was then sent to Germania Superior as legate of the *legio* XI *Claudia*, stationed at Vindonissa. All this was a fairly slow progress through the *cursus*, and one which had rather more of the minor posts than might normally be expected. It is as though he was being extensively tested, or perhaps there were doubts about his competence for the highest posts. The appointment to command a legion, though, must mean that such doubts, if they existed, had been laid to rest. He cannot have spent much time in the Senate at Rome, given that each provincial post probably lasted two years: and his posting as a legionary commander suggests that he had had a fairly serious stint, perhaps lasting more than a year, as tribune with IV *Scythica* at the beginning of his career. Perhaps the only extensive time he had in Rome was between 91 and 94, when he had charge of the Tiburtina road. On his retirement from the

Bithynian post under his father in 91, he became a brother of the Arval college, one of Rome's aristocratic priesthoods, and he would thus have been in Rome for his father's consulship in 93, as was only fitting. The promotion to a legionary command would come after this, a real compliment to his father, who himself went on to govern the important, well-garrisoned province of Moesia Inferior, probably in 96.

The son was now removed from the winter snows of Vindonissa and posted to the south coast of Asia Minor, to the hills and old cities of Lycia and the rich plain and old cities of Pamphylia, hot and sunny. The improved climate was surely a pleasure for a man brought up in Phoenicia, as was, perhaps, a posting in the civil government for which he was maybe more fitted than for military command. (The likelihood of a war on the Danube frontier may have been another reason for removing him from legionary command.) Even more welcome may well have been the fact that for his wife the posting to Pamphylia was almost a homecoming, for Julia Tertulla came from the city of Apollonia, a hundred Roman miles inland.[34]

The numerous cities in Asia Minor had had a century of peace and developing prosperity since the end of the Roman civil wars. Those cities had also during that period seen a process of developing wealth which was concentrated in relatively few hands. Some of that wealth was in the hands of long-domiciled Greek families who dominated the cities of the Aegean coast. Other cities, notably the Roman colonies planted by Augustus, were dominated by families of Italian descent, as at Antioch-by-Pisidia.[35] Still other families were descendants of the old royal families of the area – the Attalids, Galatians and others. The wealth of all these families was above all in the form of land, and it was exhibited in their monopoly of public offices, in their control over the provincial religious cults and of the cults of the emperor, and in their gifts to their cities of festivals and public buildings. It had taken some decades for these families to emerge and consolidate their positions, but one of the most notable developments of the second half of the first century AD was the simultaneous processes of interconnection between these dominating families and the appearance of representative members of them in Roman offices, and so as members of the Senate; the two processes, of course, fed each other, for local wealth was the key to success in Rome, and Roman success reinforced and safeguarded local wealth. It was exactly the same process, if somewhat delayed in time, which brought about the Spanish–Narbonensian network.

The marriage of Julia Tertulla and Julius Simplex had probably taken place in the mid-80s. By that time Simplex was seen to be a coming man, if at that time perhaps unlikely to rise any higher than praetorian rank. His new father-in-law, C. Julius Cornutus Tertullus,[36] was a member of a prominent Italian family in Apollonia, a Hellenistic city which Augustus had reinforced with Roman colonists. There they were intermarried with a similar family, the Servenii Cornuti, whose base was at the neighbouring city of Akmoneia.[37] Julius Simplex was thus joining a network of families which had developed locally and had already begun to intermarry. Cornutus Tertullus had at that stage also reached praetorian rank, and was evidently himself going no further. His son, Simplex's brother-in-law, was married to the daughter of M. Plancius Varus, from Perge in Pamphylia, the head of the most prominent local family in that city.[38] It seems that Varus also adopted Tertullus, whose full name was

C. Julius Plancius Varus Cornutus Tertullus. Varus was another of the Italian transplants, from a family probably originating in Latium, where records from Atina name several people of that name. The original migration perhaps took place in Augustus' time, and by the second half of the first century AD Varus was prominent enough at Perge – that is, he was very, very rich – to be called *ktistes*, 'founder' of the city.[39] This meant that he had spent lavishly on equipping Perge in the way the Pergeans thought their city should be equipped. His daughter, Plancia Magna (no less), Tertullus' wife, was also lavish with her money, putting up numerous statues – especially to the imperial family – in the reigns of Trajan and Hadrian.[40] The alliance of the Cornuti Tertulli and the Plancii Vari was locally very powerful.

M. Plancius Varus had been reasonably prominent earlier at Rome, for an easterner. He had gone through the early stages of a political career, reaching praetorian rank by 69, by way of a quaestorship in Pontus-Bithynia, and a tribunate. In Vespasian's reign he worked as legate to the governors of Achaia and Asia, and finally became governor himself, of Pontus-Bithynia again, where his name appears on several milestones.[41] That was the end of his official career, but he apparently maintained a connection with Rome, where there was a temple of Diana Planciana – and one of the main goddesses of Perge was Artemis, the Greek version of Diana.[42]

His son Tertullus' career, up to the death of Vespasian, had been very similar. He was favoured by Vespasian by being adlected to praetorian rank, and served as legate to the governor of Crete-Cyrenaica, then as governor of Narbonensis in about 78. This was a very rapid rise, reaching his father's status almost simultaneously with the older man. But then the process stopped. We have a full record of his career, and there is nothing between his governorship of Narbonensis and 98, when he appears in Rome again as Prefect of the Treasury.[43] He was also a great friend of Pliny.[44] When his daughter Julia Tertulla married Julius Simplex, perhaps in the early or mid-80s, all three men involved – Simplex, Varus, Tertullus – were of the same praetorian rank. And none of them advanced any further than that during Domitian's reign. This can only have been as a result of imperial displeasure, but the fact that all three were stopped at the same time shows that they were seen as a distinct group; the Asian network was developing, and was perhaps seen by Domitian as a potential problem.

However, there is yet another connection, another marriage. Julius Simplex's mother Caecilia, the daughter of Cn. Caecilius Simplex, consul in 69, had a sister, another Caecilia (referred to as 'Caecilia Minor') – though both of these women's existence has to be assumed, from their sons' names.[45] She married another multinamed politician, Ti. Julius Candidus Marius Celsus.[46] The connection here is perhaps even more overtly political, for Simplex was a consular colleague of Celsus' father A. Marius Celsus in that fraught year of 69 – when Varus was praetor, as well. Marius Celsus[47] probably came from Narbonensis, perhaps from Nemausus, and he had been a legionary commander of XV *Apollinaris* under Corbulo in the east in the 60s. Involved in the civil war on the losing side (Otho's)[48], he was quickly reconciled with Vespasian and sent to command in Germania Inferior in the aftermath of the reconquest of that area, and then to the governorship of Syria. There he seems to have died, probably in 73.[49] He was clearly valued highly by Vespasian, for in both provinces he faced considerable difficulties: in settling Germania Inferior after the war with the Batavi, and in Syria in the conquest of Commagene, the extraction of the refugee Commagenian princes from Parthia and the problems of Romano-Parthian relations. At some point he adopted Candidus as his son, who thus increased his name.

Candidus' origin is unclear, but is probably either Narbonensis or Asia;[50] adoption by Marius Celsus may be a pointer to Narbonensis. His early career is not known, but after his consulship in 86, he governed the huge double province of Cappadocia-Galatia for three years (c. 87–90), in a disturbed and difficult time in that area, which included the incursion from Parthian territory of a 'false-Nero'. The failure of the governor of Asia, C. Vettulenus Civica Cerealis, to react quickly enough to block this invasion cost him his life; Candidus survived, and his reaction may thus be presumed to have been entirely satisfactory to Domitian. Candidus' marriage to Caecilia Minor brings us back to Narbonensis, whence the bride's father, Cn. Caecilius Simplex, originated, and to AD 69, when Marius and Caecilius were colleagues as consuls. If there was ever a year when consular colleagues needed to be mutually supportive, it was 69. The marriage must have taken place before Marius' death in 73, and probably, like that of the other Caecilia, before the civil war.

In the generation of the husbands of the two Caeciliae, it was the Narbonensians who made the running, but it was in the east that the future of this aristocratic network lay, where the practices of intermarriage and adoption to form alliances and to preserve family names and properties were deployed with stunning strategic success. The Cornuti, Servenii and Plancii were an early example of the process, linking two locally prominent families in cities in neighbouring provinces. Perge and Apollonia were linked by road and Apollonia and Akmoneia were neighbours: an alliance between the prominent families in each city made good economic and political sense. But the connections ramified much further than that.

Perge's nearest neighbour was the city of Attaleia, where another Julia Tertulla had married M. Calpurnius Rufus about the end of Augustus' reign. Their son, also M. Calpurnius Rufus, had been governor in Lycia-Pamphylia in Claudius' reign, soon after the formal annexation of Lycia to the empire.[51] This alliance made even better economic sense that the Cornutus–Plancius alliance, for Attaleia was a port, through which the Cornuti could trade. The family remained senatorial for at least two more generations, right into the second century.[52] In another direction the Servenii of Akmoneia, of which family L. Servenius Cornutus reached the Senate in Vespasian's reign, were linked by marriage into an even wider network. This Cornutus was the son of L. Servenius Capito; his mother was Julia Severa, who was descended from one of the royal families of Galatia.[53] This family became senatorial in Trajan's reign in the person of C. Julius Severus, consul in 138.[54] By that time, according to an inscription,[55] he was related to the leading families of Sardis, the Julii Celsi, and of Pergamon, the Julii Quadrati, to King Alexander of Cilicia, as well as to the Servenii of Akmoneia. This last family brought them within the Plancii–Cornuti group as well, of course, and Julius Severus' daughter was adopted into the family of the Plancii of Perge. The connection is even more direct, since the Plancii owned at least one important estate in Galatia, near Juliopolis. The adopted daughter, Plancia Magna Aquillia, died young and unmarried, and was commemo-rated at another Galatian city, Tavium.[56]

These extensive connections thus linked the old Hellenistic royal families of Galatia and Pergamon, who had clearly survived in person and property, with a whole series of rich Italian immigrant families who had settled in a string of ancient Hellenistic cities, and it was the Italian families which led the Asian former royal families into participa-tion in the Roman government system. Still another link also existed, for M. Plancius Varus of Perge, the governor of Bithynia-Pontus, was married to Julia, the daughter of King Tigranes VI of Armenia. Her brother was C. Julius Alexander, king in Cilicia Tracheia, just along the south Asian coast from Perge. In turn, Alexander was married to Iotape, descended from the defunct royal family of Commagene, a kingdom annexed to the empire by Vespasian in 72, where A. Marius Celsus was Syrian gover-nor, and so linked to the dynasties of Emesa and Judaea, who formed their own net-work.[57] These dynasties may not have had royal titles any more, but their members were still rich and influential, and their old connections had remained. They were now being reinforced by these new links with the ex-Italian families.[58]

In other parts of Asia Minor, other groupings can also be discerned, though none are quite as extensive as this main one. In the larger cities there were several families who intermarried: at Antioch-by-Pisidia the Sergii Paulli had been senatorial since Claudius' time, and they intermarried with the Caristanii from the same city, who produced a consul in 90, the first from Asia Minor. L. Sergius Paullus, who reached no further up the ladder than quaestor, married his daughter to Cn. Pinarius Cornelius Clemens, of patrician rank, whose father had been consul in 70;[59] their daughter married M'. Acilius Glabrio,[60] one of the most distinguished of Roman aris-tocrats, consul in 124, whose father was Trajan's consular colleague in 90. The evi-dence from Antioch-in-Pisidia shows the existence of a dozen or more of these Italian-origin families: the senatorial ones were thus the tip of a substantial iceberg of colo-nists.[61]

Representatives of these families were increasingly to be given governing powers in the various provinces of Asia Minor, often in provinces with which they had a family connection, though not usually in their home province. L. Julius Marinus, probably from Syria and related to the Pergeans and Apollonians, governed Pontus-Bithynia; his son was his legate there and later governed both Lycia-Pamphylia and Cappadocia; C. Antius A. Julius Quadratus, from Pergamum, governed Lycia-Pamphylia; Ti. Julius Celsus Polemaeanus, from Sardis, governed Cilicia. All these are part of the net-work of Asian relationships, and all had more or less close family or marital connec-tions with the provinces they governed. There are too many examples of this here to ascribe the phenomenon to chance. Out of the thirteen governors of Asian provinces appointed under Domitian whose origins are known, seven have local connections. (This is omitting Asia itself, still the preserve of senators from Italy.)[62] It seems that the choice of governors for these Asian provinces clearly favoured those with a local connection.

For the central government in Rome this must have made sense, at least within limits. The local civic aristocracies had joined with the old royal families and, over the past century, the two groups had solidified into a crust of power and privilege, wealth and landownership – a clear regional aristocratic network, in fact. Their connections covered the whole of the peninsula, from eastern Galatia to Ephesos, and from Cilicia and Pamphylia to Bithynia and Pontus. The evidence thus amounts to an alliance between the central government and the local aristocracy. This is especially well exemplified in the reaction of C. Antistius Rusticus, governor of the great double province of Cappadocia-Galatia in 91–93, to a famine at Antioch-by-Pisidia. His reaction was to ally with the local power structure, composed of Italian-descended families, who included the Caristanii and the Sergii Paulli – and C. Caristanius Fronto had been a consular colleague of Antistius' the previous year.[63] They aimed to control both the famine and the starvation prices the rich were charging – and, of course, the population. The price he set for grain, double the 'normal' price, clearly favoured the rich, who had grain to spare.

Antioch-by-Pisidia was one of the group of Roman military colonies in Asia whose leading families were now reaching the Senate. The histories of these two intermarried families, the Sergii and the Caristanii, illustrate the rise of this aristocracy. Two brothers, L. and Q. Sergius Paullus, reached fairly lowly offices – Curator of the Tiber Banks and governor of Cyprus respectively – in Claudius' reign.[64] Lucius' son, with the same name, reached about the same rank, serving as a road curator in Italy, military tribune with *legio* VI *Ferrata* in Syria, and as quaestor in Rome.[65] His sister, Sergia Paulla, married C. Caristanius Fronto, the representative of a family which by that time was at least four generations old in Antioch, and thus probably one of the original military settlers.[66] The family was equestrian in rank until 73/74 when Sergia's future husband was adlected to the Senate in the rank of tribune. He had served as a legionary tribune and as commander of an auxiliary cavalry regiment before then, and went on to govern Lycia-Pamphylia just before Caecilius Simplex, and so to the consulate in 90.[67]

Such a network of power could also be seen as a threat to imperial control, however, and so as a source of trouble. The practice of the Roman government was still very largely to see that governors were not sent to govern in their home provinces. The exceptions which can be seen in Asia Minor are unusual, but as a concession it was limited to such a degree that any threat to the central government was minimised; in particular it is noticeable that, with the exception of Cappadocia-Galatia, none of the provinces involved had a serious military garrison, and were amongst the smallest of provinces. If this was special treatment, the emperor favouring a group of Asians, it was carefully controlled. But in the crisis it worked. The test came in 87–88, in a crisis which provoked the emperor to extraordinary measures in the Asian province. It was a difficult moment, for there had been a plot in Rome in September 87, according to a note by the Arval Brethren,[68] and there was tension on the Danube, where one Roman army had been defeated in 86 and another was being readied for the war of revenge. Then, in 88 in the east the spectre arose, for the third time in twenty years, of the 'return of Nero'.[69] Who the imposter was is not known, but he had the support of the Parthian king. It is possible he was the same man, Terentius Maximus, who had tried the same trick eight years before, in Titus' reign.[70] Then he had taken refuge in the end in Parthia; this may be his own return. The appearance of the imposter with Parthian support instantly converted the matter into an international as well as a Roman crisis.

The governors of Syria and Cappadocia-Galatia, P. Valerius Patruinus and Ti. Julius Candidus Marius Celsus respectively, were in the front line, and they are an interesting pair for such a crisis. Patruinus had been Celsus' predecessor in Cappadocia-Galatia, and he had been transferred to Syria without a break between appointments.[71] Between them these two men governed provinces that contained no less than five legions, and perhaps twenty auxiliary regiments, at least 40,000 soldiers. And, of course, Celsus was a part of that enormous network of local aristocrats which reached from his own province back to Ephesos, the capital of the Asian province. In addition Patruinus was linked to the consul of 87, L. Neratius Priscus, by the marriage of his granddaughter to Priscus' son.[72] The main Asian network was already in place, but Celsus himself was related to the Berytian Julii Marini, to the Cornuti of Apollonia, to the Plancii of Perge, to the Calpurnii of Attaleia and to the Julii Severi of Galatia. He was, in effect, by virtue of his office at the time of the appearance of the false-Nero, the leader of this network, the spider at whose plucking the whole web would resonate and tremble.

The problem for provincial governors when an imperial imposter appeared was always: 'What if he wins?' A refusal to support him early enough could then be disastrous. It was less than twenty years since the civil war, a nearly comparable situation, in which numerous governors had made the wrong decisions. Added to such fearfulness was ambition. The success of the Flavians in 69 had been the success also of their supporters, who had thereby gained unexpected power as a result. The first supporter of a successful rebel became his most valued adviser. So C. Licinius Mucianus had supported Vespasian, and had even promoted his pretensions to empire, as a result of which he became consul for a second and then a third time; M. Ulpius Traianus became consul in 70 and held a series of important governorships for the next ten years; another early supporter, Ti. Julius Alexander, prefect in Egypt, became Praetorian Prefect in the 70s.

When the false-Nero emerged in 88, therefore, the temptation existed to acclaim him and to rise with him against Domitian. Celsus in Cappadocia-Galatia, with two legions under his command, and with family and political connections throughout Asia Minor and into Narbonensis and Syria, was ideally placed, and must have been the first target of the imposter's blandishments.

It is clear that he resisted them, and so did Patruinus in Syria, whose connections were almost as important, and that the decisions of these two powerful men doomed the venture at the start. Their colleague C. Vettulenus Civica Cerealis, the governor of Asia, apparently reacted differently, however, or perhaps only more slowly. This man was even more highly connected than Patruinus or Julius Celsus, for his brother, Sex. Vettulenus Cerealis, had been one of Vespasian's legionary commanders in Palestine – the colleague of Titus and Traianus – and he had been left in command of the whole army in the east when Titus returned to Rome. The brothers were consuls in the early 70s and then were successive governors of Moesia. The elder, Sextus, may have been governor of Africa a few years before this crisis. The family originated from the Sabine lands in Italy, so it seems, which was another link with the Flavian dynasty.[73] This was a family which had done very well out of its Flavian connections, and might be expected to be automatically loyal.

But the Vettulenus in Asia did something wrong in 88. Perhaps he simply hesitated to do anything at all, assuming that the problem would go away, knowing that Celsus and Patruinus were on top of the problem; perhaps ambition touched him and he responded too positively to a false-Neronian approach – one was surely made, even before the imposter crossed the frontier. Vettulenus' connection with the Flavians may have bred jealousy in him rather than loyalty. Whatever actually happened in the gubernatorial court at Ephesos or Sardis, and whatever Vettulenus did or did not do, he suffered for it. He was executed [74] with such speed, secrecy and suddenness that the province was left completely leaderless. Domitian, it seems, felt that the whole of the governor's staff was untrustworthy – many of them may well have been Vettulenus' relations, and all of them would have been his clients. Instead of leaving the province in the hands of Vettulanus' own legate, or even his quaestor, as would normally be the case in the event of a sudden death, he transferred C. Minicius Italus into Asia as an emergency, temporary governor.[75]

Italus is an interesting figure in his own right, and was later to be Prefect of Egypt.[76] At the time he went to Asia, he was the procurator of the 'Hellespontine province', the northern part of the province of Asia bordering on the Hellespont. He was also, startlingly, an *eques*, now sent to govern the richest province, one invariably reserved for the very highest of senatorial aristocrats. He was thus part of the administration of the province, but had been appointed by the emperor, whereas Vettulenus' appointment technically originated with the Senate. Italus had had a career of military command, as prefect of a succession of four auxiliary cavalry regiments and then tribune of the *legio* VI *Victrix* before he moved over to the civil administration, where the Hellespontine post was his first. Such a man was, on the face of it, wholly unsuitable to take charge of Asia, and only an emergency can account for it. He had little civilian administrative experience: his manners were surely military and so he was not likely to appeal to the refined aristocracy of Asia; he was a mere *eques*, and so his appointment was an insult to the Senate; and his was so obviously a temporary appointment that he can have had little real authority. It was surely seen as a weak, tactless, and provocative appointment, only to be justified by an extreme emergency.

In fact, it may be simply a matter of geography. The higher ranks of the governor's staff – his legate, his quaestor – were tainted by the governor's unacceptable conduct, so a procurator, a man appointed directly by the emperor, was the first replacement who would come to mind; the emergency might require the use of troops, and so an experienced military man would be useful; and the procurator of the Hellespontine province was simply the nearest to Rome, the first official across the Hellespont whom the imperial messenger speeding along the Via Egnatia through Macedon and Thrace would reach. The next governor of Asia, L. Mestrius Florus, perhaps set out for the east earlier than he at first intended, in order to re-establish normal government, but he would need a full staff, and that might take some time to organise in an emergency: meanwhile a soldier in charge in Asia as a back-up for the military governor of

Cappadocia-Galatia was a very useful man to have in post. As for Italus' authority, it was clearly he who carried out Vettulenus' execution: this would inevitably cow the locals most effectively.

The problem of Vettulenus and Asia was subordinate to that of the 'false-Nero'. The military posture of both of the eastern governors, Celsus and Patruinus, was boosted by the transfer of auxiliary regiments to the east.[77] Neither was tarred with the brush of treason which killed Vettulenus, and, in the face of the manifest Roman preparation and resolution, the Parthian king decided that he was involved in a losing game and surrendered the false-Nero to the Roman government.[78] No doubt the hapless imposter rapidly died.

The loyalty of the Asian network was surely noted when it was contrasted with the vacillation, or worse, of the Italian senatorial governor of the Asian province, a man who owed a great deal to the Flavian dynasty. It is possible that this gained its reward in the next years, for C. Caristanius Fronto, Ti. Julius Celsus Polemaeanus and L. Julius Marinus, all easterners, became consuls in the years (90, 92 and 93 respectively) following the defeat of the eastern threat. They were a judicious selection: one from the Antioch-by-Pisidian group in the province of Galatia, one from the Ephesian group in the Asian province, and one from the Perge group in Lycia-Pamphylia. It looks very much as though Domitian and his advisers were keeping a deliberate balance between the various sections, and that the doubts which appear to have blocked the promotions of Julius Simplex, M. Plancius Varus and Cornutus Tertullus during Domitian's reign had been set to rest.

For the government, and for the senators in the Asian network, this was a most useful, even cosy, situation. The government now had a new pool of wealthy men, by definition well-educated and cultivated, and to all appearance committed to the regime, from which could be drawn new senators, governors, magistrates, even military commanders. The men themselves benefited from such preferment, gained government support for their positions locally and from its approval of their methods, and access to yet more power and privilege. The alliance between government and local aristocracy was thus based fully on mutual self-interest, to their mutual benefit.

The power of these men came from their wealth, which, like most wealth in the empire, was based on ownership of land, in particular the possession of large estates which produced food to supply the cities of south and west Asia. Estates in the interior produced wool, hides, animals and increasingly grain from the great private and imperial estates; those closer to the wetter coastlands, grain and other plant crops.[79] The families lived in and near the cities, which they controlled through the local senates. Some cities retained a formal democratic constitution, some even had popular participation in elections, but the great majority were oligarchies in both style and constitution.[80]

The non-participants were the great mass of the population. To be sure, they benefited from the employment which was generated by expenditure by the wealthy, for most rich families spent lavishly on their cities, both in buildings and in festivals, and by the doles and food distributions at festivals and games, but access to power, to landownership, perhaps even to trading opportunities, was denied them.

The alienation of the lower-class population of Bithynia, for example, was one of the causes of the widespread, if ignorant and undiscriminating, adoption of Christianity, as Pliny discovered when he went there as governor in 110.[81] It was at this time that St John the Divine, addressing Asian Christians from his exile on Patmos, called for a revolution, and in part he based his expectation of success on that same alienation.[82] And Dio Chrysostom the orator, a native of Prusa in Bithynia, travelled about as a sort of urban trouble-shooter, calming passions in various cities, including his own.[83]

Dio and John are representatives of two other aspects of the rise of the Asian aristocratic network. John's exile forced him to put pen to paper in an attempt to purge his Asian Christian audiences of their unchristian beliefs and behaviour in preparation for the expected apocalypse. But he was the last of the line of those who held that belief and expectation; there would soon be none left with personal knowledge of the message Jesus of Nazareth had tried to deliver. Other Christians at this time were busy laying the foundations of the future episcopal organisation of the church, which developed all over the east, but above all under the leadership of Polycarp, Bishop of Smyrna in Asia. It was based on the close-packed network of Asian cities, and it enabled Christians to provide the self-defence which only a proper political organisation could provide. It also enabled, even demanded, the development of the sort of orthodox beliefs which John called for – though perhaps not his own set of beliefs – and this led to the collection and selection of the required documents that became the basis of that orthodoxy, above all in the formation of the New Testament as a more or less coherent set of beliefs.

The rise of this Christian political organisation has to be seen as in part the reply of the disregarded majority of the population to the great power of the oligarchs, whose mutual support system I have here called the 'Asian network'. Inevitably the Christians mimicked the system developed by those by whom they were disregarded. Very quickly, bishops became very powerful, and thus they were rivals to the great land-owning family network. (And in the process John's revolution was rendered out of the question, since the leaders, the bishops, were far too comfortably placed.) Both bishops and oligarchs could call on the support of numbers of people – 'clients' for the landowners, 'congregations' for the bishops. The bishops thus formed a network which was as all-pervasive, but far more enduring, than the aristocratic network which was linked together above them. The difference was, of course, that the aristocrats depended too much on their links with the imperial power in Rome, whereas the church was an organisation rooted in the communities.

Dio of Prusa's representative status comes from his life's work as a travelling orator, and as an author at the heart of the revival of Greek as a literary language, which was taking place throughout the first century AD. The revival came largely out of Greece itself, quite unexpectedly. Old Greece had been wrecked in the Roman civil wars. All the decisive battles – Pharsalus, Philippi, Actium – were fought there, and the great greedy armies had crawled locustlike over it, leaving it impoverished and depopulated.[84] Slowly the imperial peace healed its wounds and restored its wealth, though not its originally teeming population, and the wealth was concentrated in relatively few hands, when not siphoned off into taxation.[85] The old Greek pride revived as well, all the stronger for its evil experiences.

Greek literature had been a major casualty of the civil wars. The only notable writing in Greek came from outside Greece proper: Strabo from Pontus, Diodoros from Sicily, Philo of Alexandria. Revival came with Nero, the philhellene, who declared Greece 'free', and participated in the Olympic Games. That revival came to fruition in Domitian's reign, when those who were educated in the time of Nero's enthusiasm became adult and active. So we have Dio – from Prusa in Bithynia – born in the 40s, receiving his higher education in the 60s, then wandering, writing, advising, orating, philosophising; and Plutarch of Chaironea in Boiotia, Dio's almost exact contemporary, writing, writing, writing and orating. These two are an intellectual counterpart of the Asian political network. In one sense, this produced one of the great cultural flowerings of the Roman empire, the 'Second Sophistic', whose later delineator, Philostratos, might claim had started in fourth century BC Athens, but which more convincingly began with Dio, the mobile orator whose style and lifestyle became the model for dozens of less serious performers in the next century and more.[86]

It also developed in a new and unexpected direction. In Nero's reign there had appeared the first of a series of novels, fantastic accounts of ancient histories, or scurrilous examinations of contemporary manners, by such men as Petronius and Lucilius, 'Dictys' of Crete and 'Dares' the Phrygian. It may be that the initial impulse for these was the appearance of the Christian Gospels, as fantasically full of impossible incidents as any novel. One of the novelists, Ptolemaeus Chemnus, dedicated his *Paradoxical History* to Julia Tertulla, probably the lady who was the wife of L. Julius Marius Caecilius Simplex. This is altogether fitting, for one of the most notable productions of the *genre*, just about this time, was Philo of Byblos' *Phoenician History*; and Byblos is the neighbour in Phoenicia of Berytos, the home city (probably) of Julia's father-in-law, L. Julius Marinus. The efflorescence of the novel in the next century was thus well founded, and ahead lay Apuleius and Philostratos and Lucian.[87]

Coming back to earth, the two more traditional prose-masters, Dio and Plutarch, were concerned not least to mediate between the imperial government and the Greek world. They had the ear of the emperors[88] – though Domitian was unresponsive – and they were heard by the Greeks of Greece and Asia. They could explain the Greeks in Rome. In the east they spelled out the requirements of the Roman government, and how the affairs of the cities should be conducted, the better to avoid the heavy Roman hand.[89] The experience of Vettulenus and his staff in 88 was a vivid reminder of the power and ruthlessness of that fist. The other side of the coin is that Plutarch's closest Roman friend, the man who made him a Roman citizen, welcomed him into his Italian home and took him on a tour of northern Italy, was L. Mestrius Florus, Vettulenus' successor in Asia.[90] The more one looks at the Asian network and its Greek and Syrian connections, the more tight-knit it seems.

That network was clearly rich, potent and extensive, linking many of the main cities and regions of several of the provinces of Asia Minor. Its link with Rome was, however, fairly weak. There was no Asian senator on hand on 19 September 96 to make sympathetic remarks to the new and unsteady emperor. Several Asians were of consular rank, and more were of praetorian or lower rank, but they were not at the heart of government.

They were, however, present in a sense. It will have been noted in this account that several of the families I have designated as members of the 'Asian network' were in fact not Asian in origin, but from Narbonensis. A. Marius Celsus, consul in 69, and his son Ti. Julius Marius Celsus, consul in 86, were from Nemausus. Cn. Caecilius Simplex, consul also in 69, was in all probability from Narbonensis. These two intermarried in the same way as, and only a little later than, the Arrii and Aurelii. But Caecilius' daughter married Julius Marinus, and their son married Julia Tertulla, thus linking this second Narbonensian group fully with the Asians.

It is impossible to locate the origin of these connections between Gaul and Asia – though there were old connections between the Galatians and the Gauls of Gaul back in the early second century BC. It is possible that governors in the Asian provinces made the connections, but it is just as likely that they met at Rome, where all ambitious men went at some point. From the point of view of this study, however, the main point is that the connection existed, not only between Asians and Narbonensians, but between the Asian network and the Spanish–Narbonensian network. And there were men who in a sense represented both groups close to the great concentration of armed might in and about Pannonia in the crisis which developed in 97.

The potency of the networks depended on their holding offices in the administration, and to do this the individual members had to climb the magistrates' ladder at Rome. But these individuals were also representatives of their families and their connections. The power of such connections in action had been demonstrated by the false-Nero crisis in Asia in 88. The Asian network was a relatively recent development, but the links it had with Narbonensis put the members in touch with the other great aristocratic network, linking Spain and Narbonensis. And at the centre of the whole was Trajan, from Italica in Spain, married to a woman from Nemausus in Narbonensis, whence came Marius Celsus. It was one of the essential bases for the elevation of Trajan to the purple.

8

CHOICE

The defeat of the conspiracy of Crassus, perhaps in November 96 and certainly about that time, together with good news from any fighting in the north – if Nerva's '*Victoria*' coins [1] of about that time are to be taken literally – meant that the new emperor was more firmly seated on his throne at the end of 96 than he had been in the days and weeks immediately after his accession.

Yet the main issue of his principate, and the issue which had predominated from the start – who would succeed him? – was now more urgent than ever. The longer the delay in choosing an acceptable successor the more likely it would be that Nerva would be compelled to choose a man who might not be acceptable to other men who could claim a voice in the discussions. Crassus' plot, amateurish and incompetent as it was, was also a warning, for Crassus' success would only have made things worse. Nerva was clearly very vulnerable to plots and to assassins. His failure to perform the essential duty of choosing a successor thus became increasingly dangerous the longer he prevaricated. The fact that he was old and decrepit, and therefore likely to be succeeded soon by someone more vigorous and active, was the main reason he was acceptable himself. And the longer he delayed, the more likely it was that another plot, one more intelligently organised than that of Crassus, would be launched. Alternatively, one of the armies might post a candidate, which would trigger a civil war for sure. Delay opened up the possibility that his decision would be pre-empted from elsewhere.

The other aspect of his problem was that an early selection of a successor might be just as dangerous, which was perhaps a good reason for continuing to delay. By choosing and naming a successor he would thereby disappoint all those others who felt they had the right qualifications for emperor and had hopes of being chosen, and this might therefore ignite the very civil war everyone was hoping to avoid. So Nerva was trapped, and would need considerable political skill to escape the trap. It is not clear he possessed such skill. The issue therefore would need to be resolved by the exercise of power by others in conjunction with the emperor. No doubt his *consilium* was the scene of frequent discussions on the subject, though it was surely a difficult matter, since the presumption was the forthcoming imperial demise.

The factors which had to be taken into account in the selection were numerous, which may well be a good reason for not reaching an early decision. It is thus necessary to locate the factors required in the candidates. But the matter was essentially political, so it is also necessary to identify the people whose actions and opinions counted. Factors involved in considering the candidates included the command of armies, the weight of senatorial influence, proximity to the emperor, personal acceptability, age, experience and perceived ability, and the influence each could exert through the political elite. These were all matters which would be taken into consideration by those who discussed the problem, and by those who pressed their views on the emperor. Yet, in the end, Nerva would have to decide himself and pronounce his decision. The period from Crassus' defeat to the adoption of Trajan, say from November 96 to October 97, was therefore filled with intrigue.

The problem, of course, is that most of the events of that period are hidden from us. Indeed, it is very likely that they were largely hidden at the time, for most of the discussions were oral, and most of the important ones would be in secret. The reconstruction of the process by which Trajan emerged as Nerva's adopted son attempted here is therefore necessarily tentative, perhaps even more so than in other episodes of ancient history. Yet, having identified the many forces and the main candidates, such a reconstruction is worth attempting. It is also worth noting that Trajan's selection came at the end of that year-long discussion; it cannot be known when his name came into the discussion, early or late.

The appointment of Trajan as governor of Germania Superior was one of Nerva's few such appointments. As argued in Chapter 3 it took place very early in his rule, that is, before the end of 96, and most likely in October. It would seem, therefore, that Trajan was in Rome during the events of 18 and 19 September, and so will have attended the meeting of the Senate which acclaimed Nerva. This all suggests that he had been an early supporter of the new emperor. He had also been a conspicuous supporter of Domitian, having marched his legion from Spain to the Rhine with exemplary speed to help suppress the insurrection of Antonius Saturninus in 89.[2] His adherence to the new regime was thus important, though hardly crucial, and as a military man he was a good choice for a province close to the Pannonian fighting. We do not know whom he replaced there.[3] If this interpretation is correct, of course, it suggests that Trajan was a smooth political operator, able to suppress any feelings of sorrow at Domitian's death, an event which will have come as a shock to him.

The importance of the man and of his new posting must not be exaggerated. Trajan may have emerged as Nerva's successor in October 97, but a year earlier he was not that, by any means, though it may be significant from Nerva's later decision that he had met and appointed Trajan late in 96. At that time Trajan was only a well-known general, of consular rank and the son of a consul, but no more powerful or prominent or important than several dozen other men of similar rank and accomplishments. Indeed it might be argued that, to the men in Rome, the posting of Trajan to the frontier province might seem to be a means of removing him from the centre of events, for they would assume that it was in Rome that the real decisions were being taken.

Once in post at his governor's seat at Moguntiacum, however, Trajan will have become aware of the general unhappiness of the army over what had happened in Rome. The German legions knew Domitian, for he had commanded them in victories more than once. The legion he had raised from new, *legio* I *Flavia Minervia pia fidelis*, was stationed just down the Rhine from Moguntiacum, at Bonna. This was in the neighbouring province of Germania Inferior, to which a new governor, L. Licinius Sura, a Spaniard like Trajan, was posted during that same year, in the normal rotation of appointments.[4] On Trajan's other flank were the garrisons of the relatively small provinces of Raetia and Noricum, consisting of a number of auxiliary regiments, but no legions. Who their governors were at this time is not known. Then came the great concentration of armed power based in Pannonia under the governorship of Pompeius Longinus, at present deeply involved in the war in Bohemia, five legions and many auxiliaries. Beyond Pannonia were the two Moesian provinces: Superior, whose governor is not known, but who commanded two legions and a large auxiliary force, and Inferior, where L. Julius Marinus had another two legions facing the Dacians across the Danube. Between them, therefore, five men – Sura, Trajan, Pompeius Longinus, Marinus, and the unknown in Moesia Superior, commanded thirteen legions and their associated auxiliaries, almost half the whole Roman army.

In this situation two things were required of the governors. The first and most important was to maintain full control over their armies. The men were inevitably upset by the news from Rome and signs of mutiny or insurrection had to be suppressed at once, lest they fester, multiply and spread – as the episode of Dio Chrysostom in the auxiliary camp demonstrated. Second, the governors had to maintain contact and agreement with each other, for any division between them would permit the restless elements to erupt. These necessities were clear and obvious, all the more so to men who had lived through the civil war of 69, and who had participated in the suppression of the hopeless attempted rebellion of Saturninus, who had begun his movement at Trajan's gubernatorial capital at Moguntiacum.

All this was surely also obvious to Nerva and his counsellors in Rome. They had also lived through 69, and Verginius Rufus could explain to any who had forgotten just how the German legions had behaved. They remembered also the close shave of 89. Nerva's choice of consuls for 97 had indicated his hope for a reconciliation of opposite opinions in the Senate and for a burial of old feuds. At the same time that list showed that the policy of promoting deserving men to the summit of the consulship would continue, particularly among men from the more highly romanised of the western provinces, such as Narbonensis and Baetica. There was also a recognition of the rights of army men to accede to that position – one of them being Atilius Agricola, Trajan's gubernatorial neighbour in Belgica. In addition, the procurator in Belgica, Sex. Attius Suburanus, was, to judge from his later rapid promotion by Trajan, an early ally.

Of course it was also the case that the main part of the army was involved in a war. It is one of the greater mysteries of our sources that almost nothing is known about the course of the fighting in this war. Indeed it is only indirectly, by the discovery of a bureaucratic document, a soldier's discharge diploma, that we know the great size of the army, and the name of its commander.[5] We also know that on at least three occasions Nerva's government used the coinage to proclaim victories.[6] But the absence of any detail about the war, from a period when a considerable amount of miscellaneous matter is known, and from a time when numerous writers were active, including the greatest of Roman historians and the blithest of Roman letter writers – Tacitus and Pliny – makes one suspicious. It may be that the victories were, if not actually phoney, then perhaps somewhat exaggerated. It is perhaps more likely that detail was suppressed to divert renown from that most unmilitary of emperors, Nerva, the *triumphator* from Nero's time. Since the war, in the end, was unsuccessful, and was brought to an end by Trajan (see Chapter 10), it is likely that a discreet veil was drawn over it. It would not do for Nerva to be thought victorious when the soldierly Trajan was not.

These possibilities are a necessary conjecture to help with the background to events in Rome during 97. The preoccupation of the great Roman army in Pannonia – or rather, in fighting beyond the Pannonian frontier – left the door open for mischief by others. They took advantage, in other words, of the fact that the main military power in the empire was unable to exert its true political weight in the capital. Yet the fact that that power existed was also inhibitory of any plots. That is, like Crassus, any plotter could be balked by reference to the Roman army.

The winter of 96/97, after the unsuccessful exploit of Crassus, apparently passed peacefully – perhaps because the Pannonian army was in winter quarters, and so, not being involved in fighting, was available to intervene in Italy if needed. But with the spring more crises began. Of them we know of two, though only one of them in any real detail. The first was some sort of a problem which arose in Syria. It is mentioned by Pliny as taking place, or at least comments about it reached him, at the time he was in the midst of an oratorical attack on an enemy in the Senate. This took place several months after Domitian's death, and so in the early part of 97; Domitius Apollinaris is identified as consul designate, and so it was before May, when he took office.[7]

The atmosphere is well conveyed by the incidents he reports. Pliny was attacking Publicius Certus over some issue in Domitian's reign. He was rebuked by a senior senator, a consular, who pointed out that Certus had friends, one of whom might well be the next emperor. It is therefore permissible to conclude that some senators were expecting that Nerva would choose his heir from among the men in Rome – or that they were expecting a coup to remove Nerva, as Nerva had removed Domitian. When Pliny persisted in his attacks, another consular remarked to him that the governor of Syria was one of those friends of Certus. The implication of this is not clear. It may be taken as indicating that the governor of Syria was a candidate, or simply that he was a powerful man.

That governor was probably P. Cornelius Nigrinus Curiatius Maternus. His career is detailed on an inscription from Liria in Tarraconensis.[8] He had been adlected to the rank of praetor by Vespasian, having served as a military tribune in the *legio* XIV *Gemina*, possibly in Britain, and possibly during the civil war of 69. He was legate of the *legio* VIII *Augusta* and then governor of Aquitania and Moesia, having served as consul in 83 between these posts. He served with distinction in Domitian's Dacian war, collecting several awards for bravery.[9] He was in his fifties as governor of Syria, a decade and a half older than Trajan (and Domitian). His qualifications for high office had been recognised by all the Flavian emperors, and his name indicates that he had been adopted by the orator Curiatius Maternus,[10] probably as an adult, an adoption which may indicate some cultural achievements in the adoptee. He was otherwise not, so far as can be seen, from a notable family.[11]

The Syrian governor was a powerful man in post because of his large army and his rich province, and in part because of memories of the part played by the Syrian governor in helping Vespasian to the throne in 69. But Pliny's memory is of trouble *in* Syria, not a threat *from* Syria. It may be that the Syrian governor was rattling his sabre because he felt that he was being ignored in the discussions which were obviously going on over the succession; such a man clearly had to be consulted: even if it was not a clear and constitutional right, it would obviously be prudent to do so. It may also be something quite different.

In the event Nigrinus did not follow through, and this suggests that it may be that he was not in fact putting forward his own claim to the succession. There are other possible explanations for what happened. It is known that A. Larcius Priscus was sent from his post as quaestor in Asia to take command of the *legio* IV *Scythica* in Syria, and in that post he also acted as governor of Syria until a new governor arrived, and so we have to account for this sudden vacancy.[12] It has been assumed that this emergency posting was as a result of the trouble in Syria mentioned by Pliny, and that the governor before Larcius Priscus (that is, Nigrinus) had had to be removed because of his imperial ambitions.[13] There is, however, no suggestion of any such emergency, nor is there any evidence for his removal. Pliny's words are relatively innocuous, and they do not require such a drastic explanation. To impute a full imperial crisis to what he said is going too far, though it is clear that something did happen. The answer may well lie in another diploma.

A recently published military diploma, dated to late 97, contains the partial names of the consuls in office. One of these is 'RICOLA', and is to be seen as the name of Q. Glitius Atilius Agricola, who is also known from the *Fasti Ostienses* to be consul in 97, holding office in September and October. His colleague's name survives only as 'TERNO'.[14] Just as no other man with a name ending in RICOLA can be found than Glitius, so the only known prominent Roman of the time with a name ending in TERNO is Nigrinus.[15]

It is, of course, necessary to justify this theory. It is unusual that a consul take up his office immediately after arriving from his province; yet this is exactly what happened with both men who became consuls in September of that year – Agricola had governed Belgica until the summer. This circumstance, given the chronology of the year, is clearly connected with the succession crisis. Both men must therefore be seen as Trajanic supporters, installed in office in Rome in order to facilitate the adoption. Both men were powerful figures, Nigrinus with a substantial military reputation, and Agricola went on to a second consulship of his own in 103. With these two in post from 1 September, the most important civil posts in the city after the emperor were in safe hands.

I suggest, therefore, that whatever problem existed in Syria in 97 was connected with Nigrinus' absence from that province in the summer. His consulship, which commenced in September, was clearly signalled in advance, and a new governor would need to travel to Syria to take up the office well before September. Something went wrong: the new governor did not arrive in time, and the legionary legate of IV *Scythica* became the temporary governor. He was replaced as an emergency measure in command of the legion by Larcius Priscus, and it was a problem caused by the temporary governor that was agitating Rome – perhaps he died,[16] perhaps he was too ambitious. At any rate he was suddenly and briefly replaced by Larcius Priscus until the new replacement for Nigrinus arrived from Rome. The identity of the new governor is unknown.[17]

There are problems with, and objections to, all this. One would expect the diploma to show 'TERNO II' if it was Nigrinus but this is perhaps not wholly necessary. One would certainly expect this also to appear on the inscription showing Nigrinus' career, but as it happens that is exactly where there is an unrestorable gap in the inscription. One would expect an iterating consul to be *ordinarius*, but Antoninus earlier in the year had been suffect, and next year there were four iterations as suffects. It is also all somewhat speculative, but if Glitius Agricola's name can be restored, so can Nirgrinus'. And it does explain the unusual work of Larcius Priscus in Syria. His transfer to command the legion is not too surprising, but his brief time as temporary governor is most odd. It did, of course, follow from the legionary command. IV *Scythica* was the legion whose headquarters, at Zeugma, were closest to Antioch of all the Syrian legions, and it was the legion whose commander would need to have diplomatic sense, being also closest to potential Parthian trouble. The commander of the legion had taken over as temporary governor of Syria in the past; it was perhaps part of his duties. In this case, no fuss was made. The event is recorded only on Larcius Priscus' own career inscription, but not noted anywhere else. If there had been real trouble in Syria it is very odd that the appointment of a man of no more than quaestorian rank was sufficient to quieten it. It may be remarked that Pliny's words on what was happening in Syria do not clearly suggest anything very serious, nor do they demand to be interpreted in the context of the imperial succession: that is a modern interpretation only.

Whatever the explanation for the events in Syria, it is clear that the Syrian governor must be eliminated from the list of candidates. This appears to have become clear some time after Pliny's conversations with the senators who were providing warning advice, perhaps late in the spring. If Nigrinus really did become consul in September 97, he would need to leave Syria two or three months before that date, and this again suggests that the Syrian crisis – if that is what it was – was over by, say, May or June.

It was immediately succeeded by another crisis, in Rome. The Praetorian Guard had only marginally been involved in the killing of Domitian, though by doing nothing, the Guard had accepted the new situation. Their new commander, Casperius Aelianus, was a man who had been a supporter of Vespasian in 69 and a previous Guard commander under Domitian. He was thus a Flavian loyalist, as were many of the army commanders. But those commanders were away from Rome, whereas he was present in the city. He was also subject to pressure from his men, who were, it seems, increasingly annoyed at Domitian's fate. In the summer of 97, with Aelianus in command, some of the guardsmen surrounded the palace. They were not in insurrection, and were not intent on a coup; instead they had certain demands, and their numbers made it necessary for Nerva to meet these. They wished Domitian's murderers to be punished.[18]

In the circumstances, where the Guard was the only real military force in the city, this demand is surprisingly moderate. It was not a demand for the punishment of those involved in the plot to kill Domitian, but only for the punishment of the actual killers, and in the event they were satisfied with only two victims. Nerva attempted to protect the two men, melodramatically baring his throat to the guardsmen and proclaiming his willingness to die rather than deliver them. Presumably he only did this once it was clear that the soldiers would not take up his offer. His bluff was called, the men insisted, and their former commander Petronius Secundus and the freedman Parthenius were handed over. The fact that they were present to be handed over suggests that they were at hand, in the palace. No doubt the Guard's unhappiness was well known, and the rising anger at the lack of punishment will have driven these men to seek refuge. But others involved – Clodianus the guardsman, the unnamed gladiator, and so on – were not sought out (Stephanus was dead already), unless they had been killed earlier.

This was an episode which could well have become more serious, and it was a clear warning of future trouble. The Guard immediately killed the two men: Petronius was executed at once, cleanly; Parthenius was killed slowly and most cruelly: first castrated, and then slowly strangled. This may have been a gesture of contempt directed at Nerva, for the emperor had issued a decree making the practice of castration illegal;[19] it echoes the refusal of the soldiers to take seriously Nerva's attempt to protect the two men, and the requirement they enforced that Nerva should publicly give thanks for the soldiers' actions. An emperor held in such contempt by his soldiers was unlikely to last very long.

The limited demands and actions of the Guard in this episode – limited by comparison with what they could have done – might well have found approval in much wider sections of the population. Their selection of victims, if it was not merely fortuitous, in the sense that they were the only ones who could be found, was interesting, perhaps even careful. Petronius, in his office as Guard commander, had been charged with the protection of the emperor's person, and had clearly failed in that duty even if he had not participated in the plot or the killing. It should have been Nerva's first duty to punish him, not merely dismiss him. Parthenius, an imperial freedman, was beholden to Domitian as a servant to a master; his participation in the plot was a personal betrayal of the most unpleasant and unsettling sort – hence, no doubt, the refined cruelty of his killing, and the preservation of its details, as a warning to others who might be tempted to plot in the same way.

But the way in which these punishments were accomplished – richly deserved as they were according to contemporary lights – was just as unsettling and dangerous as the failure to punish had been. The Guard had threatened the emperor, had defied him, had treated him with contempt. The men had thereby tasted power of the most direct sort. No one in Rome could be in any doubt now that Nerva, as emperor, was little more than a cypher. When the guardsmen realised that their potential power could be translated into actual control, they would be back. The emperor had thus only a relatively short time in which to head them off, and to do so he required military support. Though it was not directly concerned with the issue of the succession, the Guard's riot in summer 97 was the event which forced Nerva to make a decision, and a military man would need to be chosen.

The decision was made public in October. The Guard's riot took place in the summer, perhaps July or August, so there was some time, two or three months, between the riot and the publication of the decision. The riot was thus not the immediate cause of the decision, though it is clear that it had a substantial bearing on it, largely by making it even more urgent, and by eliminating the possibility of a 'civilian' being chosen.

Nor can the precise details of the adoption of Trajan, as we are informed of them, be taken as the whole story. According to Pliny in his speech of praise before the new emperor three years later, a 'laurelled letter' arrived at Rome in October with news of a victory in the war in the north. Nerva took the letter to the Capitol to proclaim the news to the gods and, having done so, turned to the assembled crowd and proclaimed also that he adopted Marcus Ulpius Traianus as his son and so as his chosen successor.[20]

If there was a way of causing still more trouble for himself it would have been for Nerva to catch everyone in Rome by surprise in this way. It would have been seen as a coup comparable with the way Nerva became emperor, and it would surely cause a row, if nothing worse. There were men who would have supported Nerva's choice, if consulted; and if not consulted, they would be annoyed, and could well oppose it. But Nerva was an insider, a man who had operated on this level for thirty years or more. He had delayed his choice because of a certain lack of decisiveness in his nature which was a result of just that history, but also because he surely appreciated the problems involved. It is beyond belief that he did this deed abruptly, taking the political world by surprise. There had certainly been consultations beforehand.

It therefore follows that Trajan knew in advance, as did Nerva's own council, whoever was on it. Considerable numbers of senators surely knew in advance, and since Trajan was only one of a fair number of senators or soldiers who could be considered to be candidates, the generals had been consulted as well. It is therefore worth considering at whose intiative Trajan's name was put forward.

The first problem is Trajan himself. He may well have become one of the most distinguished and famous of the Roman emperors after his accession, but such a destiny was by no means evident to his contemporaries beforehand. His career had been notable, certainly, but no more so than that of a dozen other men of consular rank at the time. There was, for example, A. Bucius Lappius Maximus, twice consul under Domitian, in 86 and 95, the real destroyer of Saturninus in 89. Trajan may have marched his legion all the way from Spain in that crisis, but he had arrived when it was all over. Lappius Maximus had governed Bithynia, Germania Inferior (in 87–89) and Syria (89–92).[21] Or there was Pompeius Longinus, winning victories in the Suebic-Sarmatian war – it was actually from him that the news of the victory had come – currently in command of a huge army, consul the year before Trajan, and a former governor of Judaea (86–89) and Moesia Superior (94–96).[22] There was L. Caesennius

Sospes, who had commanded in the first Suebic-Sarmatian war, earned decorations for bravery, was a widely experienced administrator, a relative by marriage of the deceased Domitian, and had been governor of the great military province of Cappadocia-Galatia in 93–94.[23] If an older, even more experienced, head was required there was Sex. Julius Frontinus, consul in Vespasian's reign, a former governor of Britannia (73–77) and Asia in 86, author and soldier, and currently *curator aquarum* in Rome, still clearly hale and vigorous.[24] Or, of the same generation, there was Q. Corellius Rufus, who had twice been consul under Vespasian and had governed in Germania Superior and in Asia.[25] And of course there was M. Cornelius Nigrinus Curiatus Maternus, though lack of ancestry might have ruled him out.

All these men, and there were others, had the same experience as Trajan or better, and had a more distinguished record in government. If it was closeness to the dead Domitian that counted, Trajan may have been a distant and approximate relative by marriage, but Caesennius Sospes was closer; if it was experience of the higher reaches of government and membership of Domitian's *consilium*, then Lappius Maximus and Julius Frontinus were very much more notable than Trajan, as was Nigrinus. Some men, like Pompeius Longinus, had the advantage of having armies under their command during 97, just as did Trajan, but Trajan was newly appointed and had not been militarily active for several years. In other words, even if Trajan's record, his connection with Domitian, and his present situation are all taken into account, he was still just one of perhaps a dozen or so men who could pretend to the succession by reason of his accomplishments and abilities. Nevertheless by October 97 Trajan had emerged as the preferred candidate.

There were, therefore, other factors involved than Trajan's military and administrative record. One was his ancestry, for, unlike the rest, his father was consular (though Pompeius Longinus' adopted father was consular). Another was his age. Some of the 'candidates' in Rome had already been considered at the time of Nerva's accession, and had declined. Often they were of Nerva's generation, and if Nerva was now considered to be too old, so were they. This would rule out such men as Julius Frontinus and Corellius Rufus. It also may have counted against Pompeius Longinus and Nigrinus, who were in their fifties. But particularly potent in Trajan's favour was the support he could call on through his personal, familial and social connections. Trajan, as already noted, was the intersecting point of the two western aristocratic networks, for his marriage to Pompeia Plotina linked the networks of Baetica and Narbonensis. He thus had connections with such powerful Rome-based men as Arrius Antoninus, Annius Verus and Julius Ursus. He also had as his neighbouring governor another Spaniard, L. Licinius Sura, consul in 93 and governor of Germania Inferior. Their neighbour in Belgica was Q. Glitius Atilius Agricola, who became consul in September 97, and so was in office at the time the adoption was announced, and who had held a judicial post in Tarraconensis when Trajan was in command of the legion stationed in that province. In the northern armies, therefore, Trajan stood out for his political connections before all the rest.

The political weight of those armies has to be taken into account. The northern commanders were especially significant since they apparently worked together, and they were all candidates. Pompeius Longinus, with the most powerful army, was surely on most men's lists. He was a distinguished man, the adopted son of the consul of 71 or 72, and was later to demonstrate his loyalty to both Rome and Trajan in the most drastic fashion in the Second Dacian War.[26] But he was, like Nigrinus, in his fifties, closer in age to Nerva than to Trajan, and this seems likely to have counted against him. One of the motivating factors in all the intrigue was to replace, not Nerva, but Domitian, who had been only forty-four when killed – just about Trajan's age. To enthrone another older man than the murdered emperor was not a replacement; and, of course it could only continue the problem of the succession into another reign, since the new 'older man' would also be expected to die soon, like Nerva.

In the question of age, therefore, Trajan was one of those with about the right number of years; but he was by no means the only one – his neighbours Sura and Glitius Agricola were about right as well. Any of the consuls of the late eighties and early nineties could qualify – a category which included the recently exiled Crassus. One of these was the governor of Britannia, P. Metilius Nepos, who had been in office for the past two years.[27] He was close enough to the German armies to be consulted on the succession by their commanders; since he commanded three legions, it would clearly be prudent to do so.

In the other direction, easterly, was a much more significant figure, in the person of the governor of Moesia Inferior, L. Julius Marinus. He had also been in that office two years, and had been consul in 93, and so he had been a consular colleague of Sura's. He was also a central figure in the network of aristocrats linking Narbonensis with Asia: his wife was the daughter of Caecilius Simplex of Narbonensis (and not just Narbonenis, but specifically Nemausus, the home city of Trajan's wife Plotina) and his son was married to Julia Tertulla of Apollonia in Asia Minor. Furthermore, that son was currently governor of Lycia-Pamphylia, the province whose aristocrats were one of the hubs of that network in Asia.

Of the possible candidates, therefore, Trajan was best placed to command these networks of support. And it was as one of the generals on the northern frontier that he could best do so. That is, his name is unlikely to have come seriously into consideration until he arrived in post as governor at Moguntiacum late in 96. It was only there that he would be in regular communication with Sura and Agricola and Pompeius Longinus, and, through Longinus, with Marinus. The central man of this group was clearly Longinus, with his great army. He was also the man who, because he was conducting the war, was in more frequent conmmunication with the emperor than were any of the others.

So this is what I suggest was going on in the year between Trajan's appointment to Germania Superior in the autumn of 96 and the arrival of the news of the victory in the Suebo-Sarmatian war at Rome in October 97: Pompeius Longinus and the nearby generals were consulting on their attitude to the choice of successor; in that process Trajan's name emerged as their preferred choice because of his record, his ancestry, his connections, and his age; the eastern and western networks, those in Asia and in Narbonensis and Spain, and their members in Rome, were consulted and mobilised. Trajan himself could speak to some extent for the Hispano-Gallic nexus, though he will have had to check through it to ensure his support; he would surely consult Arrius Antoninus, for example, or Annius Verus, both of whom were consuls in 97, and both are likely to have been members of Nerva's *consilium*. Julius Marinus in Moesia Inferior and his son in Lycia-Pamphylia are the obvious conduits for consultations between the Danubian generals on the frontier and the Asian network. It is also necessary to assume that Nigrinus in Syria was consulted and gave his support; in exchange it would seem that he gained a second consulship.[28] This process would take some time, and would not necessarily be easy. It seems likely that the Suebic-Sarmatian war would have taken a distinctly secondary place in the face of these intrigues.

In all this Nerva would also be consulted and informed. How powerful his voice was in the matter is not clear, but it is doubtful if he had a power of veto in the face of the united voice of the generals and the networks. Of course, he did know Trajan, having seen him off to his province late in 96 with special ceremony; there is no need to doubt that he approved the choice, though his personal preference might well have lain elsewhere. If he had any objections, the Guard's riot in the summer of 97 will have driven them away, and will have brought the discussions to the point of decision.

I am therefore suggesting that Trajan's name emerged from a period of consultation lasting several months, that the events at the Capitol in October 97 were prepared beforehand, were carefully stage-managed, and that the announcement of the victory was made at that time because the consultations had been completed. Reading Dio's account, for example, the impression is given that Nerva's adoption was the result of the Guard Riot;[29] yet in reality several months passed between the two events. We have then to account for the peculiar coincidence of the arrival of the declaration of victory at Rome with Nerva's public adoption of Trajan, since there is no obvious connection between them. Reading Pliny's account, it is easy to make the assumption that Trajan was adopted because he had been the victor in the war.[30] But the 'laurelled letter' did not come from Trajan in Moguntiacum, and Trajan as governor of Germania Superior was not involved in the war. His province was several hundred kilometres from the fighting, and he was separated from it by two provinces (Raetia and Noricum) into which he could not go without imperial permission, and by a large and friendly German tribe, the Hermunduri.

The letter was in fact sent to the emperor by Pompeius Longinus in Pannonia, perhaps from Carnuntum, or perhaps from the seat of war, somewhere north of the Danube. If the arrival of the news was followed immediately by the announcement of the adoption of Trajan, as is clear from Pliny did happen, it follows that Trajan had been selected as Nerva's successor well before the arrival of the news of the victory, and that the news of the victory itself was expected at Rome. Nerva, Pompeius Longinus and Trajan all knew what was going to happen, and the *Epitome* also notes the involvement of Licinius Sura;[31] we have seen that Julius Marinus was a probable player in the game as well.

The involvement of Licinius Sura is another detail which provides corroboratory evidence. If he was involved then so was Q. Glitius Atilius Agricola, for Domitian's positioning of the German provinces' treasury in Belgica meant that the three governors had to co-operate.[32] Agricola was suffect consul in September and October of 97, or so the reconstruction of that year's list shows,[33] so he was in Rome from some time before September at least until after the end of October, by which time Trajan's adoption had taken place. His positioning in Rome at that time was thus utilised with opportunist imagination by the intriguers for Trajan's succession, for his fortuitous presence meant that he could co-ordinate the events of October – indeed one might even suppose that it was the fact of his consulship which determined that the event should take place then.

This reconstruction of events is, of course, to a degree speculative, as are all reconstructions of Trajan's emergence as emperor. Support of a kind is, however, forthcoming from one of the less tendentious sources, the consular lists of the early part of Trajan's reign. As with Nerva's lists, these may supply information about the support Trajan enjoyed in his first years, and the lists of those years are very odd, as has been remarked more than once. In particular a comparison of Nerva's with Trajan's first lists shows that the latter included members of the Asian aristocratic network, a group which was noticeably absent from Nerva's 97 list.

Trajan's adoption was announced in October 97, and he had been Nerva's choice for some time before that, so he will have been consulted over the composition of the consular list for 98; he was also wholly responsible for the list of 99. These two lists will thus give some indication of the sources to which Trajan looked for support during his consultations in 97, just as Nerva's list for 97 was a good indication of his own support, and of his policy towards the Senate.

The list for 98 is probably known in full,[34] and as argued in Chapter 2, it is very oddly constructed. Nerva and Trajan began the year as joint ordinary consuls, a post reigning emperors usually held for perhaps a fortnight, and Nerva duly resigned half way through January (and died at the end of the month), but Trajan continued in office (in his absence, in Germany) until June, a full six months. This was something only occasionally indulged in; the last time had been by Vespasian, in holding his first consulship as emperor; before that the only example seems to be Augustus. Trajan – it must have been his idea, for Nerva would have used it himself the year before – was making a serious political point, that he was, like Vespasian and Augustus, restoring the state to stability after an uncomfortably disturbing period; the previous two years were being likened to the civil wars.

This six-month consulship thus provided Trajan with particular distinction, but it also allowed him to be partnered with a succession of men, who would be given honour by him, and whose own distinction would provide him with good political support. A notable series of suffects were thus Trajan's partners through to the middle of the year, men who were in fact in all probability Nerva's supporters originally; their presence with Trajan was a strong signal that Trajan had Nerva's full support. Their distinction has been noted already, but a few more remarks may be made here.[35] Four of these men were receiving second consulships. Two were from Narbonensis, Cn. Domitius Tullus, who had been consul in 84, and Domitian's counsellor Sex. Julius Frontinus, consul for the first time in 73. L. Julius Ursus was from either Spain or Narbonensis, but more important, he was a family connection of both Trajan and Domitian. The other two colleagues of Trajan were T. Vestricius Spurinna, a poet who had his first consulship as long ago as 72, and C. Pomponius Pius; Spurinna was from northern Italy, Pomponius' origin is not known.

By contrast the rest of the list for 98, three pairs holding office for two months each, is much less distinguished and had all the appearance of a normal list, from which one might suspect that it was the original list produced by Nerva and his people, with consuls reduced to two months in office from the usual four so as to accommodate the special, perhaps emergency, list for the first half. It contains two men from Italy, L. Maecius Postumus and A. Vicirius Martialis, and two whose origin is unknown, C. Pomponius Rufus Priscus Coelius Sparsus and Cn. Pompeius Ferox Licinianus. Of these men only the career of Maecius Postumus is known in any detail;[36] these four men can muster only a single (later) governorship between them, that of Coelius Sparsus in Africa about 112/113;[37] the others appear to be the usual aristocratic drones. The last two, in office in November and December, are not securely attested, but two names have been advanced by Syme:[38] Q. Fulvius Gillo Bittius Proculus, who went on to govern Asia in 115,[39] and P. Julius Lupus, who was probably the brother of Julius Ursus, second husband of Arria Fadilla, the daughter of Arrius Antoninus; he was also probably from Spain or Narbonensis, though nothing but his consulate is known of his career.[40] The predominance of non-Italians in the early part of the list is very notable: four out of seven (for Trajan himself was a Spaniard) is perhaps a record up to that time, and those four were all heaping up extra prestige by receiving second consulships. The second-half men are a great contrast: generally Italian nonentities, the professional senators who gained their posts by virtue of their wealth and lived on long enough to become governors of Asia or Africa when their turn came; only Julius Lupus' connections are very noteworthy.

This pattern is repeated, so far as can be seen, in the consuls for 99, though only seven names are known out of, presumably, twelve. The *ordinarii* are a pair who emerged with distinction in Trajan's reign: Q. Sosius Senecio,[41] whose origin is uncertain, and A. Cornelius Palma Frontonianus [42] from Italy. Both of these were military men, became important generals and governors under Trajan, and both went on to acquire second consulships; further, Senecio was Sex. Julius Frontinus' son-in-law. Another Spaniard on the 99 list is Senecio Memmius Afer,[43] who was also related by marriage to Caesius Fronto, the consul in office during the assassination of 96; Q. Fabius Barbarus Valerius Magnus Julianus was from either Spain or Narbonensis.[44] Of the rest, one of the consuls was an Italian, T. Julius Ferox, active in government throughout Trajan's reign.[45] The same can be said of A. Caecilius Faustinus.[46] The last man is a mere name, perhaps incomplete, Sulpicius Lucretius Barba.[47] This is, on the whole, a more workmanlike set than the ancient and Italian group of 98, at least so far as can be judged – there are five names missing.[48] It seems clear that this was the result of the influence of Trajan being now paramount.

Several easterners reached the consulship in the next few years. In the next year, 100, one of the suffect consuls was C. Julius Plancius Varus Cornutus Tertullus, Pliny's friend, and a fully participating member of the Asian network.[49] A year later, 101, another easterner, L. Julius Marinus' son, L. Julius Marinus Caecilius Simplex, was consul.[50] The increase in eastern participation of the later years of Domitian, halted by the Italian predominance under Nerva, had been resumed.

The emergence of Trajan as successor to Nerva was by no means a foreordained matter. If he was *capax imperii*, no one had noticed it before 97.[51] His nomination was therefore the result not of his personal qualities – it has to be said that even as emperor, these were not noticeably special – but to the political situation in that year. The early failure of Nerva to nominate an heir, for whatever reason, opened the field to a larger choice. The successive crises of his first nine months – Crassus, Syria, the Guard riot – made the choice a matter of increasing urgency. The concentration of armed forces in Pannonia, and the continuing war, which Nerva could not dominate as Domitian had, or as Trajan would, lent even greater weight than usual to the opinions of the generals, and the existing connections between the governors and commanders of the northern frontier – commanding between the five of them no less than thirteen legions – meant that they could put forward their man with every likelihood that their wishes would be respected.

The man they chose had certain advantages of which his nominators were obviously aware. His ability as a soldier was on a par with theirs, a fact important since a war was being waged as they discussed the problem; his age, experience and Flavian loyalty made him generally acceptable to the soldiers; above all, his familial connections meant that he could command wide senatorial and civilian support, in Spain, in Gaul, in Asia and in the Senate, where his ready acceptance in September and October of Nerva's accession provided him with support later. Given that his age, experience and ability were more or less standard for several men at the time, it was Trajan's connections which made him the choice of the generals; their deftness of political touch is evident in that choice, as in their ability, mediated no doubt by the presence of Glitius Agricola in Rome at the right moment, to persuade the emperor and to mount a remarkable display to publicise the announcement.

9

HEIR

When Nerva announced the adoption of Trajan in the Forum in late October 97 he gave him his new name: Marcus Ulpius Nerva Traianus, and he sent his new son a diamond ring, which would seem to have been a method of authenticating the news which it accompanied – the same ring was handed on to Hadrian later. It was accompanied by an apt quotation from Homer, and, presumably, a full account of events.[1] This was, however, only the first stage in the adoption process. The legal measures to make Trajan Nerva's imperial successor as well as his personal heir had to be gone through as well. For the adoption, even if publicly announced, was essentially a private matter, making Trajan the legal inheritor of Nerva's goods and chattels – and his name – whereas for him to become the designated successor to the imperial power he had to have various offices and titles conferred on him by the Senate.

Nerva confirmed his choice and his intentions by the other acts which were within his prerogative. One was another addition to Trajan's name, whereby he became 'Caesar' as well. This had become less a name than a title by now, borne by emperors and their heirs since Tiberius.[2] Then, or perhaps at the same time, he and Trajan were both hailed as *imperator* and both adopted the honorific Germanicus, in recognition of the victory which Nerva had used as a peg to hang his adoption on.[3] These three awards were perhaps made one at a time, providing cumulative evidence of Nerva's favour. It would certainly seem that this was all done before the Senate was summoned to consult on the legal measures needed,[4] in order to present the Senate with a group of *faits accomplis*. Yet there is no sign that the Senate was in any way reluctant. This meeting may well have been one summmoned to meet by Tacitus the historian, who was one of the consuls in the last two months of the year, taking up the office only a few days after Nerva's public announcement.

The next stage was for the Senate to confer the imperial powers on Trajan. At a formal meeting, Trajan was given the *tribunicia potestas*, making his person sacrosanct as a protection, and *imperium maius*, giving him superior authority over other magistrates. This was accomplished by a combination of Nerva's imperial authority and votes in the Senate.[5] This made him Nerva's near equal, except that Nerva was clearly the senior of the two, not only in age but also by virtue of his superior number of consulships, his extra year of tribunician power, his two salutations as *imperator* (to

Trajan's one) and his office as *pontifex maximus* – 'you were subject, legate, and son', said Pliny, summarising his continuing subordination to the old man.[6]

This was quite enough to make Nerva out as having greater *auctoritas*, particularly from the point of view of the Senate and Rome, and towards Trajan's erstwhile senatorial equals. It is clear, however, that comparative youth and greater physical vigour could well counter-balance all these formal and institutional advantages in the provinces and on the frontier. Trajan remained on the frontier but with an expanded remit.[7] Nerva stayed in Rome. After all, both places needed imperial attention, and the competent Domitian was no longer around to provide that attention to both in one person. Trajan's presence in Germany also made it wholly clear that he was the army's imperial nominee. He was also in contact with the legions he had recently commanded, and which could be expected to be his supporters. At the same time his presence with the troops would help suppress any movement of dissension and would put him at one of the danger spots when Nerva died.

There is no hint of an argument over any of this. Admittedly the sources are scarcely voluminous, yet the whole process seems to have gone through without any fuss or even much discussion.[8] This argues that the ground had been well prepared, and that Nerva's pre-adoption consultations had been careful, wide and convincing. It also implies that no one in Rome, or in the army, was surprised by any of these events, from the adoption onwards. For such an important matter, this apparent unanimity is perhaps disturbing; there were surely other men who could have been considered, and it is simply not reasonable to believe that Trajan was unopposed; the absence of dispute, however, is the main evidence for the well-prepared nature of the process.

After the evils of the previous thirteen months, it is perhaps an index of the fear that had developed among the senators that everything went smoothly, and any opposition remained unheard. There had been plots, conspiracies, disturbances, the Guard riot and murders, all following on the assassination, a sequence of disturbances which were spreading outwards in their effects from the fight in the emperor's bedroom in the palace to threaten senators in a seemingly inexorable process. Pliny comments on rioting and mutiny in the army and widespread violence and terror,[9] though this is notably unspecific and might well simply refer to the Guard riot. These events were far too reminiscent of the civil war less than thirty years before for anybody's comfort. All this had so worked on the Senate that a clear answer to the question of the succession was surely welcome, even if Trajan himself was not necessarily everyone's choice, and whose indecisiveness probably mirrored the inability of the Senate to decide collectively on a successor. The uncertainty had been compounded by the indecisiveness of the emperor, who was in a sense the Senate's own choice. The very fact that his successor was seen as a military man was a criticism of the Senate and of Nerva. It will have become clear that only with the army's agreement and participation could the succession be settled; and a younger man than the sick and elderly Nerva was clearly needed. As Pliny put it in his panegyric: 'The country reeled under the blows to take refuge in your embrace; the empire which was falling with its emperor was put into your hands at the emperor's word.'[10]

All this took time. Starting from the announcement of the adoption in late

October,[11] there then took place the Senate meeting at which imperial powers were conferred on Trajan, perhaps a day or two after the public announcement of adoption. The conferral of the title and offices may have taken place all at one meeting, but of course there will have been much discussion and speechmaking, and so perhaps it is more likely to have been spread over several days. The senators were entitled to their ceremony, and a series of meetings and measures was much more impressive to doubters than a swift single act. It will have been in this period that Nerva and Trajan organised, or reorganised, the consular list for the next year, with its exceptionally long consulate for Trajan and its notably distinguished list of suffects as his partners. They will also have divided the imperial responsibilites between them, a process which needed discussion with others. It is unlikely that all this took much less than a month – Trajan in Germany and Nerva in Rome will have needed repeated messages, carried by hand, for everything to be worked out. It seems impossible, no matter how detailed the pre-adoption negotiations, that it was finished before the end of November. Two months later Nerva was dead.

During that time Trajan was in Germany.[12] Governors of both Germania Inferior and Superior are known at this time, so Trajan's presence in the area was in his capacity as emperor (and not as governor of his former province, which was a possibility). Colonia Agrippinensis was the normal headquarters of the governor of Inferior; Trajan would thus appear to have been operating as supervisor of the whole German Rhine frontier. He had the two governors under him, and each of them had three legions in his province. Trajan therefore controlled an army of six legions, three of which he already knew from his time as governor of Germania Superior in the past year. The two governors were his fellow Spaniard L. Licinius Sura in Inferior, probably in office since 96, and L. Julius Servianus, who was Trajan's replacement in Superior; Sura was replaced by L. Neratius Priscus during 98.[13] In the delicate period of joint-*imperium* Trajan was therefore in command, more or less directly, of a fifth of the Roman army. He also – and this was perhaps more for prestige reasons than for security – commanded a larger army than Pompeius Longinus in Pannonia.

It may be that this locating of Trajan in Germany provides some indication of the problems of the moment, and of the internal dynamics of the joint regime. Given that there was a war going on in Pannonia, and that Trajan was to some degree a military man, it has to be asked why he did not go to take charge of the operations in Pannonia. Putting to one side for the moment a discussion of the war itself, which will occupy some space in the next chapter, one obvious reason is that it would not be sensible to change commanders in mid-war, when Pompeius Longinus had commanded in the field for two years. But it may also be that Pompeius Longinus who, by virtue of his post, had to have been one of the most important of Trajan's supporters as candidate for the purple, was too powerful to be moved; it was possibly one of his conditions for supporting Trajan that he be left in command. This could explain the rather odd positioning of Trajan in Germany where, so far as we know, there was no urgent need for full imperial attention at the time, and of his command of even greater forces than Pompeius Longinus. It may also be noted that Trajan, for all his military credentials, had no experience, so far as we can see, of large-scale command in war. He may have commanded detachments in minor conflicts in Syria or Spain, but his one noted military exploit – the rapid march by his legion from north-west Spain to the Rhine in 89 – was essentially a logistical exercise and a route march. Perhaps Trajan deliberately ceded the command to Pompeius Longinus because he himself was not competent to exercise it.

This was, after all, a time of considerable difficulty for everyone. Trajan, surely to many a surprise choice as imperial successor, would need to establish himself as emperor, above all with the soldiers. His authority was clearly only indefinite and potential until he could actually enforce it in person, hence perhaps his presence in Germany, where he was already known. Being associated with Nerva was not necessarily a recommendation to the army, and there were surely impatient soldiers who wanted him to seize power at Rome and get rid of Nerva right away; he may also have had military and diplomatic work to do in Germany. The war along the Danube frontier was still going on, and the problems of the imperial power in Rome will have alerted the German tribes to the possibility of a weakening of the Roman vigilance on the frontier. They too could remember the Roman civil war of thirty years before, when the frontier suddenly became porous, and invasions became possible. And perhaps the continued fighting on the Danube was unsettling to those more distant tribes, for it involved several tribes besides those who were actually fighting. It was, despite their claims of victories, not a wholly successful war from the Roman point of view, and a Roman defeat on top of the imperial governmental problems would clearly spell opportunity for the German tribes. The presence of a new and military emperor on the German frontier would obviously be a steadying influence.

There had been one major recent event close to the Roman frontier which will have drawn Trajan's attention, as it did that of all Romans in Germany. According to Tacitus, not long before he wrote his brief ethnographic essay on Germany and the Germans, a major German tribe, the Bructeri, had been defeated and destroyed by their German neighbours.[14] The *Germania* was finished, it seems, during 98, for there is a reference to Trajan's second consulship in 98,[15] but to nothing later; the fighting had thus happened no more than a year or two before. The Bructeri had inhabited the valley of the Lippe, eastwards of the old Roman legionary fortress at Vetera. Their destruction came when the tribe was attacked by two (at least) of its neighbours, the Chamavi and the Angrivarii. Tacitus claims the Bructeri suffered 60,000 casualties, and that they were totally destroyed as a community, though neither of these claims need be accepted as literally true. He congratulated Rome on a victory by proxy, where no Roman casualties were suffered, and drew the conclusion that Rome was still favoured by god.

Tacitus' own fierce satisfaction on Rome's behalf is clear in the passage, but that was hardly the end of the matter. One of his purposes in the short treatise was to deny the dead Domitian's claim to have conquered and pacified Germany, which he had celebrated by triumphs and in his coinage,[16] by detailing the large numbers of Germans still outside the empire and un-Romanised. Yet his work in fact tends to vindicate Domitian, by standing at the point where, for the next century and a half, 'free'

Germany began a long period of peace. The irony is perhaps one which Tacitus himself might have enjoyed.

This was Domitian's work, and that of his family. In a series of wars from the great civil war onwards the Roman frontier along the middle Rhine had been advanced in several stages, by Vespasian and by Domitian, and the most dangerous tribes had been vanquished or destroyed: the Chatti in particular, whose defeats by Domitian in 83 and 89 began the long peace. The elimination of the Bructeri was the final blow in removing the last of the tribes which were both powerful and hostile. The Chatti had dominated the centre of the frontier, and their defeat had allowed the frontier to be advanced into the Taunus hills, where a carefully fortified line was established effectively protecting the whole frontier line as far south as the Danube. Partly as a result, to the south of this newly fortified area the eastern plain of the Rhine rift valley was annexed and was now being settled from Gaul, and the frontier line was pushed forward twice more without trouble; in the north the Batavian rebellion in 70 was defeated, and the Bructeri's destruction removed the last of the formidable tribes. The only other major tribe facing the Roman Rhine was the Hermunduri in Bavaria, and they were consistent Roman allies.[17]

Trajan's tenure of the German frontier therefore allowed him to appreciate the new situation as perhaps it was not fully understood in Rome – Tacitus certainly does not seem to have understood it, if the *Germania* is any guide. Trajan knew of the middle Rhine frontier from his year as governor of Germania Superior before his adoption; now at Colonia Agrippinensis he could appreciate the effect of the destruction of the Bructeri, and gain a good understanding of the north. Nowhere along the Rhine frontier was there any more an active enemy of Rome, nor any prospect of one arising in the foreseeable future. This was the background to his later reduction in the strength of the Rhine garrison. Domitian had already been able to take away two legions, out of the eight which had been there when he acceded, and Trajan was able soon to move two more, XI *Claudia* and X *Gemina*, to the Danube, leaving their former bases at Vindonissa and Noviomagus without legions.[18]

It was only after his personal inspection of the Rhine frontier that Trajan was able to make these decisions. In 98 at Colonia Agrippinensis, fifty miles south of Vetera and the junction of the Lippe with the Rhine, he could be briefed by Licinius Sura on the situation to the east after the Bructeri's destruction. Briefly the destroyer tribes would now have had more territory into which to move, and any population pressures they suffered were clearly much reduced. As a result they would not feel the need to challenge Rome. And, of course, the general inactivity of the Roman army along the Rhine was another pacifying factor: the Germans did not feel threatened, and so had less need to feel hostile.

Trajan's time in Germany during his period as joint-emperor will have given him much to think about. In Rome, meanwhile, Nerva lived on until the end of January 98. We have absolutely no information about anything he did, said or thought during that time. The general atmosphere in the city had presumably calmed down with Trajan's installation as his heir. There was no longer any point in senatorial plots against Nerva when success would only mean having to tackle Trajan and the army.

The Guard could take satisfaction from the successful elimination of their enemies and their humiliation of Nerva; had the men wished to repeat their riot, they were no doubt deterred from it by the knowledge that Trajan commanded a large army. From subsequent events it is clear that they had no idea of Trajan's own attitude to their actions. Trajan's adoption was, as Pliny pointed out later, calming: 'every disturbance died away at once', he claimed, no doubt exaggerating the calm as he had exaggerated the trouble.[19]

The new year opened with the installation of the new magistrates, Nerva and Trajan being the *ordinarii*, Trajan taking up the office in his absence. Nerva was replaced on 13 January or thereabouts by the first of five suffects who would hold the office jointly with Trajan until the end of May. This was Cn. Domitius Tullus, consul for the second time, another of those elderly senators with a career stretching back to Nero's time, a friend and crony of Nerva's, a man who had been virtually inactive since his governorship of Africa about 85.

Before Tullus' brief consulship was over – he was succeeded on 1 February by Sex. Julius Frontinus – Nerva was dead. He died on 27 January [20] in his house in the Sallustian Gardens in Rome. He had been angered by something done by a man called Regulus, suffered a fever and died as a result.[21] Whatever the precise medical details, the overall cause was age and general ill-health, which made his body unable to cope with the fever.[22] He had been emperor for sixteen and a half months.

10

NEW EMPEROR

In mid-February 98 Trajan was given the news of Nerva's death by his cousin P. Aelius Hadrianus (Hadrian), who is said to have arrived from Moguntiacum in advance of the official messenger sent by the governor, L. Julius Servianus.[1] The story of his journey, as preserved in the *Historia Augusta*, is probably taken from Hadrian's own account.[2] It is scarcely believable, and may hide the fact that Hadrian was in reality the official messenger himself.[3] He had already been employed as a messenger of congratulations on the occasion of Trajan's adoption.[4]

Hadrian had begun a military career in 95 by appointment as a military tribune in *legio* II *Adiutrix*, stationed at Aquincum in Pannonia. The transfer to that province of Pompeius Longinus in mid-96 had involved considerable transfers and interchanges of officers, and Hadrian went on to be a military tribune in *legio* V *Macedonica* at Oescus in Moesia Inferior.[5] The influence of the governor there, L. Julius Marinus, was no doubt involved in his new appointment, and it was presumably by Marinus' choice that Hadrian was sent with his and the legion's congratulations from Moesia in the autumn of 97.

Hadrian was then retained in Germany, possibly by Trajan's order, his new posting being as military tribune of *legio* XXII *Primigenia* at Moguntiacum. This may in fact have been the work of the new governor of Germania Superior, Servianus, who was married to Hadrian's sister, Domitia Paulina.[6] (No doubt Trajan gave the order, and Servianus found the place.) It is of interest that Trajan's arrival as joint-emperor was accompanied by the gathering of these relations of his in the provinces he was supervising. He was thus hedged about by friends and relations in both provinces as well as commanding familiar troops; if this was not simply nepotism, it was for reasons of security. Nerva, after all, was emperor by reason of his predecessor's murder, and there had been more than one candidate for the succession before Trajan's adoption. Nerva's age and debility meant that his designated successor would become sole emperor fairly soon: it made Trajan an assassination target rather more than was Nerva. This was another reason for the two emperors to be separated and for Trajan to be with friends, relations and troops he could trust.

Hadrian's news of Nerva's death was perhaps not wholly unexpected, certainly not a surprise, but one would have thought that Trajan might have wished for a longer period as heir to work himself into the part. On the other hand, any possibility there had been of conflict between the two emperors was now ended. And no length of time as heir can have adequately prepared him for the deluge of work which descended on him soon after Hadrian's arrival.[7]

His first instruction was for the full elaborate funeral ceremonies for the dead emperor to be carried out. This involved many senators in a variety of ceremonies spread over nearly two weeks; the process of deification then had to be gone through, taking more time and involving the whole Senate. The instructions cannot have reached Rome until late February, and the ceremonies will have continued into March.[8] During that time it will have gradually dawned on the senators in Rome that Trajan was not on his way to the city, that he intended to stay on at the frontier for some time, and gradually more men will have made their way from Rome to the north, to the temporary imperial court at Colonia Agrippinensis. The procession will have begun with officials of the court; hangers-on and importunates a little later.

After Nerva's obsequies the Senate met to deal with any loose ends in the succession. Formal confirmation of Trajan as the new emperor was made, and he was elected the new *pontifex maximus*. In addition extra honours were awarded him. He was given the title *pater patriae* and his wife and sister were voted the name Augusta. The bundle of honours began an odd dispute between emperor and Senate, whereby Trajan selected one of the new honours – *pontifex maximus*, which gave him extra real powers – but refused the rest; the Senate pressed him, he refused, the Senate insisted, and he at last, late in 98, agreed to take the title of *pater patriae*, although the ladies had to wait for some years for their own titles. Trajan's motives were perhaps modesty, but *pater patriae* was a title usually taken late in an imperial career, when it had been earned by some major and solid achievement; awarding it at the start was clearly cheapening it, so modesty might have been Trajan's reaction. To be *pontifex maximus* was, however, useful and not merely decorative, so he accepted that position at once.[9]

Appointments within the court had to be made. This would provide emperor-watchers with an early indication of the direction of imperial policy in the short term. The reappointment of C. Octavius Titinius Capito as *ab epistulis*, however, was perhaps less a sign of a continuity of policy than a recognition of the need for a professional secretary close to the emperor.[10] More important was the way Trajan dealt with the problem of the Praetorian Guard.

A guardsman had been involved in Domitian's assassination; the Guard as a whole had acquiesced in that deed for at least nine months, but some of the men had then rioted and committed murders in defiance of the new emperor – who was now Trajan's adoptive father. This was a body of men who were supposed to be the emperor's bodyguard; they had now failed one emperor, and become an active threat to another. Trajan clearly could not trust them. To be on the safe side, it seems he co-opted the governor's horseguard at Colonia Agrippinensis as his own guard, and organised its recruitment from the original 500 men to 1,000 from local men.[11]

This guard, the *equites singulares Augusti*, was composed of men from several local German tribes: Batavi, Baesatei, Ubii and Frisiavones. Their historian, M.P. Speidel, points out that the customs and traditions of this area of Germany were thus well established in the force for the rest of its existence. This was also the area from which the horseguards of the Roman rulers from Julius Caesar to Nero had been recruited; later a strong loyalty to Nero, and a rebellion by other Batavians in 70, tarnished their enviable reputation for loyalty and military skill in the eyes of the Flavian emperors, but the governors of Germania Inferior had recruited them as their gubernatorial guard, and Trajan trusted them. This very fact, of course, made them loyal. (He had presumably had such a guard when governor of Germania Superior.)

As heir and as joint-emperor Trajan was clearly entitled to a large guard, certainly one at least double that of a provincial governor, and so it seems probable that his takeover of the governor's guard as his own took place on his arrival at Colonia Agrippinensis, and the process of doubling its size will have begun at once. (The governor – Licinius Sura – will also have then needed to recruit a new guard for himself and his successor; maybe Servianus in Superior had to do the same.) If this is so, Trajan will have also needed to appoint the commander of his new guard at the same time. This would seem to have been Sex. Attius Suburanus Aemilianus.[12]

The existence of his own guard made it easier for Trajan to deal with the Praetorians. A decision was apparently made that the riot should be punished, and that since the rioters had been led by their commander, whether or not he initiated their actions, it was the commander who should bear the main punishment. Casperius Aelianus was called to Colonia Agrippinensis along with 'the Praetorians who had mutinied against Nerva'.[13] Exactly how many this meant is not known, but it is unlikely to be a large number; M.P. Speidel has suggested that it was the small group known as the *speculatores*, who provided the closest guardians of the imperial person, who were thus summoned.[14] According to Dio, these men were decoyed north by a pretended purpose. If they were the *speculatores*, this can only have been to be the new emperor's own guard. Instead they were 'put out of the way', which is assumed to be a euphemism for execution.[15]

The new Guard Prefect, Suburanus, had already had a lengthy career in a series of equestrian posts in Rome, Spain, Gaul and Egypt, as governor of the Alpes Cottiae, procurator in Judaea and, most recently as procurator in Gallia Belgica the year before. This posting put him at the centre of affairs at the time of Trajan's adoption, and it may be assumed that he was one of those giving Trajan his support. Now, perhaps by way of a brief command of the new imperial horseguards, he was promoted to Guard Prefect. Trajan is reported to have remarked as he appointed him that he was giving him a sword to use for the emperor, or against him if he tyrannised[16] – a most apposite remark in the circumstances, and perhaps not one quite so earnestly meant as is sometimes assumed. Both men, after all, had been complicit in the killing of Aelianus and his colleagues.

Suburanus had an appallingly difficult task. The men of his new command were surely very resentful at the execution of their officers and colleagues and at the deceitful way it had been accomplished; he would need time to enforce his authority, time to rebuild confidence in a unit probably confused and demoralised, time to weed out those men he could not trust. This may well be one of the reasons for Trajan staying away from Rome for the next year and a half.[17] Only when the Guard was under control would it be safe for him to go to the city; no repetition of Nerva's experience was required in this new regime. That Suburanus was successful, perhaps beyond expectations, is indicated by his adlection to praetorian rank in 100 and his two consulships in 101 and 104.

In that year and a half, from February/March 98 to September/October 99, Trajan was in Germany and then on the Danube frontier. It was in that time that he worked out that his policy would be aggressive, and this decision was inevitably based on the situation he found on the northern frontier, a situation which had been produced as a result of Domitian's work in the previous twenty years. It was above all in this area that Trajan could claim to be Domitian's true successor, but only so long as their policies were not examined too closely. For a careful examination suggests that Trajan deliberately shifted the focus of Roman policy in the north towards a relatively easier conquest, and that by doing so he destroyed what might have been the real aim of Domitian.

Domitian had conducted a whole series of wars all along the Rhine and Danube.[18] None of them, until the last, was lengthy, but the cumulative results were decisive. Along the Rhine his two wars against the Chatti, in 83 and 89, broke the power of that strong tribe. The frontier could then be pushed forward across the river and a new fortified line developed to hold the heights of the Taunus and the lower valleys of the Main and Neckar. This allowed the occupation of the eastern Rhine rift valley and the Schwartzwald – the area called by Tacitus the *agri decumates*.[19] Rather more importantly, it also scotched the hostility of Germany. At the same period the Bructeri in the north were compelled to accept a king forced on them by Rome, in the person of the governor of Germania Inferior in the mid-80s, A. Vestricius Spurinna.[20] This action was clearly part of the overall policy of forward control beyond the old frontier line. A decade later, that tribe was destroyed by its neighbours; perhaps the fact that the tribe was perceived to be under Roman influence was one cause of this; either way the Romans, as Tacitus pointed out, gained.

The overall results of all this took time to work themselves out, but by 90 it will have become clear that the Rhine frontier had settled down. With the Bructeri under control with a Roman-appointed king, the Chatti broken and the Hermunduri firmly allied to Rome, there was little to fear. By that time, therefore, Domitian was beginning to concentrate his full attention on the Danube frontier. He had fought two brief wars against the Dacians in the 80s, but in 89 trouble developed in the central section of the frontier, that area which faced the Pannonian province, and more fighting occurred in 92. The enemies of Rome here were the Suebi and the Sarmatae. Suebi is a general term for a group of German tribes inhabiting a large area of the centre of Europe from Bohemia to the Baltic.[21] In fact it was the Marcomanni and the Quadi (both Suebic tribes), who inhabited Bohemia-Moravia, who were the precise enemies. The Sarmatae involved were in fact only a branch of that tribe, the Iazyges, a nomadic group who lived on the Hungarian plain east of the Danube, between that river and Dacia. This was a huge territory, a land the size of Italy, a thousand kilometres in length from western Bohemia to the Danube facing Singidunum.

This was the general background to the war which had begun shortly before Domitian's assassination. The three years or so since the second of his Pannonian wars

(93 to 96) had been devoted to extensive military and diplomatic planning and organisation. The signal for the final preparations for the war was the transfer of Domitian's chosen commander, Pompeius Longinus, from Moesia Superior, where he had been governor since 93, to Pannonia in the summer of 96. He is known, from a military diploma, to have still been in Moesia in July 96,[22] and the attack across the Danube would necessarily take place before the harvest, in August or September. Pompeius Longinus' three years in Moesia Superior and then his transfer to Pannonia imply that he had been Domitian's choice for war-commander all along, and that it had been his task since 93 to oversee the logistical and planning preparations. No doubt the overall strategy and the diplomatic preparation were the emperor's, as was the timing. It was the preoccupation of Pompeius Longinus' huge army with this war which was one of the factors determining the moment of Domitian's assassination.

In Pannonia, Pompeius Longinus had under his control a force of no less than five legions. The exact stations of all of them are not certain, but XIII *Gemina* and XV *Apollinaris* were definitely at Vindobona and Carnuntum, facing the Quadi: XIV *Gemina* had probably been stationed at Musellae, a little south of the river, and was moved to Ad Flexum on the river. The two legions originally raised in the 60s, I and II *Adiutrix*, had also been stationed away from the actual frontier, in south-east Pannonia, and were also moved to the river, at Brigetio and Aquincum. There were by that time five legions positioned in a line along a river frontage of only 200 kilometres. Further east along the river, in Moesia Superior, there were two more legions, IV *Flavia Firma* at Singidunum, and VII *Claudia* at Viminacium; both of them were within 60 kilometres of the Pannonian border, the first indeed only separated from it by the River Save. In addition but more distant, L. Julius Marinus in Moesia Inferior had two legions, V *Macedonica* at Oescus (to which legion Hadrian was moved in 96), and I *Italica* at Novae, conveniently close together,[23] and clearly intended to guard against any trouble from Dacia: Oescus was at the southern end of the major route into that kingdom. Auxiliary regiments were similarly concentrated in the frontier area. Those listed in the diploma which records units in Moesia Superior in 96, include some which had earlier been in Pannonia, and perhaps been moved out to accommodate the heavy legionary concentration. It is calculated that Moesia Superior held three cavalry *alae* and twenty infantry *cohortes* – a force of at least 25,000 men – as well as its two legions.[24] Pannonia's five legions were supported by a proportionate number of auxiliary units: at least six *alae* and forty *cohortes* perhaps, unless some of those in Moesia were to be used. In 96 Pannonia and Moesia Superior thus held seven legions and up to sixty auxiliary regiments – at least 70,000 soldiers.

The cause of the enmity of the three tribes towards the empire is not clear. For a long time, the Marcomanni had been friends and allies of Rome, and both they and the Iazyges had assisted Vespasian in the civil war of 69. The archaeological evidence suggests that both the Marcomanni and the Quadi were peacefully absorbing Roman influences – trade, bathhouses, villas and all,[25] but by 89 this peaceful accommodation had changed to enmity, and in that year, at the time of the rebellion of Antonius Saturninus and Domitian's second war with the Chatti, it is most unlikely that the aggression was Rome's. The destruction of XXI *Rapax* by the Iazyges in the war of 92 no doubt fixed both sides into attitudes of full enmity, and the marshalling of five legions for the war of 96 indicates that Domitian was intent on more than a mere war of revenge. A force that size clearly implies an intention to conquer and annex territory.

The Iazyges were a fragment of the great Sarmatian nation, whose main body was spread over the south Russian steppes from the Carpathians to the Volga; the Iazyges themselves were scarcely much of a threat to the empire.[26] The Marcomanni and the Quadi in Bohemia and Moravia, however, had an extensive and fertile territory and were linked by ties of kinship and religion with the Suebic tribes beyond them, to the north. At least two of those northern tribes, the Lugii of modern Silesia and the Semnones in the middle Elbe valley, had been contacted diplomatically and were persuaded into some sort of an alliance with Rome. The Semnones in particular had a strong influence on other groups as the senior Suebic tribe, and had a notable religious influence on them; the Lugii were provided with both weapons and troops by Rome.[27] The Iazyges, who were perhaps more at enmity with the Dacians than the Romans, automatically became Roman enemies when Rome and Decebalus of the Dacians became allies at the end of their war in 89. Apparently, they allied themselves with the threatened Suebians; they had nowhere else to go, and if the Quadi and Marcomanni were attacked and defeated, they would clearly be next. But the disposition of the Pannonian legions indicate that it was not the Iazyges who were the immediate targets of the Roman attack.

The involvement of the Iazyges necessarily concerned the Dacians, who were the Iazyges' eastern neighbours, and whom Domitian had also fought twice. The result of the second Dacian war had been a peace agreement by which the Romans provided substantial technical and financial aid to the Dacian kingdom. The Dacians had been a formidable foe: ensconced in their mountains, numerous and with a large territory, they may, it seems, have been responsible for the destruction of another legion, V *Alaudae*.[28] The generous peace terms were hardly popular in Rome.[29] The Dacian problem and its solution had repercussions on the middle Danube frontier, since it successfully sowed enmity between the Dacians and the Iazyges, and opened the way to make an anti-Sarmatian alliance with Decebalus, the Dacian king, an alliance which was already in operation in the war of 92.[30] Domitian had therefore successfully organised a series of alliances which isolated and encircled the three central tribes. Romans, Hermunduri, Semnones, Lugii and Dacians surrounded them.

It was a system that had been constructed piecemeal during the early 90s, and was probably not originally designed for an assault on the central tribes, but more to keep them quiet. The alliance with the Hermunduri went back decades,[31] and that with the Dacians dated from 89. The contacts with the Lugii and the Semnones were clearly the final blocks to be added to the circumvallation in the early 90s. This diplomatic work – no doubt both Hermunduri and Dacians had to be constantly reassured – was the essential complement to the great military concentration in Pannonia and Moesia Superior. It was also a diplomatic constraint that was unlikely to survive for long; the ties between the Suebic tribes were probably stronger than any attractions of a Roman alliance, and a long war would put intolerable strains on it.

The strategic situation on the whole northern frontier in 96 thus becomes clear. Since 89 the Roman frontier in southern Germany had been stabilised on an advanced line, approaches to which were blocked by the alliance with the Hermunduri, and the northern end blocked by the Roman near-control over the Bructeri. At the eastern end, the Dacians had also been Roman allies since 86, and this had stabilised the frontier from Viminacium to the Black Sea, helped by the presence of the two legions at Novae and Oescus. The remaining section was that between Viminacium and the border of Noricum, facing the Iazyges, the Quadi and the Marcomanni, the area where the war began in 96.

The question, therefore, is what exactly were Domitian's aims in the coming war? He had put in a major diplomatic effort, and such a large concentration of force was scarcely defensive. The only conclusion must be that he was intending an invasion and conquest of the trans-Danubian lands of the three tribes. The imperial frontier was to be moved northwards, probably to the mountain line along the northern edge of the Marcomannian–Quadian lands, the Sudeten and Erzgebirge, and perhaps across the Hungarian plain to the western border of the Dacian kingdom. This was the aim that Marcus Aurelius stated in a smaller way eighty years later,[32] and it made powerful strategic sense, rather more so than the line along the Danube. To the west of Bohemia the allied Hermunduri, surrounded on three sides, could then be peacefully absorbed, at which time the northern boundary of the empire would run from Colonia Agrippinensis on the Rhine due east to the Erzgebirge and the Sudeten mountains, with the allied Semnones of the middle Elbe and the allied Lugii of the Upper Oder valley as absorbable allies north of the mountains. To the east, the Dacian kingdom, a more formidable military proposition but coming under increasingly strong Roman influence, would be flanked on both west and south by Roman territory. It is not beyond conjecture that Domitian was ultimately aiming to absorb these as well. The result would be to move the Romano-German frontier to a line up to 300 kilometres north of the Danube line, and to include several populous tribes; the prestige of emperor and empire would be enhanced, and the stage would be set for still more conquests into Germany and eastern and northern Europe.

This war is little known.[33] In part, as usual, this is because of poor sources, and what sources there are have gross distortions of one type or another. But the main reason is because it falls across three reigns: it began under Domitian, continued under Nerva and concluded under Trajan. Neither Nerva nor Trajan come out of the episode with any prestige, and neither had any wish to give any credit to Domitian. The senatorial damnation of Domitian's memory expunged any appreciation of his intentions. Nerva's necessary concentration on events in Rome removed attention from the frontier problems, and Trajan's deliberate abstention from involvement on the Danube until the war was effectively all over, coupled with his refusal to take responsibility for the war, left it all in an ahistorical limbo. Tacitus deliberately and selectively hid it,[34] and later historians fell victim to the contemporary determination to forget the war ever happened. All this is unfortunate, but enough hints survive, and enough evidence has come to light in non-literary sources, to show that the war was on, that it was a

great war, and the fact that the Romans wrote it out of their histories is sufficient dem-
onstration that they lost.

None of the assumptions I am making about Domitian's intentions can be proved,
in part because the murder of the emperor will have dislocated all plans, but it fits with
the great efforts Domitian had made in preparation for the fighting. This had clearly
begun in the late summer of 96, and Nerva was able to claim a victory later in the year,
and another in October 97.[35] He was not, however, able to claim a peace, and in coins
of 98 (that is, issued in January of that year) he was still proclaiming victory.[36] The
war, therefore, was still going on when Nerva died and Trajan, on the German frontier, became sole emperor: during that time Pompeius Longinus had remained in
office as governor of Pannonia,[37] and so as commander of the expeditionary force.

Despite victories claimed by the emperor at Rome, it is evident from the overall
results that Domitian's intentions were not being carried out. This may be because the
resistance to the Roman attack was too strong, though it seems unlikely that the
Roman forces were being defeated; more likely it was because Domitian's plans and
intentions died with him, and his diplomatic preparations unravelled. Nerva's experiences and background did not include anything military, and his problems during his
rule were much closer to home, requiring his full attention. Without the vigorous support of the preoccupied emperor even the great Pannonian army would be in difficulties; some decisions, for example, would require the emperor's participation or
ratification, and with Nerva always in Rome, that process would take disablingly long.
The alliances that Domitian had concluded might well have collapsed with his death –
within two years Trajan was contemplating war with the Dacians, for example, which
is suggestive – and without the support, active or passive, of the German neighbours
of the Suebic-Sarmatian alliance, the Lugii and the Semnones, it is unlikely that the
war could be concluded quickly.

Trajan left Pompeius Longinus in command not only during his period as joint
emperor in the winter of 97/98, but throughout 98 as well. The emperor himself
remained in Germany all that year. There were tasks for him to do there, no doubt,
and some suggestions have been made: it has been suggested, for example, that he was
responsible for an extension of the fortified frontier between the Main and the
Neckar, the 'Odenwald *limes*'.[38] In the north the lands from which many of the men in
his new horseguard came were enhanced by the foundation of a *colonia*, Ulpia
Traiana, probably arranged while Trajan was in Germany. It was close to the legionary
fortress at Vetera, which was abandoned briefly during the movement of legions in
connection with the Dacian wars. The process was no doubt the same as at Glevum
and Lindum in Britain, where similarly abandoned fortresses were the scenes of new
coloniae.[39]

These developments were no doubt significant, but neither of them – nor any other
work which could be imagined – can have taken up Trajan's time for most of 98, and
they scarcely compared in importance with the war on the Danube. But the war was
not being won, and the new emperor would not wish to be directly associated with a
lost war right at the start of his reign. In the end, however, in the winter of 98/99, he
could no longer hold aloof. He went to the Danube himself. It may be that Pompeius

Longinus had already achieved some sort of agreement and that it needed Trajan's ratification. Pliny appears to indicate that hostages were taken from the enemy (if this
actually refers to this war) and this would suggest a sort of Roman victory.[40] There is
an anecdote which seems to apply here, of Trajan parading his army on the banks of a
frozen river to both deter and impress an enemy army that looked like attacking.[41]
Pliny does his best to make this seem like a victory; but in the context of the Suebic-
Sarmatian war, where victories had been proclaimed for three years without the war
ending, it looks more like a determination to make the enemy stop fighting, and, if the
river was the Danube, to prevent an invasion of Roman territory. There was certainly
no annexation of territory as a result of the peace agreement. The result can thus only
be described as a defensive victory for the Roman enemies.

After this three-year war, which was – if Domitian's aims have been elucidated correctly – a strategic defeat for Rome, the setback could be disguised by such means as
Pliny's circumlocutory words without much difficulty, and if anyone penetrated
through the spin to the truth, it could then all be passed off as Domitian's war or
Nerva's fault. Neither of his predecessors was present to contradict, and neither's reputation could be damaged any further by such stories. But it would seem to have had a
major effect on Trajan. Perhaps because of such incidents as the dispute over the title
pater patriae, which he could not feel he had earned, Trajan spent his whole reign
searching for victory. The one area where a strategic success could have benefited the
empire in the long run was by annexing Bohemia-Moravia, as Domitian had come to
appreciate. But Trajan could only see a defeat there. Where Domitian had learned
from defeats – by the Dacians, by the Iazyges – and had developed new policies and
methods to reverse those defeats, and gone on to do just that, Trajan recoiled instead
and tried another place without changing his methods: after the lack of success on the
central Danube, he shifted to an easier target. First he attacked Dacia, a well-organised
kingdom that could be conquered by a formal and relatively brief military campaign,
and then he turned on Parthia, where an established polity, in this case pretty far gone
in desuetude, was another inviting target. But neither of these targets was strategically
useful, and in fact both were costly and wasteful enterprises. Dacia, a salient surrounded on three sides by enemy territory, required a large permanent garrison to
hold and protect it; the Parthian conquests were hopelessly indefensible and those that
had not been already lost before Trajan died were abandoned with relief by Hadrian.
In neither area can Trajan be seen as an intelligent commander; he was not a patch on
Domitian in strategic imagination. To stand at the head of the Persian Gulf and
mutter about Alexander and India was about Trajan's style: neither of these commanders had much political sense.

Trajan may have spent two years on the German and Danube frontiers, but he certainly kept in touch with events in Rome. The to-and-fro argument over his titles is
evidence enough of that. But the longer he stayed away, the more obvious it became
that power was where the emperor was, not at the Senate, and not at any particular
place, not even Rome. Trajan was accompanied in the north by much of the executive
branch of the government of the empire – that is, his court – and it was from this
group of men that the administrative decisions flowed. Just as in 68 and 69 it had

become clear that the emperor could be made elsewhere than at Rome,[42] so in 98–99 it became clear that the empire could be governed from elsewhere than Rome. The nervousness displayed by emperors such as Claudius (in his visit to Britain in 43) and Domitian (in his various wars) at being away from Rome for any length of time, was clearly no longer appropriate.

In addition, Trajan, was necessarily accompanied by his *consilium*, the group of men with whom the emperor habitually discussed imperial problems, normally men with whom he could socialise in a fairly informal context.[43] Who the members were at the start of the reign can only be guessed at, but the number of those whom Trajan called on is fairly limited for the whole two decades of his reign.[44] It may be assumed that while in Germany he was advised by the German governors, L. Licinius Sura and L. Julius Servianus, both of whom are known to have been his friends and supporters before his accession. Sura's successor in Germania Inferior, L. Neratius Priscus,[45] was close enough to Trajan to be thought of as his successor later in his reign [46] and can be assumed to have been part of his *consilium* from the start. Suburanus the Prefect was another until he was sent to Rome to discipline the Guard. The governor of Belgica, Q. Sosius Senecio, who was rewarded with an ordinary consulship in 99, was probably another, if he was able to leave his province. The *ab epistulis*, C. Octavius Titinius Capito, was certainly on hand, and may have been consulted, though he worked discreetly and left no mark on the sources. It seems probable also that Sex. Julius Frontinus, who had advised Nerva and was to be given a third consulship in 100, was also called on from the start. Several of these men were military experts, and all of them knew a good deal about provincial matters: several were experts on Germany in particular.

When Trajan moved to the Danube some of these men went with him. Servianus was transferred from the governorship of Germania Superior to Pannonia during 99;[47] his successor in Germania Superior is not known, but he will no doubt have arrived soon enough to allow Servianus to move to Pannonia along with, or soon after Trajan. In Pannonia Pompeius Longinus will have joined the group. Since Trajan's journey was concerned with the Danube frontier, and Pompeius Longinus was both a supporter of his candidature and had held successive governors' posts in Moesia Superior and Pannonia for the past six years, he was an obvious source of advice.[48]

Many of the emperor's advisers were also men who had held the various magistracies and offices in the emperor's gift, and were often rewarded with others, so that the membership of the *consilium* must have changed constantly: Sosius Senecio, for example, had to go to Rome for his consulship – he was *ordinarius* – in the first part of 99. It is clear that individual expertise was recognised and called on where appropriate, not only in military, provincial and frontier matters, but also in legal ones. Indeed it was these awkward, local, legal matters that were possibly the most numerous of the many minor problems that came up to the emperor for decision, and it was useful for him to be able to delegate to others the power of judgement on the spot. But it may be that the emperor did not always have a free choice of his advisers: men of consular rank will surely have been able to claim a place by right, and be able to tender advice unasked. There were not so many men of both rank and expertise in the empire that the emperor could afford to neglect any offer of help and participation in the burdens of administration. At the same time it was clearly possible for men to absent themselves from the governing and advisory circle if they did not wish to participate. Several men who had been prominent in the early Flavian years faded away during Domitian's time only to re-emerge during Nerva's and Trajan's early years – Julius Frontinus was one of them.[49]

Before moving to the Danube in late 98 Trajan will have made up his list of men to be consuls for 99, a list which would probably need to be made known by October. He apparently declined to take up a third consulship for himself, on the grounds, so it is said, that he would be absent from Rome at the time. This is strange because he had held his second consulship in 98 – for six months – while in Germany.[50] He was going to be away from Rome *again*, and a second consulship held in absence might be construed as an affront. But Trajan was never so greedy for consulships as the Flavians, who had amassed thirty-three between them in less than thirty years, and the accumulation of titles he had already acquired was quite enough to give him power and authority. Absence from Rome did not diminish that power; possession of the consulship was thus really only important when the emperor was personally in Rome.

The consular lists were, as ever, a useful means of promoting and rewarding friends and deserving men. The list for 99 is the first for which Trajan alone was responsible – that of 98 was obviously in part Nerva's work – and it can be examined, as was Nerva's, to provide some indication of Trajan's preferences and intended policies. The list as we have it is probably not complete. Six names are known, which might give a complete list if each pair was in office for four months, handing over at the end of April and August. One of the second pair is recorded in office in June, but one of the third pair is known to have been in office in August.[51] This suggests a list of at least eight – each pair being in office for three months – or possibly twelve, for two months each. It is no help to look at others of Trajan's lists, for there seems to be no real consistency, and they vary between three and four pairs, often with a seventh or a ninth name as well to be suffect for a short *ordinarius*.[52] The balance of probability suggests a total of eight men for the year, two names being unknown.

The final two consuls have been recently identified from a fragmentary military diploma as Q. Fulvius Gillo Bittius Proculus and M. Ostorius Scapula.[53] Of these the second is reasonably certain, since most of his very idiosyncratic cognomen survives; the first is a good deal less certain, his name having been deduced from a general survey of those whose names should have been included on the consular *fasti* at some point yet were missing. Both had actually been suggested for consulships in the late 90s on the basis of their holding the office of proconsul of Asia in 114 or 115 (Scapula) and 115 or 116 (Proculus). They do fit rather well into the list for 99 as we have it, since they seem to be much the same sort of minimally active senators as Barba and Faustinus. The date of the diploma, however, presents a problem. In part this is because it is uncertain. What remains on the diploma is 'K OCTOBR', with a substantial space before it in which a number and the formula '*a.d.*' (indicating the date) would fit nicely.

This is all very well, but such a restoration puts the term of office of these two consuls into September. This in turn means that the two previous consuls, who are attested in office in August by another inscription, were in office only two months, because the two previous consuls (Barba and Memmius) are known to have been in office in June. If two suffects were in office for two months, then presumably all pairs in that year were, and the *ordinarii* no doubt also. This leads to the conclusion, therefore, that there were *six* pairs of consuls in 99, not three or four as previously thought. The paradoxical result of identifying two missing names is that there are now four more missing names, two immediately following the *ordinarii* for March and April, and two for November and December.

The *ordinarii* are the best known of the eight men, and the most distinguished (though these categories are not necessarily synonymous): A. Cornelius Palma Frontonianus and Q. Sosius Senecio. Both went on to receive second consulships, and both of these were *ordinarii* as well; in other words, these men were particularly close to Trajan. Palma came from Volsinii in Etruria, and his first known post was as praetorian legate in Asia sometime during Domitian's reign, a post in a senatorial province requiring tact and care, as well as honesty and efficiency. He went on to command a legion – which one is not known – in 94–97, before reaching the consulship on 1 January 99. Immediately following that post he went to Spain as governor of Hispania Citerior (that is, Tarraconensis), taking up the position later in the same year. He was later to be governor of Syria and annexer of the Nabataean kingdom, and then consul again. The intensity of his loyalty to Trajan and his memory may be judged from the fact that he was one of the four consulars summarily executed by Hadrian soon after his accession in 117.[54]

Q. Sosius Senecio's origin is unclear. A damaged inscription from Rome has been interpreted as listing his career, beginning with a quaestorship in Achaia and through the tribune of the plebs and praetorship in Rome, where he was Domitian's preferred candidate for both posts. Command of Domitian's own *legio* I *Minervia* was followed by the post of governor of Belgica in 97–98.[55] Both of these posts put him in or close to Germania Superior when Trajan was governor. He went to Belgica in succession to Q. Glitius Atilius Agricola, and from that position (where he had Sex. Attius Suburanus as his procuratorial colleague), he gave early support to Trajan. His consulship was followed after a year by the governorship of Moesia Superior, commencing during 101. This was, of course, a key province in Trajan's Danube frontier policy, and it was one of a series of appointments in the Danubian provinces which help reveal the emperor's new policy. Perhaps as important for his consulship in 99 was Senecio's marriage to Julia Frontina, the daughter of Sex. Julius Frontinus, who was to receive a third consulship next year. Frontinus was old by now,[56] and the marriage had presumably taken place some time, perhaps decades, before. Their daughter, Sosia Polla, was married to Q. Pompeius Falco, who seems to have come from Cilicia and been so well connected that he collected a whole series of extra names in the next forty or fifty years by one means or another, including those of the last king of Sparta.[57] Falco was not particularly favoured by Domitian in his posts (a decemvirate and then a military tribunate in Germania Inferior, a quiet area at the time) but in Trajan's first year he was made legate of *legio* V *Macedonica* and commanded that legion in Trajan's first Dacian

120

war.[58] His marital connections with Frontinus and Senecio were surely decisive in this unexpected promotion.

Senecio's familial link to a distinguished man, while it might help to a consulship, would scarcely be sufficient on its own, and surely not for an ordinary consulship. Senecio had other qualities to recommend him: he had the ability Trajan looked for; he even reached his second ordinary consulship two years before Palma, as the colleague of L. Licinius Sura (receiving his third). Senecio also had wider connections in the intellectual world: he was a member of the circle with whom both Pliny and Plutarch corresponded, and he was the dedicatee of Plutarch's major works, *Parallel Lives* and *Table Talk*.[59] Palma does not seem to have shared such interests, but both men would seem to have been valued by Trajan for their administrative and military skills most of all. Senecio may have served his military tribunate in *legio* XXI *Rapax*,[60] the legion destroyed by the Iazyges in 92; no doubt in that case revenge for that would be one of his motives.

The other four identifiable consuls of 99 are less well known, and certainly much less distinguished, though only one of the men is wholly mysterious. This is Sulpicius Lucretius Barba, whose praenomen is not known, and whose attested career is limited to his consulship.[61] We have rather better information about his colleague, Senecio Memmius Afer. An inscription from Tibur gives two other offices he held: governor of Aquitania and proconsul of Sicily, which are assumed to have been held in the mid-90s and 97 respectively.[62] He was probably from Spain, and he had distinguished connections, his son being married to the daughter of Caesius Fronto, the consul of 96 who was deeply involved in the accession of Nerva, and son of the poet Silius Italicus. (Memmius may also, at least eventually, have been a connection of Pompeius Falco, one element of whose collection of names was 'Silius Decianus', who was Fronto's brother.)

The pair of consuls in office in July and August includes another man from Spain, or perhaps Narbonensis, Q. Fabius Barbatus Valerius Magnus Iulianus, whose ancestry, despite his collection of names, is not clear. He had served as commander of *legio* III *Augusta* in Africa in 96–97, a post which was combined with that of governor of Numidia. His subsequent career, like his ancestry, is unknown; a posting to Numidia did tend to go to men whose careers ended with either that post or the consulship, however, and Fabius might well be finished by 99.[63] His colleague was A. Caecilius Faustinus, who went on to be governor of Moesia Inferior in 103–104, in the peaceful period between Trajan's two Dacian wars, and was then governor of Africa in 115, with no known offices in between.[64] Neither man thus made a significant impact on events and must be assumed to have risen up the magistrates' ladder by the usual combination of wealth, ancestry, unspectacular competence and the lapse of time; they were certainly not selected by Trajan for his *consilium* or for special tasks, nor posted to problem provinces, so far as can be discovered.

Six of these consuls were the sort of men one might expect to find holding the office in a normal year; the exceptions in the list are the two *ordinarii*, who are very different. (Incidentally, there is no indication that the four missing names were of anybody exceptional, for no notable men of the time seem to be missing from the list; four more aristocratic drones, perhaps.) But Palma and Senecio were exceptional men, and their presence as *ordinarii* so early in the new reign, and similarly so early in their careers, suggests that they were particular Trajanic friends and colleagues, and that their abilities were especially valued by the new emperor. Both were notable in later life for governing awkward provinces (such as Syria) and for carrying out difficult military and gubernatorial tasks (such as Palma's annexation of Nabataea). It may be assumed that their promotion provided a clear indication of the direction of Trajan's intentions to those who noted such things – especially when combined with his extended stay on the northern frontier. He had, of course, arrived at the conclusion that the Dacians would need to be dealt with first, a decision the strategic rationale of which is highly questionable, but whose origin probably goes back to the murder of Domitian, the emperor who had made the peace with Dacia which Trajan was soon to denounce. The payment of 'tribute' to Dacia was not a popular practice, and one would suppose that the soldiers in particular were repelled by the idea. Certainly it was something Trajan detested and stopped.[65]

The governorships of important provinces were other positions Trajan had to attend to. Given his preoccupation in 97–99 with the northern frontier it is obviously significant who was posted at this time and in the next few years to the provinces along that frontier from Germania Inferior to Moesia Inferior. Raetia, Noricum and Germania Superior were the quietest sectors, and the names of their governors are not known for several years after Servianus was moved from Germania Superior to Pannonia in late 98 or early 99. Germania Inferior, facing the somewhat disturbed area where the Bructeri were destroyed about this time but which did not present any danger to the empire, was governed by Trajan's friend L. Neratius Priscus from 98 to 101, when he was succeeded by Q. Acutius Nerva, fresh from the consulship in 100, who was in the post for at least two years.[66]

Along the Danube, Servianus stayed in Pannonia only a year or so, and was then succeeded by Q. Glitius Atilius Agricola,[67] another very experienced and able man, who was clearly put in post in preparation for Trajan's first Dacian war. In Moesia Inferior Q. Pomponius Rufus had succeeded L. Julius Marinus during 97.[68] Rufus was another very experienced soldier-cum-administrator, having commanded *legio* V *Alaudae* before its destruction, and governed in Spain and Dalmatia; but he was no longer young, having held his first office early in Vespasian's reign, or perhaps even before, and having held his consulship in 95, some years later than the expected date, in all probability.[69] He was succeeded in Moesia by October 100 by M'. Laberius Maximus, consul in 89, whose career is otherwise not known but who was a successful commander in the first Dacian war.[70] Both Laberius and Agricola were given second consulships in 103, after the relative success of the first war. Laberius, however, became involved in another of P. Calpurnius Crassus Frugi's careless plots, and was exiled to an island for the rest of the reign.[71] He had been consul before Trajan; he may have been jealous. His appointment to Moesia, though, was surely on account of his ability. Next door, in Moesia Superior, the new governor, taking office in 99, was C. Cilnius Proculus, who had been governor of Dalmatia and who went straight on from Moesia to his consulship in 100 or 101;[72] in the province he was succeeded by Q.

Sosius Senecio: the contrast in seniority between the two men is striking. The arrival in the Danubian provinces during 100 and 101 of Laberius, Senecio and Agricola has all the appearance of the emperor's deliberate choice. During 100 and 101, it would seem, Trajan was ensuring that competent generals were put in post in all those provinces; his war in Dacia was clearly planned well in advance.

One further indication of such planning might be the construction work done at the Iron Gates of the Danube, where a towpath along the Roman bank that had existed for some time was rebuilt before 100, and a canal dug to bypass the Gates altogether. This was work which had begun under Domitian, and was in fact a repair of the original construction done in Tiberius' reign; digging a navigable canal to bypass the Gates was certainly Trajan's initiative, but neither of these measures can be said to be obviously undertaken to prepare for an attack on Dacia; the appointment of active military men as governors of neighbouring provinces facing Dacia is rather more convincing.[73]

No such careful selection and placing of men may be discerned in provinces elsewhere. In the east no governor of Syria is known between A. Larcius Priscus' emergency tenure in 97 and the arrival of a new governor in 100. T. Pomponius Bassus, Domitian's last governor of Cappadocia-Galatia, took up office in 94 and stayed in post until 101,[74] when he was replaced in the normal way by Q. Orfitasius Aufidius Umber, consul in 97, who stayed in office for the usual three years.[75] In Egypt, the prefect in office when Domitian died, M. Junius Rufus, remained there until 98, and was replaced by C. Pompeius Planta by October of that year.[76] Planta was described by Trajan as his 'prefect and friend' in a letter to Pliny over a decade later;[77] it would seem that Trajan had carefully placed a man loyal to him in that vital province. In the west the governor of Britannia from 98 was T. Avidius Quietus who stayed until 101 and was followed by L. Neratius Marcellus (brother of Priscus).[78] Generally, these were men who achieved their offices in the normal way, by seniority; without a crisis in either area there was no need to be too carefully selective.

Trajan completed his Danube tour in the autumn, and returned to Rome before the Central European winter closed in. He reached the city in September or October,[79] two years after his adoption, and three since the murder of Domitian, which had been the ultimate cause of his elevation. The welcome he received was ecstatic, all the more so as he ostentatiously entered the city on foot – though he was accompanied by Praetorian Guardsmen and preceded by twelve lictors, their *fasces* wreathed in the laurel of an *imperator*.[80] It was the entry of a highly confident man who had overcome any initial diffidence at his swift elevation.

The Roman welcome was, of course, partly one that signified relief at the effective end of the crisis which had begun with the murder of the emperor. When Trajan greeted the senators, then the knights, and accepted the plaudits of the commonalty – and all this before even approaching the imperial palace – he was concluding the crisis by a display of political and communal unity which had been missing for the past three years, or perhaps for a decade, since the revolt of Antonius Saturninus that he had helped to suppress, but which had so affected Domitian that he became ever more suspicious.[81]

What the welcoming politicians and crowds did not yet realise, however, was that Trajan had begun to develop a policy which, in its way, was as much a reaction to the personal insecurity of any Roman emperor as was Domitian's dark suspiciousness. Emperors lived their lives in public, meeting and greeting, talking, arguing, discussing, speaking, listening; it was politically and governmentally impossible for them to do otherwise. Unless universally popular – a political and personal impossibility – they were always vulnerable. The murder of Domitian and the experiences of Nerva in the past three years showed that. It was partly to avoid such experiences, no doubt, that Trajan had resolved on war, during which he would be able to camp out with his army, in active command, and so well away from the febrile politics of the city; he was to spend nearly seven years of the next eighteen on campaign. Having collected the prestige of victories, as he had by 102, he was then able to dominate city affairs without difficulty. But this was scarcely the emperor the senators expected when he embraced them one by one, addressing them by name, on his triumphal entry in late 99.

He had been emperor for a year and a half by the time he returned to Rome, and there were some outstanding tasks to be accomplished. The donative to the army and the *congiarium* to the citizens in commemoration of his accession had not yet been agreed and paid, though, since one of each had been distributed by Nerva late in 96 there was perhaps an excuse for delay. Certainly by waiting some time the treasury will have been able to prepare. Both gifts were distributed forthwith on his return, and commemorated with a coin issue. Pliny claims the distribution was done with unusual care.[82]

It was in this early period also that the new governors who took up their posts in the next year or so were appointed, and, of course, the consular list for the year 100 was drawn up. This time Trajan took up one of the *ordinarius* posts himself, with old Sex. Julius Frontinus as his colleague, both of them for the third time. This was a singular honour for Frontinus, who may well have begun life as an *eques*; repeated consulships were, however, only to be expected of an emperor. During January, Trajan resigned and was succeeded by L. Julius Ursus, another *tertius*, and another link with Domitian's reign.

The rest of the list, which appears to be complete, comprised ten first-time consuls, each holding office for two months only; one name is not fully preserved.[83] The two striking aspects are first, the geographical range of their origins, and second, the generally active involvement of most of them in public affairs, so that the proportion of aristocratic drones was very low. The three men who were *tertii* gave a taste of the geographical range of the rest, for they comprised one each from Spain (Trajan), Narbonensis (Frontinus) and Narbonensis or Spain (Ursus). The origin of five of the others is not known; of the rest one was from northern Italy, two from Spain, and two from the Greek east, a most unusual spread.

The work they had done was equally varied. Macer's colleague in March and April was C. Cilnius Proculus from Arretium in Etruria, who had been governor of Dalmatia and went on to govern Moesia Superior after his consulship; he won awards for bravery in Trajan's wars.[84] L. Herennius Saturninus, the one whose origin is unknown, had been governor of Achaia and was also to govern Moesia Superior in the period between the two Dacian wars;[85] not, it seems, a military man. His colleague was T. Pomponius Mamilianus Rufus Antistianus Funisulanus Vettonianus, a Spaniard; he had commanded *legio* XX *Valeria Victrix* at Deva in Britain, and went on to govern a military province in 107–108, though which one is not known.[86] In July two consuls of unknown origins took office – Q. Acutius Nerva went on to govern Germania Inferior next year; his colleague L. Fabius Tuscus (whose name implies an Etrurian origin at least for the family) is wholly unknown, both as to family and achievements.[87] In September the two friends Pliny and Cornutus Tertullus took over, giving the former the opportunity to make his *Panegyricus* speech when Trajan returned to Rome. He was, of course, from northern Italy; he had gone through the civil and military offices in sequence to reach his consulship, and was to be curator of the Tiber Banks and then governor of Pontus-Bithynia in 110.[88] His colleague was from Pamphylia, C. Julius Plancius Varus Cornutus Tertullus; his career had begun under Vespasian, and had included governing Crete-Cyrenaica and Narbonensis, in addition to the normal city offices, and he was to follow Pliny in Pontus-Bithynia and then go on to govern Africa in 116. Tertullus' career had not advanced under Domitian, who may well have distrusted him in part because he was guardian to the daughter of Helvidius Priscus. The advance his career took under Trajan is a sign of Trajan's alliance with the easterners.[89]

One of the last pair was L. Roscius Aelianus Maecius Celer who had, like Mamilianus, served in a British legion (military tribune in IX *Hispana*), a vexillation of which he had commanded in the Chattan war in Germany in 83, under the immediate command of Julius Frontinus. Like Tertullus, Roscius went on to govern Africa in 117 or 118; he may well have been the son of L. Roscius Coelius, who had commanded XX *Valeria Victrix* in Britain in 69 and became consul in 81, and his last two names show a connection with one of the consuls in office the next year; clearly a well-connected man.[90] He was the third Spanish consul in the year, and his colleague was the second from the east, Ti. Claudius Sacerdos Julianus, probably from Greece, but fully integrated into Roman society: a *frater Arvalis* and a *pontifex*.[91] These last two are not recorded as being particularly active – a governorship of Africa could come to a senator more or less automatically if he wanted it. These last two would seem to be the make-weights in an unusually vigorous and active set of consuls, yet even they were not as drone-like as some of the previous year's list.

This list may be seen as a sign that this was to be an active principate, with an emphasis on military matters, but also with a will to bring to the centre of affairs the developing aristocratic groups in the provinces. With three of the consuls from Spain and two from the Greek lands, in addition to the usual Italians, the list provides clear evidence of the sources of Trajan's support: the old colleagues of Nerva, the Spanish–Narbonensian aristocratic network and the Asian network. With these groups and the army supporting him, and with eight or nine consulships available every year to reward his people and to entice others, Trajan could revel in his welcome to the city, and the city could be wholehearted in its cheers. The succession crisis was over.

CONCLUSION

The question of the Roman imperial succession had been an ever-present problem since the dictatorship of Julius Ceasar finally broke the elective method used by the Republic. The death of every emperor raised the issue again, and only the most careful advance preparations could prevent serious trouble. The contempt that had been generally felt for Nero among the Roman aristocracy had legitimised the successful rebellion of Galba, but civil war, as in the 40s BC, 30 BC, and AD 69, was a clear warning of the dangers. The succession problem could however be evaded by familial inheritance. The Julio-Claudian dynasty had used such a method, in its way, and that had become the accepted practice under the Flavians.

Galba's precedent to some degree legitimised the assassination of Domitian, but it brought out again the threat of another civil war. It was this spectre which hung over the political events of 96–99 like a black cloud. The accession of Nerva was an act accomplished by a small group of self-appointed conspirators for their own diverse public and private reasons, which was then ratified by the Senate. But the events of 69 had shown that ratification by the Senate was insufficient: the army had to give its consent as well. The Senate had then ratified the successive accessions of Galba, Otho, Vitellius and Vespasian, but only the last had been successful – because he had the biggest and best army.

The Roman army was, however, commanded by Roman senators, who therefore reacted to events both as senators and as army commanders. In the September of 96 the main part of the Roman army was involved in a great war, and this imposed a delay on their reactions, which provided the commanders with time for reflection. From that time on two parallel sets of events were taking place in the empire. In Rome Nerva was seated on his throne, where he was buffeted repeatedly by problems and threats and plots, through which he only just held his own. At the same time the senator-officers were in a more leisurely way consulting over who should be his successor. These men accepted Nerva only because he was not expected to last long; as soon as they had agreed on a candidate of their own – Trajan – he was imposed on Nerva and the Senate. The timing of this was due more to their lengthy consultations than to the activities of the Guard in Rome, whose riot had taken place two or three months before Trajan's adoption. And then Trajan carefully stayed away from Rome for the next two years. During that time the Senate perforce became used to the idea of an absent, soldier emperor.

The process of consultation among the senator-officers is largely invisible to us, but the choice of Trajan reveals what were the considerations which operated in their discussions. He was a military man, though his experience of command in war was very limited. He was, of course, a senator, but one who had made no obvious mark on events in Rome. He was a generation younger than Nerva, being about the same age as Domitian – a clear slap at the plotters. Most crucially – for there were plenty of men with those qualifications – Trajan was the man at the hinge of three extensive and powerful provincial aristocratic networks: the Spanish (through his birth), the Narbonensian (through his marriage) and that of Asia Minor (through his Narbonensian connections). It was these connections that distinguished him from his contemporaries, and it was this factor which led to his selection.

The actual mechanism of succession was by adoption, with the odd result that a childless old man adopted as his son a married homosexual in his early forties who had no children. It may have been one of Nerva's recommendations to the Senate that he had no son to succeed him; it was surely no coincidence that the Senate so willingly accepted another childless man as emperor. The succession would thus cease to be hereditary – the system which had brought both Nero and Domitian to the throne. And so it was, for the next eighty years. When it became overtly hereditary once more, the products were Commodus and Caracalla; one cannot dispute that the Senate's preference was correct.

It may have been a preference, but the succession was not *designed* in any way. Only in retrospect was there any pattern or policy discernible in these events. The succession of Nerva came about by a crime and because several other men more acceptable to the plotters as emperors had refused to become Domitian's nemesis; the succession of Trajan happened by the decision of a different group of men, probably even fewer in number than the accession-plotters. In each case the choice was largely coincidental. In August 96 neither Nerva nor Trajan could be considered worthy of, or eligible for, the throne. If by February 98 Trajan was sole emperor, after the brief reign of Nerva, it was the result of a wholly unpredictable series of events. And if by that date a new method of choosing an emperor had emerged, it can only be described as such in retrospect.

For the central method was not, as some history books may have it, a process by which the existing emperor selected his successor and made his choice public by adoption, nor was it a careful process of choosing the best available man. It was in fact succession by *coup d'état*: Nerva became emperor by an overt *putsch*. Trajan was imposed on him by the army commanders, with the implicit threat of civil war if he was refused, after the Praetorian Guard had showed up his and his senatorial supporters' weaknesses – that is, by a covert coup. In the future, the determination of the succession would proceed in very similar ways: Hadrian seized power when Trajan died because he was on the spot, like Nerva; and like Trajan, he forthwith killed a group of men who were an apprehended threat to him; at the end of his reign he cleared the way for his successor Antoninus by a series of forced suicides and murders, marriages and adoptions; the succession of Marcus Aurelius and Lucius Verus was thus assured by Hadrian's actions – a coup projected into the future; at the same time these two took power because, like Hadrian, they were on the spot when their predecessor died; but then Marcus permitted his son to succeed, though he left the choice until less than three years before his own death, and Commodus also had to use force to establish himself. The Nero–Galba pattern of assassination, coup and civil war was then repeated even more unpleasantly.

What was thus revealed in the crisis of 96–99 was the absolute centrality of the army in the affairs of state; and the absolute necessity of controlling the army through its commanders. Since these commanders were aristocrats it was their particular concerns which had to be addressed: in Trajan's reign they could be appeased by honours and offices, and by access to power. The pattern of the next decades was thus set: Trajan's campaigns and Hadrian's travels both came from a need to use the army and to honour the provincial aristocrats.

What was not settled in 96–99, except in the crudest way, was the method of succession to the throne. Without a clear system the empire could only relapse into a crisis every twenty years or so. Sooner or later the civil war which had been evaded in 96–99 would break out, as it eventually did in 193 – though there had been rebellions more than once in that period, designed to put their head on the throne. It was not that it was beyond the wit of Romans to devise a workable system to provide a smooth and peaceful, and accepted, system of succession: they were familiar, after all, with the two obvious and most efficient methods: heredity and elections; instead they used a mixture of the two, a compromise which was inherently unworkable. By failing to determine clearly on one or other of these, they ended up with *coups d'état*, civil wars and the collapse of the empire.

NOTES

1 ASSASSINATION

1 Suetonius, *Domitian*, 16–17; Dio Cassius 67.1–17.2; shorter and much later accounts are in Europius, 8.1 and *Epitome de Caesaribus* 12.1; there are few modern accounts of the assassination other than brief and passing mentions: Jones, *Domitian*, 193 – 196; B.W. Henderson, *Five Roman Emperors, Vespasian–Trajan AD 69–117*, Cambridge 1927.

2 This meeting follows from the wording of the *Fasti Ostienses* which dates Domitian's death to 'XIIII K Oct' and Nerva's accession to 'XIII K Oct', i.e. 18 and 19 September (Vidman *FO*, frag Fb = Smallwood 15). Nerva later took 18 September as his *dies imperii* (*ILS* 275 = Smallwood 27(a), and Smallwood 148(d), an extract from the *Feriale Duranum*).

2 CONSPIRACY

1 *Epitome de Caesaribus* 11.11–12.

2 Dio's account is also informed by the assassination of Commodus, of which he was a contemporary, cf. F. Millar, *A Study of Cassius Dio*, Oxford 1964, 133.

3 The central figure for them both is Casperius Aelianus, killed by Trajan, after manipulating the Guard.

4 It is at Dio Cassius 67.15.4–4. It is repeated, with varying degrees of astonishment and doubt, by most moderns: e.g., most recently, Bennett, *Trajan*, 33, but he omits the boy's role; Jones, *Domitian*, 194, emphasises Dio's phrase, 'it is said that'.

5 I know of no comprehensive discussion of the possible candidates: Jones, *Domitian*, 195, perhaps suggests one (Lappius Maximus); Bennett, *Trajan*, none; Syme, *Tacitus*, none; Henderson, *Five Roman Emperors*, ignores the issue, and so on.

6 *PIR*(2) C 248; Jones, *Senatorial Order*, no. 67; Garzetti, *Nerva*, *certi* 31.

7 *PIR*(2) C 194; Jones, *Senatorial Order*, no. 64; Garzetti, *Nerva*, *certi* 37.

8 Pliny, *Letters*, 2.11.3, 4.3.15, 6.15.3.

9 Juvenal, *Satires* 1.7–13.

10 *PIR*(2) C 194, by Groag.

11 R. Syme, *Roman Papers*, IV, 163, 381, and V 642, suggested adopted son, but in *Some Arval Brethren*, 79, opted for nephew; O. Salomies, *Adoptive and Polyonymous Nomenclatures in the Roman Empire*, Helsinki 1992, 95–96.

12 Jones, *Senatorial Order*, n. 165; Syme, *Tacitus*, 1.71, note 4.

13 This has occasioned much study: cf. E. Wistrand, 'The Stoic opposition to the principate', *Studii Classice* 18, 1979, 92–101, for an example and references; textbooks discuss the issue, e.g., M. Goodman, *The Roman World 44 BC–AD 180*, London 1997, 169–171.

14 Cf. Jones, *Domitian*, 121–123, for the treason trials of 93, and their effects on Domitian.

15 Dio Cassius 67.14.5, says he 'died after entering upon the consulship' which might mean either during or after, particularly since he was the ordinary consul, and as such often had his name used all the year; if he died during his term of office, there should be another suffect consul for the year 96, unless one of the next pair took over early.

16 *PIR*(2) M 163; Jones, *Senatorial Order*, no. 188; R. Syme, 'Governors dying in Syria',

ZPE 41, 1981, and id., 'Domitian, the last years', *Chiron* 13, 1983, 134, referring to Manlius Valens as a 'relic'.

17 *PIR*(2) A 774; Jones, *Senatorial Order*, no. 20; Garzetti, *Nerva, certi* 10.

18 Vidman, *FO*, frag Fb, and 89; *PIR*(2) F 54 and P 934; Jones, *Senatorial Order*, nos 105 and 242; Garzetti, *Nerva, certi* 57 and 128.

19 Illustrated by the collection of names borne by Q. Roscius Coelius Murena Silius Decianus Vibullius Pius Julius Eurycles Herclanus Pompeius Falco: Jones, *Senatorial Order*, no. 230; Garzetti, *Nerva, certi* 134; Birley, *Fasti*, 95–100; his names indicate at least three adoptions, including Caesius Fronto's brother.

20 Martial, *Epigrams* 1.8.

21 Martial, *Epigrams* 8.66.

22 See references at note 6.

23 *PIR*(2) C 474; Pliny, *Letters* 3.7; Jones, *Senatorial Order*, no. 266; Garzetti, *Nerva, certi* 38.

24 D.J. Campbell, 'The birthplace of Silius Italicus', *Classical Review* 90, 1936, 56–58; Syme, 'Eight Consulars from Patavium', *PBSR* 1983, denies this, but accepts Transpadana.

25 The other was Q. Asconius Pedianus.

26 Tacitus, *Annals* 16.21.1; A.R. Birley, 'The life and death of Cornelius Tacitus', *Historia* 49, 2000, 230–247, argues also a relationship between Tacitus and Thrasea Paetus.

27 Strabo 5.1.7.

28 These are: L. Arruntius Stella, praetor in 93, consul perhaps in 101 (Jones, *Senatorial Order*, no. 31); C. Ducenius Proculus, cos. 87 (no. 98) and (presumably his brother) P. Ducenius Verus, cos. 95 (no. 99); M. Arruntius Aquila, cos. c. 77 (probably father of Stella) (no. 333); another P. Ducenius Verus was a pontifex by 101/102, and was presumably a relative of the other Ducenii (no. 383); the last is [Po]mponius Secundus P. Cest[ius] … ius Priscus Ducenius Proc[ulus], a military man perhaps adopted into one of the families his name commemorates (no. 476).

29 Silius Italicus, *Punica* 12.212–267.

30 Pliny, *Letters*, 3.7; Italicus starved himself to death in 101.

31 Talbert, *Senate*, 185–186 and 225–226.

32 See Chapter 1, note 2.

33 Domitian's list of senatorial victims is a good deal longer than this, and the ex-consuls amongst them are listed by Jones, *Domitian*, 183–188. His quite reasonable conclusion is that, generally speaking, they deserved what they got.

34 Suetonius, *Domitian* 15.1; Jones, *Domitian*, 48.

35 Fronto's colleague, M. Calpurnius [---]icus, may well, for all we know, have been involved; however, not only does he not appear in the sources, but we know nothing about him to provide a basis for the conjecture I am making about Fronto. Yet he must have gone along with events – as did all other senators present.

36 Note also the unusually long list for 90, in the wake of the Saturninus crisis the year before; there were thirteen consuls in the year (including Nerva).

37 Talbert, *Senate*, 202–205.

38 Of course, consuls and other magistrates had to stand for election, a process which involved considerable time and senatorial energy. Yet the elections had largely ceased to have any real effect. Only at lower magistracies was there any real competition, and then only if among candidates not favoured by the emperor. For the consulship no emperor was going to permit a candidate he did not approve of being elected. Magistrates made speeches of thanks for their election – in the Republic addressed to the people, but by AD 100 they addressed the emperor (Pliny, *Panegyricus*); cf. Talbert, *Senate*, passim.

39 Vidman, *FO*, frags Fg, Fh; only nine names are known for certain, with one more sure (Tacitus); two are unattested, though I have a suggestion later; there were thus twelve altogether.

40 Vidman, *FO*, frag Fj.

41 *CIL* XVI, 42.

42 Syme, *Tacitus*, 642 makes the identification; the *cognomen* is not recorded.

43 *PIR*(2) J 322; Jones, *Senatorial Order*, no. 152; Garzetti, *Nerva, certi* 72; Birley, *Fasti*, 69–72, suggests he may have begun as an *eques*.

44 *PIR*(2) D 167; Jones, *Senatorial Order*, no. 97; Garzetti, *Nerva, certi* 52.

45 *PIR*(2) J 630; Jones, *Senatorial Order*, no. 164; Syme, *Tacitus*, 55 and 635–636; Jones, *Domitian*, 40–42; Garzetti, *Nerva, certi* 80 and *incerti* 165.

46 He was also his nemesis: Servianus was executed, with his son, by Hadrian in 136.

47 *PIR*(1) V 308; Jones, *Senatorial Order*, no. 298; R. Syme, 'Vestricius Spurinna', *Roman Papers* VII, 541–550.

48 Syme's splendid, if cruel, characterisation, *Tacitus*, 1.

49 Jones, *Senatorial Order*, no. 239; Garzetti, *Nerva, certi* 125; cf *PIR*(2) P 746.

50 See note 20 in Chapter 10 on this date.

51 E.g., Pliny, *Letters* 9.13.2.

52 F.G. d'Ambrosio, 'End of the Flavians: the case for senatorial treason', *Rendiconti dell'Istituto Lombardo, Classe di Lettere, Scienze morali e Storiche*, 114, 1980, 232–241, is too vague and general to be taken seriously.

53 Martial, *Epigrams*, 5.6.2.

54 Even from Apollonia the ex-slave Epictetus lamented that to get to the emperor one had to bribe a freedman, cf. F. Millar, 'Epictetus and the imperial court', *JRS* 55, 141–148; also C.G. Starr, 'Epictetus and the tyrant', *Classical Philology* 44, 1949, 20–29.

55 Suetonius, *Domitian*, 14.4; Cassius Dio 67.14.1.

56 This practice started tentatively with Claudius, but Domitian seems to have been a good deal more systematic about it than earlier emperors – and so more of a threat to the freedmen, of course: Jones, *Domitian*, 61–69; for Abascantus, cf *PIR*(2) F 494.

57 S. Applebaum, 'Domitian's assassination: the Jewish aspect', *Scripta Classica Israelica* 1, 1974, 116–123, only succeeds in demonstating that there was no 'Jewish aspect' to the assassination.

58 Dio Cassius 67.15.4; Suetonius, *Domitian*, 14.1.

59 Suetonius, *Domitian*, 3.1; Dio Cassius 67.3.1; cf. Jones, *Domitian*, 32–38 on all this.

60 *CIL* 15.548a–6a, stamped bricks from a brickyard she owned – though there is no evidence that Domitia knew she was being characterised as Domitian's wife on these bricks.

61 R. Syme, 'Prefects of the city: Vespasian to Trajan', *Roman Papers* V, 608–621.

62 A. Garzetti, *From Tiberius to the Antonines, A History of the Roman Empire, 14–192*, trans. J.R. Foster, London 1974, 277.

63 Syme 'Prefects of the city'.

64 On the Vigiles, see P.K.B. Reynolds, *The Vigiles of Imperial Rome*, Oxford 1924; on the *annona*, see G.E. Rickman, *The Corn Supply of Ancient Rome*, Oxford 1980.

65 Jones, *Domitian*, 96–97.

66 *PIR*(2) P 308.

67 *PIR*(2) N 162; G. Winkler, 'Norbanus, ein bisher unbekannter Prokurator von Raetien', 1972, *Akten des VI internationalen Kongresses für greichische und lateinische Epigrafik* 495–498; P. Brunt, 'The administrators of Roman Egypt', *Roman Imperial Themes*, 1990, 248–249; his full name is not known; H.G. Pflaum, *Les Carrières procuratoriennes équestres sous le haut-empire romain*, supplement, Paris 1984, 17–18.

68 Martial, *Epigrams* 9.84.

69 Norbanus may have held another post between Raetia and the Guard – Jones, *Domitian*, 149, suggests Egypt.

70 Dio Cassius, 67.15.2; Eutropius 8.1.

71 Dio Cassius 68.3.3; John of Antioch III, p. 760 (Boissevain).

72 Clodianus vanishes from the sources afterwards. What happened to him? If the troops

killed Petronius for being involved in Domitian's death, one must assume Clodianus also died, perhaps sooner – killed by Petronius, perhaps, as a belated precaution. Unless, that is, Clodianus got away rapidly into anonymity and civilian life.

73 Dio Cassius 67.5.

74 There were seven children in all (*ILS* 1839).

75 Dio Cassius 67.15.5.

76 *PIR*(2) C 1227; Jones, *Domitian*, 52–53l C.T.H.R. Ehrhardt, 'Nerva's background', *Liverpool Classical Monthly*, 12, 1987, 18–20, argued that Nerva was Domitian's secret police chief, a suggestion owing more to the time of writing (late Cold War paranoia) than to any evidence; A. Berriman and M. Todd, 'A very Roman coup: the hidden war of imperial succession AD 96–8', *Historia* 50, 2001, 312–331, appear to take it seriously.

77 *PIR*(2) L 84 and A 944 and A 949; Jones, *Senatorial Order*, no. 174; Garzetti, *Nerva, certi* 86; J. Assa, 'Aulus Bucius Lappius Maximus', *Akten des IV Internationalen Kongresses für griechische und Lateinische Epigraphie 1963*, 31–39; Jones, *Domitian*, 59.

78 *PIR*(2) A 1510; Jones, *Senatorial Order*, no. 41; Garzetti, *Nerva, certi* 27; Syme, *Tacitus*, 605, 793;

79 *PIR*(1) V 284; Jones, *Senatorial Order*, no. 297; Garzetti, *Nerva, certi* 147.

80 *PIR*(2) A 1086; *Epitome de Caesaribus* 12.2; Jones, *Senatorial Order*, no. 29; Garzetti, *Nerva, certi* 17.

81 Jones, *Domitian*, 150–153; K. Ströbel, *Die Donaukriege Domitians*, Bonn 1984.

82 *PIR*(2) P 623; Jones, *Senatorial Order*, no. 233; Garzetti, *Nerva, certi* 117.

83 *CIL* 16.33; Eck, 'Statthalter', 312–315.

84 Eck, *Senatoren*, 61; P.A. Gallivan, 'The *Fasti* for AD 70–96', *Classical Quarterly* 31, 1981, 186–220; but Jones, *Senatorial Order*, 35–45.

85 Dusanic and Vasic, 'Moesian diploma', a fundamental text and article for these events.

86 Eck, Statthalter', 321; Dusanic and Vasic, 'Moesian diploma', 301–303; B. Lörincz, 'Some remarks on the history of the Pannonian legions in the late first and early second centuries AD', *Alba Regia* 19, 1982, 265–288.

87 Dusanic and Vasic, 'Moesian diploma', 303–304.

88 Ibid.

89 Tacitus, *Germania* 38.

90 Jones, *Domitian*, 128–131 and 150; H. Schönberger, 'The Roman frontier in Germany: an archaeological survey', *JRS* 59, 1969, 144–164.

91 Tacitus, *Germania*, 41.1.

92 Jones, *Domitian*, 138–143; J.J. Wilkes, 'Romans, Dacians, and Sarmatians in the first and early second centuries', in B. Hartley and J. Wacher (eds), *Rome and her Northern Provinces*, Gloucester 1983.

93 *ILS* 92 (= McCrum and Woodhead 372).

94 Dio Cassius 67.5.3.

95 Tacitus, *Germania* 39; Dio Cassius 67.5.2.

96 Dio Cassius 67.5.2.

97 The governors of Moesia Superior, who succeeded Pompeius Longinus, and of Pannonia, who preceded him, are not known; clearly they had much to do with preparing for and conducting the war.

98 Syme's comment: 'Legates of Moesia', *Danubian Papers*, Bucharest 1971, 206.

99 I assume that the transfer of Pompeius Longinus, a proven general, was the signal to start the war; Jones, *Domitian*, 153, suggests that the war began the previous year ('?95'). This is quite possible, but the essential point here is that this great army was, by September 96, fully occupied in hostilities in enemy territory, and so unavailable for intervention in Italy; similarly Ströbel, *Die Donaukreige Domitians*, dates the start of the war to 97, though he agrees that the preparatory work took place before Domitian's death; but if the

army and the supplies had been gathered, the war would not have been delayed until after the winter.

100 F. Millar, *The Emperor in the Roman World*, London 1977, 26–29, with an emphasis on the cost to local communities of an imperial journey; Pliny, *Panegyricus*, 20, contrasts Trajan's lack of demands with Domitian's costliness. But an imperial journey to a war on the northern frontier need not be particularly expensive to local communities: he would not linger.

101 Suetonius, *Augustus* 45.1.

102 Suetonius, *Domitian* 17: 'one of the imperial gladiators'.

103 Suetonius, *Domitian* 17, Jones, *Domitian*, 85–86.

104 Suetonius, *Domitian* 5: Eutropius 7.23; M. Platner and T. Ashby, *A Topographical Dictionary of Ancient Rome*, Oxford 1929, 371.

105 Suetonius, *Domitian* 5.

106 H.H. Scullard, *Festivals and Ceremonies of the Roman Republic*, London 1981, 186–187.

107 Suetonius, *Domitian* 15; Jones, *Domitian*, 100.

108 T.V. Buttrey, *Documentary Evidence for the Chronology of the Flavian Titulature*, Beitrage für Klassische Philologie 112, Meisenheim, 1980, 30; Jones, *Domitian*, 20.

109 Dionysius of Halicarnassus 6.13.4; Suetonius, *Augustus* 38.3; Scullard, *Festivals and Ceremonies*, 164, 188.

3 NERVA

1 R. Syme, *The Roman Revolution*, Oxford 1939, 500, suggested this, but qualified it as 'no doubt'.

2 Two certainly: M. and L. Cocceius Nerva; the third had the cognomen Balbus, and his fraternity is only assumed; he could be a cousin.

3 See references in Syme, *Roman Revolution*. The connections of the family and its descent were sorted out by E. Groag, 'Prosopographische Beitrage V: Sergius Octavius Laenas', *Jahreshefte* 21/22, 1924; it is repeated in essentials by Garzetti, *Nerva*, 17–30, and with some expansion by Syme, *Tacitus*, 627–628.

4 *PIR*(2) C 1225; Tacitus, *Annals* 4.58, and 6.26; Dio Cassius 68.2.1; Syme, *Tacitus*, 627–628.

5 *PIR*(2) 0 41.

6 Syme, *Tacitus*, 628.

7 Tacitus, *Annals* 14.58.

8 Tacitus, *Annals* 16.10.

9 Tacitus, *Annals* 15.72.

10 Ibid.

11 McCrum and Woodhead, 4.

12 He was Sergius Octavius Laenas Pontianus, the Rubellian and Claudian relationship apparently suppressed in his name: Smallwood, 10; *PIR*(2) O 46, with *stemma*; not listed in Lambrechts.

13 He is included at *PIR*(2) O 45, but does not seem to be on record anywhere: it is only an assumption that he was 'Octavius Laenas'.

14 McCrum and Woodhead omit him; R. Syme, 'The Ummidii', *Historia* 17, 1968, 72–108 at 81; accepted by Jones, *Senatorial Order*, no. 25; *PIR*(1) S 110; *AE* 1998, 419.

15 Suetonius, *Domitian*, 10.3; Jones, *Domitian*, 185–188.

16 P.A. Gallivan, 'The *Fasti* for AD 70–96', *Classical Quarterly* 31, 1981, 191.

17 C.T.H.R. Ehrhardt, 'Nerva's background', *Liverpool Classical Monthly* 12, 1987, 18–20, used the absence of evidence as the basis of his theory of Nerva as Domitian's secret police chief.

18 See the list and discussion in Jones, *Domitian*, 182–192.

19 J.A. Crook, *Consilium Principis*, Cambridge 1955, 48–52.
20 *Epitome de Caesaribus* 12.11; Syme, *Tacitus*, 653, n.5 – but Garzetti, *Nerva*, 17.
21 Syme, *Tacitus*, 1.
22 *ILS* 274 (= Smallwood, 27a); see Chapter 1, note 2.
23 L. Casson, *Ships and Seamanship in the Ancient World*, 1971, 282–286.
24 Tacitus, *Histories* 1.12.1.
25 K. Wellesley, *The Long Year, AD 69*, 2nd edn, Bristol, 1989; P.A.L. Greenhalgh, *The Year of the Four Emperors*, London 1975.
26 Dio Chrysostom, *Orations* 36.
27 Philostratus, *Lives of the Sophists* 1.7.2.
28 Jones, *Senatorial Order*, 52.
29 Suetonius, *Domitian* 23.1.
30 Tacitus, *Germania*, 29; see also Chapter 10.
31 *BMC* III Nerva 4–7.
32 *PIR*(2) L 253; Jones, *Senatorial Order*, no. 279; Garzetti, *Nerva*, *certi* 89; the date of the first consulship is disputed: 97 is now discounted. C.P. Jones, 'Sura and Senecio, *JRS* 60, 1970, 98–104, argues strongly for 93; G. de Vita-Evrard, 'Des Calvisii Rusones à Licinius Sura', *Mélanges de l'École française de Rome* 1987, 320–323, argues for 96. The beginning of his governorship of Germania Inferior is also a problem, being mixed up with the theory of the governorship of Vestricius Spurinna. But the latter is best located at 86 or thereabouts, and Sura thereby has a full term of two or three years. Eck, 'Statthalter' 326–329 puts Sura in Germany from 96/97 to 97/98, but later in *Die Statthalter der germanischen Provinzen von 1–3 Jahrhundert*, Köln/Bonn 1985, 155–156, he changed his mind and put Spurinna in 97, or under Domitian, and Sura at '97?/98?'. I am more comfortable with Sura as consul in 93 and a full term as governor in 96–98.
33 Bennett, *Trajan*, 46, argues for a governorship in Pannonia in Domitian's last years.
34 Pliny, *Panegyricus* 5.2–4
35 Dio Cassius 68.1.3.
36 Suetonius, *Domitian*, 23; Dio Cassius 68.1.1.
37 Dio Cassius 68.2.3; Suetonius, *Domitian* 23.3; A.R. Birley, 'The oath not to put senators to death', *Classical Review*, 12, 1962, 197–199.
38 Dio Cassius 68.1.2.
39 *Epitome de Caesaribus* 12.2–3.
40 I.A. Carradice, *Coinage and Finances in the Reign of Domitian*, BAR S 178, 1983.
41 M. Hammond, 'The tribunician day from Domitian through Antoninus: a reexamination', *Memoirs of the American Academy at Rome*, 19, 1949, 35–76.
42 *BMC* III Nerva 1–21.
43 *BMC* III Nerva p. 14.
44 Dio Cassius 68.1.2.
45 Dio Cassius 68.1.1–3; Syme, *Tacitus*, 7; Garzetti, *Nerva*, 46–48.
46 *PIR*(2) A 1510; Jones, *Senatorial Order* no. 41; Garzetti, *Nerva*, *incerti* 27; R. Syme, 'Prefects of the city: Vespasian to Trajan', *Roman Papers* V, 608–621, discussing and correcting id., *Tacitus* 645–646, and G. Vitucci, *Ricerche sulla prefectura urbi in eta imperiale*, Rome 1956.
47 Dio Cassius 68.3.3.
48 Suetonius, *Domitian* 23.1.
49 R. Syme, 'Verginius Rufus', *Roman Papers* VII, 518–520; Jones, *Senatorial Order*, no. 297; *PIR*(1) V 284; Garzetti, *Nerva*, *certi* 147.
50 *PIR*(2) A 1086; Jones, *Senatorial Order*, no. 29; Garzetti, *Nerva*, *certi* 17; Antoninus, in fact, may be from northern Italy, which would extend this particular aristocratic network even wider.
51 Not in *PIR* or Garzetti, *Nerva*; Vidman, *FO*, frag Fg and 96.

52 Syme's characterisation, *The Augustan Aristocracy*, Oxford 1989, 378.

53 *PIR*(2) A 695; Jones, *Senatorial Order* no. 18; Garzetti, *Nerva, certi* 9; Lambrechts 9.

54 *PIR*(2) N 60; Jones, *Senatorial Order*, no. 207; Birley, *Fasti*, 87–91; L. Vidman, 'Die Familie des L. Neratius Marcellus', *ZPE* 43, 1981, 377–384.

55 *PIR*(2) D 133: Jones, *Senatorial Order*, no. 95; Garzetti, *Nerva, certi* 53; R. Syme, 'Domitius Apollinaris', *Roman Papers* VII, 588–602.

56 *PIR*(2) H 143: Jones, *Senatorial Order*, no. 128.

57 *PIR*(2) G 181; Jones, *Senatorial Order*, no. 120; Garzetti, *Nerva, certi* 60.

58 *PIR*(2) C 1467; Syme, *Tacitus*, 63–72 and ch. 45; A.R. Birley, 'The life and death of Cornelius Tacitus', *Historia* 49, 2000, 230–247.

59 *PIR*(2) C 1407; Jones, *Senatorial Order*, no. 97; G. Alfoldy and H. Halfman, 'M. Cornelius Nigrinus Curiatius Maternus, General Domitians und Rivale Trajans', *Chiron* 3, 1973, 331–373; see further discussion in Chapter 6; also Alfoldy's 'Nachtrage' in *Römische Heeresgeschichte*, Amsterdam 1987, 195–201.

60 *RMD* III 140, with references. B. Lörincz and Z. Visy 'Bemerkunden zu einer neuen Civitasurkunde aus dem Jahre 97', *ZPE* 69, 1986, 241–248, discuss the various names on this fragment of diploma. There seems no reason to conclude, as does K.-H. Dietz (in a comment noted by Roxan at *RMD* III, 256) that the [...]TERNO of the diploma refers to the son of the consul of 97; I prefer the father.

61 Curiatius Maternus is one of the protagonists in Tacitus' early *Dialogue on Oratory*.

62 E. Dabrowa, *The Governors of Roman Syria from Augustus to Septimius Severus*, Bonn 1998, 75–78.

4 REACTIONS

1 Suetonius, *Domitian*, 23.

2 Dio Cassius 68.1.1; Suetonius, *Domitian*, 23

3 Dio Cassius 68.1.3.

4 Dio Cassius 68.1.2; the man Seras is not known otherwise; the three other names are noted in a *scholium* on Juvenal 4.53 (Wessmer, p. 57).

5 Dio Cassius 68.3.2; see Chapter 6.

6 Z. Yavetz, 'The urban plebs: Flavians, Nerva, Trajan', in *Opposition et Resistances à l'Empire d'Auguste à Trajan, Entretiens sur l'Antiquité Classique* 33, Geneva 1986, 135–186, is virtually the only discussion on this subject for this period, as Yavetz himself explains at the start of the article.

7 Yavetz (previous note) 186.

8 As an example, Smallwood 64(c).

9 The murders of Galba and Piso and several of their supporters were followed by an assault on a banqueting party held by Otho in the palace, where a massacre of many senators was only prevented by Otho's tears: Tacitus, *Histories* 1.80–82.

10 Suetonius, *Domitian*, 23.

11 The coins are detailed in *RIC* and *BMC*; a most useful discussion of the coins is by D.C.A. Shotter, 'The principate of Nerva: some observations on the coin evidence', *Historia* 32, 1983, 215–226.

12 Shotter (previous note) puts the period of 'Desig III' into December.

13 '*Victoria Aug*' appears from the very first issue and so it is not a celebration of an actual victory, but a hope; the campaign in the north was still continuing, and the war did not end until the next year. It follows that '*pax*' did not mean a restoration of external peace, but the imposition of internal peace: i.e., the murder of Domitian. One wonders, therefore, if the *Victoria* coins celebrate the Senate's victory over that same enemy.

14 *BMC* III Nerva 87.

15 Philostratos, *Lives of the Sophists* 1.7.2.

16 Plutarch, *Moralia*, 828 A; J.A. Notopoulos, 'Studies in the chronology of Athens under the empire', *Hesperia* 18, 1949, 12; C.P. Jones, *Plutarch and Rome*, Oxford 1971, 27.

17 Dio Chrysostom, *Or.* 18; B.W. Jones, 'Domitian and the exile of Dio of Prusa', *La Parola del Passato*, 1990, 348–357.

18 R.H. Barrow, *Plutarch and his Times*, London 1967, 12.

19 Dio Chrysostom, *Or.* 1–4; C.P. Jones, *The Roman World of Dio Chrysostom*, Cambridge, Mass, 1978.

20 J.H. Oliver, 'Roman emperors and Athens', *Historia* 30, 1981, 412–423.

21 Dio Cassius, 67.18.1–2; Philostratos, *Life of Apollonios of Tyana* 8.26–27.

22 A. Martin, *Le titulature épigraphique de Domitien*, Beitrage zur klassischen Philologie 181, Frankfurt-am-Main 1987.

23 Birley, *Fasti*, 83–85.

24 P. Bureth, 'Le Préfet d'Égypte (30 av. J.-C.–297 ap. J.-C.): État présent de la documentation en 1973', *ANRW* II, 10, 1, 472–517.

5 THE EMPEROR'S WORK

1 Do Cassius 68.2.4.

2 Dio Cassius 67.2.3; Suetonius, *Domitian* 7.

3 The rumour is probably not true; Jones, *Domitian* 37 calls it 'a farrago of nonsense' and 'standard *vituperatio*', though neither comment is, of course, direct refutation.

4 *BMC* III 88 (= Smallwood 28).

5 Dio Cassius 65.7.2

6 Dio Cassius 68.1.2.

7 M. Goodman, 'Nerva, the *fiscus Judaicus* and Jewish identity', *JRS* 79, 1989, 40–44, which contains references to other studies.

8 Dio Cassius 55.25.5.

9 Pliny, *Panegyricus* 37.6; for an explanation of the tax see Bennett, *Trajan*, 77–78.

10 Pliny, *Panegyricus* 38.2 and 6–7.

11 Pliny, *Panegyricus* 36.4; *Digest* I.2.2.32.

12 Jones, *Domitian*, 79–98, for Domitian's buildings; chapters 6 and 7 for his wars.

13 The basic discussion of finances remains R. Syme, 'The imperial finances under Domitian, Nerva and Trajan', *JRS* 20, 1930, 55–70, though the case is somewhat overstated.

14 Dio Cassius 68.2.2; Pliny, *Panegyric* 51.1: he was *frugelissimus princeps*.

15 Pliny, *Panegyricus* 46.2.

16 *BMC* III 132 (= Smallwood 31).

17 H.H. Scullard, *Festivals and Ceremonies of the Roman Republic*, London 1981, 168.

18 Pliny, *Panegyricus* 46.3–4 and 56.2.

19 *BMC* III 119 (= Smallwood 30).

20 *ILS* 214.

21 *BMC* II Domitian, p. 406 n. – not necessarily a palace, maybe a temple, and possibly a forgery.

22 Pliny, *Panegyricus* 47.4.

23 Forum Transitorium: Suetonius, *Domitian* 5.1; generally, Jones, *Domitian*, ch. 4; Syme, 'Imperial finances', did not have the benefit of the archaeological evidence cited by Jones when he argued that Domitian's building programme had declined in his last years.

24 Jones, *Domitian*, ch. 4, for the details and references.

25 Smallwood, 412 (Casus in Pannonia); *AE* 1995, 1153 (Germania Superior); D.H. French, *Roman Roads and Milestones in Asia Minor: 1 The Pilgrim's Road*, BAR S 392, Oxford 1981 (Asia Minor); Smallwood 409 (near Cordoba, Baetica, dated 98 – in Trajan's reign, but presumably the work, or much of it at least, was done earlier.)

26 Smallwood 413 (Moesia Superior), 416 (Miletos), 417 (Galatia), 424 (Cyrene) are all dated to 100.
27 Smallwood 412; the Via Domitiana was part of this whole scheme.
28 Frontinus, *De Aquis* 88.
29 Syme's argument in 'Imperial finances' is that there was no real shortage, only inefficiency in 'the new anarchy' which is his description of Nerva's regime. But he had underestimated Nerva's expenses, as in the building programme, so one of the motives for the commission may well have been a shortage. Inefficiency no doubt also applied – it was a government, after all.
30 Pliny, *Letters*, 2.1.9; *Panegyricus* 62.2.
31 Pliny, *Panegyricus* 62.2.
32 Syme, *Tacitus*, 629.
33 As argued by Syme, 'Imperial finances', and *Tacitus*, 150 and 416–417.
34 The direct connection between the commission and these measures (Dio Cassius 68.2.3) is not explicit, and Dio in fact makes Nerva responsible for the abolitions; this, if these were the commission's recommendations, would be the case, since Nerva would be implementing them on his authority.
35 Syme, 'Imperial finances', 62 and 68, claimed this amounted to 62 1/2 *denarii*, almost another *congiarium* – so it would be if it had been handed out to all, right away.
36 Pliny, *Panegyricus* 25.2–3.
37 *Epitome de Caesaribus* 13.12.
38 *ILS* 1627 (= Smallwood 171).
39 Chronographer of 354.
40 *BMC* III 115 (= Smallwood 29).
41 This coin has been condemned as a forgery by A. Merlin, 'Le grand bronze *Tutela Italiae*', *Revue Numismatique* 10, 1906, 296–301, and this is accepted by some authorities, though not by all.
42 *Epitome de Caesaribus* 12.4.
43 *Digest* 35.2.1–3.
44 Pliny left a large legacy to his local city of Comum, having given various other sums during his lifetime: R. Duncan-Jones, *The Economy of the Roman Empire*, Cambridge 1982, 17–32, for a discussion of Pliny's wealth and his benefactions.
45 Dio Cassius 68.2.1
46 Duncan-Jones, *Economy*, 296, assumes the allocation was from *ager publicus*.
47 P.M. Rogers, 'Domitian and the finances of state', *Historia* 33, 1984, 60–78; Jones, *Domitian*, 73–74.
48 Based on a *congiarium* of 300 *sesterces* for each of 150,000 citizens; cf. R. Duncan-Jones, *Money and Government in the Roman Empire*, Cambridge 1994, appendix 1. The figures are, of course, only very approximate. Indeed, the 60 million may be itself no more than a notional figure.
49 Dio Cassius does not specify the area, but Nerva's other sources seem to be very Italian.
50 Duncan-Jones, *Economy*, 48–52, remarking that Columella's price of 1,000 *sesterces* per *iugerum* is 'unreliable', and too high: clearly land prices will have varied with quality, accessibility, distance from Rome and the sea, and so on.
51 Pliny, *Letters* 7.31; *PIR*(2) C 966.
52 *ILS* 5750 (= Smallwood 477).
53 This has been the subject of much study, because of the survival of detailed inscriptions, in particular Duncan-Jones, *Economy*, ch. 7; a briefer discussion is in Bennett, *Trajan*, 81–84; see also K.A. Woolf, 'Food, poverty and patronage: the significance of the epigraphy of the Roman alimentary schemes in early imperial Italy', *PSBR* 58, 1990, 197–228.
54 Pliny, *Letters*, 1.8.10 and 7.18.2, and *ILS* 2927 (= Smallwood 230).

55 Cf. Duncan-Jones, *Economy*, 291.

56 '*Alimenta*' originally meant either food or maintenance; its extension to schemes of charity came during the empire; one scheme is known from Augustus' reign (*CIL* 10.5055).

57 Suetonius, *Domitian* 7.2; Jones, *Domitian*, 77–79.

58 *CIL* 9.1455 (= *ILS* 6509 = Smallwood 435 (extracts)).

59 *BMC* III 378.

60 *CIL* 11.1147 (= *ILS* 6675 = Smallwood 436 (extracts)).

61 Cf. Duncan-Jones, *Economy*, 291–295.

62 Ibid., 294–295.

63 *Epitome de Caesaribus* 12.4.

64 As pointed out by Duncan-Jones, *Economy*, 291–292.

65 *CIL* XI 1149; cf. Duncan-Jones, *Economy*, appendix 3.

66 Only at Ostia were there both private and government schemes recorded; the other private schemes are marked on the map. They are listed by Duncan-Jones, *Economy*, 241.

67 Listed by Duncan-Jones, *Economy*, 340, where references are given.

68 W. Eck, *Die Staatliche Organisation Italiens in der höhen Kaiserzeit*, Vestigia 38, Munich 1979, lists six more, none of which is accepted by Duncan-Jones, *Economy*, 385; they have been ignored here as well.

69 Pliny, *Letters*, 10.8.

70 Pliny was certainly aware of a developing economic and social problem in Italy: his comments are usefully collected by Bennett, *Trajan*, 80.

71 J.C. Mann, 'The raising of new legions during the principate', *Hermes* 19, 1963, 483–489.

72 Bennett, *Trajan*, 79.

73 J.C. Mann (ed. M.M. Roxan), *Legionary Recruitment and Veteran Settlement during the Principate*, London 1983.

74 Pertinax is said to have acted to shake up the system (*SHA Pertinax* 9.3), and administrators of the scheme are recorded at that time (*SHA Pertinax* 4.1 and *Julianus* 2.1; H.-G. Pflaum, *Les Carrières procuratoriennes équestres*, Paris 1960, 1006, 1037, 1041); one inscription (*CIL* 10.5398) of Severan date shows the scheme still in operation.

75 Duncan-Jones, *Economy*, 319, points out that it had finished by the time of Constantine.

76 Mann, 'Raising of new legions'; A.R. Birley, *Marcus Aurelius*, London 1966, 194–196.

77 E. Birley, 'Septimius Severus and the Roman army', *Epigraphische Studien* 8, 1969, 63–82; A.R. Birley, *Septimius Severus*, London 1988, 107.

78 *Epitome de Caesaribus*, 12.4.

79 Bennett, *Trajan*, 126, on the basis of a papyrus which is dated later, but thought to be a copy – the matter must be considered uncertain. Hadrian remitted part of the payment (*SHA Hadrian* 6.5).

80 C. Caristanius Fronto (cos. 90) from Pisidian Antioch, Ti. Julius Celsus Polemaeanus (cos. 92) from Asia, L. Stertinius Avitus (cos. 92) from Africa, L. Julius Marinus (cos. 93) from 'the East', perhaps Berytus in Phoenicia, and C. Antius A. Julius Quadratus (cos. 94) from Asia; other men had reached the praetorship in the Flavian period. The numbers from the east in the Senate by 96 were considerable; cf. J. Devreker, 'La Composition du senat romain sous les Flaviens', and A. Chastagnol, 'Les homines novi entres au senat romain sous la règne de Domitien', both in W. Eck, K. Galstere and H. Wolff, eds, *Studien zur antiken Sozialgeschichte, Festschrift Friedrich Vittinghoff*, Köln 1980, pp. 257–268 and 269–281, but, above all, H. Halfman, 'Die Senatoren aus den kleinasiatischen provinzen des Römischen Reiches vom 1 bis 3 Jahrhundert (Asia, Pontus-Bithynia, Lycia-Pamphylia, Galatia, Cappadocia, Cilicia), *Tituli* 5, 1982, 603–650.

81 From Narbonensis, Cn. Arrius Antoninus and P. Cornelius Tacitus in 97 and Cn. Domitius Tullus and Sex. Julius Frontinus in 98; from Spain, M. Annius Verus and M.

Cornelius Nigrinus in 97 and Trajan and C. Pomponius Rufus ... Sparsus in 98; L. Julius Ursus was from either Spain or Narbonensis. The origins of two other senators is not known.

82 R. Syme, 'Prefects of the City, Vespasian to Trajan', *Roman Papers*, V, 608–621.
83 Frontinus, *de Aquis*, 1.1.
84 For example, Cn. Octavius Titianus Capito, *ab epistulis*, *PIR*(2) O 62; Pflaum, *Carrières*, 143–145.
85 Dio Cassius 68.3.4; *SHA Hadrian* 2.5: Trajan was in office in 97; Eck, 'Statthalter', 287–362.
86 Eck, 'Statthalter', shows large gaps.
87 Eck, 'Statthalter', 328; *SHA Hadrian* 2.6; Pliny, *Letters*, 8.23.
88 The governor in 96–97 was Sex. Carminius Vetus; his next-but-one successor was Cn. Pedanius Fuscus Salinator in 98–99; the dates of their consulships are not clear, but *c.*83 and *c.*85 are about right; cf Eck, 'Statthalter', 328–331.
89 Pliny, *Letters*, 2.11 and 3.9; Juvenal, *Satires*, 1.49.
90 Pliny, *Letters*, 3.4 and 3.9; on both of these see P.A. Brunt, 'Charges of provincial maladministration under the early principate', *Historia* 10, 1966, 189–227.
91 *PIR*(2) M 337.
92 Jones, *Domitian*, 149.
93 *PIR*(1) S 560; the origin of this man, for some time thought to be Cilicia, is now doubtful – Spain, Italy and Sicily are now in the frame as well.
94 *RMD* III 140.
95 By B. Lörincz and Z. Visy, 'Bemerkunden zu einer Civitasurkunde aus dem Jahre 97', *ZPE* 63, 1986, 241–249, as reported in *RMD* III 140.
96 *CIL* XVI 41; Syme, *Tacitus* 646.
97 *CIL* XVI 37; Eck, 'Statthalter', assumes he had been governor since 88, a rather long tenure. Martial praised him as a soldier (1.55.2).
98 *ILS* 9485; Birley, *Fasti*, 233–234.
99 D. J. Breeze, *The Northern Frontiers of Roman Britain*, London 1982, ch. 4.
100 J. Wacher, *The Towns of Roman Britain*, London 1974, 120–122; A.L.F. Rivet and C. Smith, *The Place Names of Roman Britain*, 393.
101 Wacher, *Towns* 137–141; Rivet and Smith, *Place Names*, 368–369.
102 *BMC* III Nerva p.3.
103 *BMC* III Nerva 50 and 51.
104 *RIC* II Nerva 45 and 46.
105 Pliny, *Panegyricus* 8.2.3; Dio Cassius 68.3.4; Nerva and Trajan assumed the title 'Germanicus' as a result.
106 Trajan remained on the Danube throughout most of 99, ostensibly to restore discipline to the legions, and acquaint himself with the frontier situation (Pliny, *Panegyricus* 18.1 and 10.1–2); persuading the Suebi and Sarmatae to keep the peace was thus also involved (see Chapter 10).

6 THE SUCCESSION PROBLEM

1 R.P. Duncan-Jones, 'Roman life-expectancy', in *Structure and Scale in the Roman Economy*, Cambridge 1990, 97–104; K. Hopkins, 'On the probable age-structure of the Roman population', *Population Studies* 20, 1966, 245–264, and, even more to the point here, 'How long did senators live?' in *Death and Renewal, Sociological Studies in Roman History 2*, Cambridge 1983, 146–148.
2 The ages and fates of the emperors until Alexander Severus (though omitting Augustus) are helpfuly listed by B. Baldwin, *The Roman Emperors*, Montreal, 1980, viii.
3 R.M. Geer, 'Second thoughts on the imperial succession from Nerva to Commodus',

Transactions of the American Philological Association 67, 1936, 47–54, points out some problems with the Nerva–Laenas connection in his note 9.

4 *PIR*(2) C 1318 and 1352; Jones, *Senatorial Order*, no. 84; Garzetti, *Nerva, certi* 55 and 56; P. Tansey, 'The perils of prosopography: the case of the Cornelii Dolabellae', *ZPE* 130, 2000, 265–271.
5 *PIR*(2) C 246 and 259; Jones, *Senatorial Order*, no. 66; Garzetti, *Nerva, certi* 32.
6 Vidman, *FO*, Frag Fg and 90.
7 Dio Cassius 68.3.2; *Epitome de Caesaribus* 12.6.
8 Ibid.

7 THE ARISTOCRATIC NETWORKS

1 *PIR*(1) U 574; Syme, *Tacitus*, 30–31; Bennett, *Trajan*, 11–19.
2 Bennett, *Trajan* 19, discusses this; an interpretation of Pliny, *Panegyricus* 89.2, suggests he had died before 100.
3 Bennett, *Trajan*, 11–12; Raepsaet-Charlier 521 (Marcia).
4 *PIR*(2) A 185; Raepsaet-Charlier 821 (Ulpia).
5 *PIR*(2) M 365; Raepsaet-Charlier 821 (Ulpia).
6 Neither man is in *PIR*; Raepsaet-Charlier 533 (Matidia).
7 Raepsaet-Charlier 802 (Vibia Sabina); *PIR*(1) V 414.
8 Raepsaet-Charlier 12 (Aelia Domitia Paulina).
9 *PIR*(2) J 389, 630 and (1) V 688, (2) J 112, 569 and 631; Jones, *Senatorial Order*, nos 154, 164, 165; Garzetti, *Nerva, certi* 77, 80 and 81, and *incerti* 165; Syme, *Tacitus*, app. 7, 635–636, connects Ursus and Lupus as brothers by their names.
10 Raepsaet-Charlier 99 (Arria Fadilla).
11 *Epitome de Caesaribus* 12.2–3.
12 *PIR*(2) A 1513.
13 Raepsaet-Charlier 62 (Annia Galeria Faustina).
14 Raepsaet-Charlier 328 (Domitia Lucilla).
15 Appian, *Iberian Wars* 38; Eutropius 8.2.1; *Epitome de Caesaribus* 13.1.
16 L.A. Curchin, *The Local Magistrates of Roman Spain*, Toronto 1990, nos 140 and 975.
17 *SHA, Hadrian*, 1.1.
18 *SHA, Marcus*, 1.2.
19 *SHA, Antoninus*, 1.1.
20 *PIR*(2) D 167; Syme, *Tacitus*, 605.
21 *PIR*(2) J 389; Syme, *Tacitus*, 636.
22 *SHA, Hadrian* 12.2.
23 *PIR*(2) C 605, A 1408; and (1) C 352; R. Syme, 'Antonine relations: Ceionii and Vettuleni', *Athenaeum* 35, 1957, 306–315.
24 See *Tituli* 5, 1982, particularly the articles by Etienne, Castillo and Le Roux on senators from Lusitania, Baetica and Hispania Citerior respectively; L.A. Curchin, *Roman Spain, Conquest and Assimilation*, London 1991, 79–81; Syme, *Tacitus*, 786–788.
25 Syme, *Tacitus*, 590, 786–788.
26 Jones, *Senatorial Order*, 70 (Table 9).
27 H. Halfmann, *Die Senatoren aus dem ostlichen Teil des Imperium Romanum bis zum Ende des 2Jh. n. Chr.*, Gottingen 1979, and 'Die Senatoren aus dem Kleinasiatischen Provinzen …', *Tituli* 5, 1982, 603–650.
28 Jones, *Senatorial Order*, 69–72.
29 *PIR*(2) J 408; Jones, *Senatorial Order* no. 156; Garzetti, *Nerva, certi* 74.
30 *PIR*(2) J 401; Jones, *Senatorial Order* no. 155; Garzetti, *Nerva, certi* 73; the date of his consulship is not certain: cf. Gallivan, 'The *Fasti* for AD 70–96', *Classical Quarterly* 31, 1981, 212.

31 J.D. Grainger, *Hellenistic Phoenicia*, Oxford 1991, 177–179.
32 G.W. Bowersock, 'Roman senators from the near east...' *Tituli* 5, 1982, 653.
33 Raepsaet-Charlier 153 (Caecilia).
34 *PIR*(2) J 706; Raepsaet-Charlier 462 (Julia Tertulla).
35 S. Mitchell, *Pisidian Antioch*, London and Swansea 1998.
36 *PIR*(2) J 273; Syme, *Tacitus*, 82, n. 6; Jones, *Senatorial Order* no. 158; Garzetti, *Nerva, certi* 80.
37 *PIR*(1) S 1043; B. Levick, *Roman Colonies in Southern Asia Minor*, Oxford 1967, 106; S. Mitchell, 'The Plancii in Asia Minor', *JRS* 64, 1974, 37–38.
38 Mitchell (previous note); S. Jameson, 'Cornutus Tertullus and the Plancii of Perge', *JRS* 55, 1965, 54–58; R. Merkelbach and S. Sahin, 'Inschriften von Perge', *Epigraphica Anatolica* 11, 1988, 97–170.
39 Merkelbach and Sahin (previous note), nos 28 a–b.
40 Ibid., nos 29–34.
41 Mitchell 'Plancii', 26–29.
42 C.P. Jones, 'The Plancii of Perge and Diana Planciana', *HSCP*, 80, 1976, 233–237.
43 *ILS* 1024.
44 Pliny, *Letters* 5.14, and 7.21.
45 Raepsaet-Charlier 154 (Caecilia Minor).
46 *PIR*(2) J 241; Jones, *Senatorial Order* no. 149; Garzetti, *Nerva, certi* 68.
47 *PIR*(2) M 223; Jones, *Senatorial Order* no. 440.
48 Tacitus, *Histories* 1.90.
49 R. Syme, 'Governors dying in Syria', *ZPE* 41, 1981, 133–134.
50 R. Syme, *Some Arval Brethren*, Oxford 1980, 51.
51 *SEG* XVIII 568; Halfmann, *Senatoren*, 101.
52 In the persons of L. Calpurnius Longus (not in Jones, *Senatorial Order* or Garzetti, *Nerva*) and L. Maecius Celer M. Calpurnius Longinus (Jones, *Senatorial Order* no. 189; Garzetti, *Nerva, incerti* 92); the first part of the latter's name indicated a connection (by adoption?) with Kadyanda: Halfman, 'Senatoren', 640–642.
53 Halfmann, 'Senatoren', 634: Raepsaet-Charlier 458bis (Julia Severa).
54 *ILS* 8826; *AE* 1923, 4; *PIR*(1) S 404; Lambrechts 258 (without detail).
55 Smallwood 215.
56 Mitchell 'Plancii'.
57 R.D. Sullivan, *Near Eastern Kings and Rome*, Toronto 1990.
58 R.D. Sullivan, 'The dynasty of Commagene', *ANRW*, II, 8, 1977, 794–795: Merkelbach and Sahin, 'Perge', no. 57.
59 *ILS* 1043; Raepsaet-Charlier 703 (Sergia Paullina); Halfmann, 'Senatoren', 445.
60 Raepsaet-Charlier 286 (Cornelia Manliola).
61 H.P. Saffrey, 'Un nouveau duovir à Antioche de Piside', *Anatolian Studies* 38, 1988, 67–69.
62 Jones, *Senatorial Order* no. 68.
63 Gallivan, '*Fasti*', 191.
64 *ILS* 5926; *SEG* XX, 302; *PIR*(1) S 375.
65 Halfmann, 'Senatoren', 645.
66 G.L. Cheesman, 'The family of the Caristanii at Antioch-in-Pisidia', *JRS* 3, 1913, 253–266; *PIR*(2) C 423; Raepsaet-Charlier 702 (Sergia Paulla).
67 *ILS* 9485.
68 *CIL* VI 2065.
69 B.W. Jones, 'C. Vettulenus Civica Cerealis and the "false-Nero" of AD 88', *Athenaeum* NS 61, 1983, 516–521.
70 Dio Cassius 66.19.3.

71 B. Krieler, 'P. Valerius Patruinus: Statthalter in Galatien-Kappadokien 83–87 n. Chr.', *Chiron* 4, 1974, 451–452; *PIR*(1) V 19 and 104; Jones, *Senatorial Order* no. 290.

72 Raepsaet-Charlier 333 (Domitia Vettilla).

73 R. Syme, 'Antonine relations'; Jones, *Senatorial Order*, nos 302, 303; *PIR*(1) V 351 and 342.

74 Suetonius, *Domitian* 10.

75 *ILS* 1374; V. Maxfield, 'C. Minucius Italus', *Epigraphische Studien* 9, 1972, 243–254.

76 *PIR*(2) M 614; Maxfield, 'Minicius Italus'.

77 *CIL* 16.35; *RMD* I 3; Jones, *Domitian*, 158–159.

78 Suetonius, *Nero* 57.2.

79 Mitchell, 'Plancii'; cf. Dio Chrysostom, *Orations* 35.16–17; S. Mitchell, *Anatolia, Land, Men and Gods in Asia Minor*, vol. 1, *The Celts and the Impact of Roman Rule*, Oxford, 1993, ch. 14.

80 D. Magie, *Roman Rule in Asia Minor*, Princeton 1950, 639–651.

81 Pliny, *Letters* 10.96.

82 This is the most obvious meaning of the Book of Revelation.

83 E.g., Dio Chrysostom, *Orations* 33, 34, 35, 38; C.P. Jones, *The Roman World of Dio Chrysostom*, Cambridge, Mass, 1978, ch. 10.

84 S. Alcock, *Graecia Capta*, Cambridge 1993, 13–16.

85 Ibid., 19–22.

86 G.W. Bowersock, *Greek Sophists in the Roman Empire*, Oxford 1969, 47–48, 110–112.

87 G.W. Bowersock, *Fiction as History: Nero to Julian*, Berkeley and Los Angeles, 1994.

88 Jones, *Dio Chrysostom*, ch. 13; C.P. Jones, *Plutarch and Rome*, Oxford 1971, *passim*.

89 Plutarch, *Precepts of Government*, *Moralia* 798 A onwards.

90 *PIR*(2) M 380; R.H. Barrow, *Plutarch and his Times*, London 1967, 12.

8 CHOICE

1 *BMC* III Nerva p.3.

2 Pliny, *Panegyricus* 14.5.

3 *SHA, Hadrian* 2.5; Dio Cassius 68.3.4; Eck, 'Statthalter', 326–327. Trajan's latest biographer, Bennett, *Trajan*, 45–46, persists in the old assumption that Trajan went to govern Pannonia; this is decisively refuted by the diploma *RMD* III 140. The province was thus in all likelihood Germania Superior.

4 *AE* 1923, 33; Eck, 'Statthalter', 326–327.

5 Dusanic and Visy, 'Moesian diploma'.

6 *BMC* III Nerva p.3 50 and 51 and *RIC* II Nerva 45 and 46.

7 Pliny, *Letters* 9.13.10.

8 *CIL* 2.3788, improved and discussed by G. Alfoldy and H. Halfman, 'M. Cornelius Nigrinus Curiatius Maternus, General Domitians und Rivale Trajans', *Chiron* 3, 1973, 331–373; *AE* 1973, no. 283 (wrongly listed under 'Bétique'); E. Dabrowa, *The Governors of Roman Syria from Augustus to Septimius Severus*, Bonn 1998, 75–78; A. Berriman and M. Todd, 'A very Roman coup: the hidden war of imperial succession AD 96–8', *Historia* 50, 2001, 312–331.

9 V. Maxfield, *The Military Decorations of the Roman Army* London 1981, 148, 151.

10 T.D. Barnes, 'Curiatius Maternus', *Hermes* 109, 1981, 382–384, on the father.

11 He would need to be from a rich family, but no antecedents (other than his adopted father) are traceable. His father, according to the inscription from Liria, was M. Cornelius Nigrinus.

12 *AE* 1908, 237; *ILS* 1055 (= *CIL* 8.17891); both are reprinted, with commentary, in Birley, *Fasti*, 235–237.

13 Syme, *Tacitus*, 631–632.

14 V. Gerasimova-Tomova, *Arkheologiya* 26, 1984, 81–84; B. Lörincz and Z. Visy, 'Bemerk-unden zu einer neuen Civitasurkunde aus dem Jahre 97', *ZPE* 69, 1986, 241–242; *RMD* III 140; *AE* 1985 764 and 1987, 856. Agricola is attested as consul in the *Fasti Ostienses*; cf. Vidman, *FO* Frag Fh.

15 The diploma does not indicate that [...]TERNO's consulship was an iteration, which may be thought to count against this interpretation. H. Solin and O. Salomies, *Repertorium nominum gentilicum et cognominum Latinarum*, Hildesheim 1994, list the possible expansions of ... terno: Aternus, Maternus, Paternus, Fraternus, Aeternus, Veliternus, of which only Maternus and Fraternus are recorded more than twice, and only Maternus has ever appeared in the consular lists.

16 R. Syme, 'Governors dying in Syria', *ZPE* 41, 981, 125–144, pointed out that Syria was a posting which proved to be lethal for many Roman governors, in part because they were appointed at a fairly advanced age, no doubt on the assumption that the power of the position would not tempt them to ambition.

17 C. Octavius Tidius Tossianus L. Javolenus Priscus has been suggested, based on *CIL* 3.2864 (= *ILS* 1015) and Alfoldy and Halfman, 'M. Curiatius Maternus', argue for his appointment to Syria in 97; Eck, 'Statthalter', places him in Syria in 92–95; Birley, *Fasti*, accepts 97; Jones, *Senatorial Order* no. 142, has 'ca. 98–99'; *PIR*(2) O 40 and J 14; Dabrowa, *Governors of Roman Syria*, 73–74, argues strongly for 93–96; Berriman and Todd, 'A very Roman coup', tend to dither.

18 Pliny, *Panegyricus* 6.1; Dio Cassius 68.3.3; *Epitome de Caesaribus* 12.6–8; Syme, *Tacitus* 10, begins his account with the over-dramatic sentence, 'The Guard rose'; this is to mischaracterise what happened.

19 Dio Cassius 68.2.4.

20 Pliny, *Panegyricus* 6.3, 6.1–5, 10.1 and 6, 46.5; Dio Cassius 68.2.3, 3.3–4; Eutropius 8.1.1–2; Victor, *Caesaribus*, 13.1; Orosius, *Adversos Paganos* 7.11.1. The very number of these sources indicates the popularity of the idea. The date, according to the *Epitome de Caesaribus*, was three months before Nerva's death, which puts it in late October – but greater accuracy is not possible. A 'laurelled letter' according to Pliny *NH* 15, 133–134, meant a victory. It did not mean an end to the war, as Bennett, *Trajan*, 41, assumes; the war was still on next year.

21 J. Assa, 'Aulus Bucius Lappius Maximus', *Akten des IV Internationalen Kongresses für griechische und lateinische Epigrafik*, Vienna 1962, 31–39; Jones, *Senatorial Order*, no. 174.

22 *PIR*(2) P 623; Jones, *Senatorial Order*, no. 233; Garzetti, *Nerva*, *certi* 117.

23 *PIR*(1) S 567; Jones, *Senatorial Order*, no. 62; Garzetti, *Nerva*, *certi* 135; R. Syme, 'The Enigmatic Sospes', *JRS* 67, 1977, 38–49.

24 *PIR*(2) J 322; Birley, *Fasti*, 69–72; Jones, *Senatorial Order*, no. 152; Garzetti, *Nerva*, *certi* 72.

25 *PIR*(2) C 1294: Jones, *Senatorial Order*, no. 93; Garzetti, *Nerva*, *certi* 49.

26 He was captured by Decebalus by a trick, and when it became clear that Decebalus would demand an extortionate ransom for his release he committed suicide (Dio Cassius 68.12.2); this can be interpreted either as extreme loyalty to the emperor, or despair that Trajan would never pay the ransom.

27 *PIR*(2) M 381 and N 32; Birley, *Fasti*, 83–85; Jones, *Senatorial Order*, no 62; Garzetti, *Nerva*, *certi* 106 and *incerti* 97; Nepos had an advantage over Trajan, for he had an adult son, who reached the consulship in 103.

28 This is a guess, of course, on top of the assumption that 'TERNO' is Nigrinus. Let me add one more layer of speculation: that Nigrinus' second consulship, as an emergency measure, displaced a man already designated, and that man was C. Pomponius Pius, who became consul next year, thus explaining his unusual position in 98's list.

29 Dio Cassius 68.3.3–4.

30 Pliny, *Panegyricus* 6.3–4 and 8.2.

31 *Epitome de Caesaribus* 13.6.

32 This had not been the intention. The treasuries of the two Germaniae were moved to Belgica to make it more difficult for the German governors to rebel after Antonius Saturninus had used the combined savings and treasuries of two legions at Moguntiacum to finance his rebellion. Technically the treasury was under the control of the procurator at Augusta Trevirorum who at this time was Sex. Attius Suburanus. The arrangement must have made it necessary for the various officials to consult more often than usual.

33 Vidman, *FO*, Frag Fh and 91–92; R. Syme, 'Consulates in absence', *JRS* 48, 1958, 1–9, suggests that Agricola was one who was absent from Rome during his consulate; in the circumstances of the adoption, it would seem highly unlikely.

34 G. Calza, 'Due nuovi frammenti de Fasti Ostiensi', *Epigraphica* 1, 1939, 151–159; *AE* 1940, 93; Syme, *Tacitus* appendix 11, 642–643; Vidman *FO*, Frag Fjk and 93–94.

35 See Chapter 2; for references see notes 47–49, 51 and 53.

36 *PIR*(2) M 46; Jones, *Senatorial Order*, no. 187; Garzetti, *Nerva, certi* 93.

37 *PIR*(2) P 750; Jones, *Senatorial Order*, no. 241; Garzetti, *Nerva, certi* 127.

38 Syme, *Tacitus*, 642–643.

39 *PIR*(2) F 544; Jones, *Senatorial Order*, no. 115; Garzetti, *Nerva, certi* 58.

40 *PIR*(2) J 389; Jones, *Senatorial Order*, no. 155; Jones, *Domitian*, 42; Garzetti, *Nerva, certi* 73; Syme, *Tacitus* 642; Vidman, *FO* 84, accepts them.

41 *PIR*(1) S 560; Jones, *Senatorial Order*, no. 268; Garzetti, *Nerva, certi* 141; W.C. MacDermott, '*Stemmata quod faciunt?* The descendants of Frontinus', *Ancient Society* 7, 1976, 229–261.

42 *PIR*(2) C 1412; Jones, *Senatorial Order*, no. 88; Garzetti, *Nerva, certi* 46.

43 *PIR*(2) M 337; Jones, *Senatorial Order*, no. 192; Garzetti, *Nerva, certi* 96.

44 *PIR*(2) F 23; Jones, *Senatorial Order*, no. 103; Garzetti, *Nerva, certi* 55.

45 *PIR*(2) J 114; Jones, *Senatorial Order*, no. 151; Garzetti, *Nerva, certi* 71.

46 *PIR*(2) C 43; Jones, *Senatorial Order*, no. 55; Garzetti, *Nerva, certi* 26.

47 *PIR*(1) S 727; Jones, *Senatorial Order*, no. 271; Garzetti, *Nerva, certi* 142.

48 There is no fragment of the *Fasti Ostienses* for this year.

49 *PIR*(2) J 273; Jones, *Senatorial Order*, no. 158; Garzetti, *Nerva, certi* 70; W.C. MacDermott and A.E. Orentzel, *Roman Portraits*, London 1979, 108–119.

50 *PIR*(2) J 308; Jones, *Senatorial Order*, no. 156; Garzetti, *Nerva, certi* 58.

51 Tacitus, *Agricola*, 44.5 claims that Agricola foresaw Trajan's rule; one may take leave to assume this to be a biographer's and politician's invention.

9 HEIR

1 *SHA, Hadrian*, 3.7; Dio Cassius 18.3.4.

2 Pliny, *Panegyricus*, 9.3; B. Parsi, *Description et investiture de l'empereur romain*, Paris 1963. Bennett, *Trajan*, 48, and note 26, cites two inscriptions to show Trajan holding the name Caesar before Nerva's death, but only one can be accepted, i.e., Smallwood, 185. The inscription from Ephesos in P.C. Weaver, 'Two freedman careers', *Antichthon* 14, 1980, 143–156, shows Trajan as Germanicus and Dacicus: it must therefore be much later than 97.

3 Although Nerva had IMP II on his coins (on the last group, in his fourth consulship, i.e., early in 98), he did not have GERMANICUS on them. Perhaps he did not have time.

4 Pliny, *Panegyricus* 9.3 is explicit that all were awarded before Trajan came to Rome.

5 Pliny, *Panegyricus* 6.4, 8.6.

6 Pliny, *Panegyricus*, 8.6.

7 This follows from Eutropius 8.2 and *Epitome de Caesaribus* 13.2, though not from Pliny, *Panegyricus* 9.2, which refers to Trajan's previous post as governor of Germania Superior.

8 As Bennett, *Trajan*, points out, 48–49; it is an argument from silence, of course, and so not wholly reliable; but one might have expected a hint to be preserved by Pliny, either in his *Panegyricus* or his *Letters*, had there been any opposition.

9 Pliny, *Panegyricus*, 5.7.

10 Pliny, *Panegyricus*, 6.3.

11 The exact date is not clear. Bennett, *Trajan*, ix, says 25 October (classified as 'conjectural') but it will be better to claim only 'late October', as does Garzetti, *Nerva*, 85–86: 'Verso la fine di ottobre del 97'. The only ancient indication is that it was three months before Nerva's death (*Epitome de Caesaribus* 12.9), which, if precise, would be 28 October, but which is, in reality, inexact.

12 See note 7.

13 Eck, 'Statthalter', 330.

14 Tacitus, *Germania*, 33.1

15 Tacitus, *Germania*, 37.2.

16 Tacitus, *Germania* 37: 'in recent times the Germans were more triumphed over than conquered'.

17 On the Roman frontier in Germany, H. Schönberger, 'The Roman frontier in Germany: an archaeological survey', *JRS* 59, 1969, 144–164, is still a reliably good account.

18 H.M.D. Parker, *The Roman Legions*, Cambridge 1958, 157–158; I *Minervia* went to the Danube and then returned to Germany; XI *Claudia* went to Moesia Inferior; X *Gemina* was permanently moved to Pannonia Inferior.

19 Pliny, *Panegyricus* 8.5.

20 R.O. Fink, A.S. Hoey and W.F. Snyder, 'The *Feriale Duranum*', *Yale Classical Studies* 7, 1940, 41 and 76–77; other dates are given by Eutropius 8.1 and Dio at 68.4.2, but the formal commemoration of Trajan's *dies imperii* on 28 January by the Dura garrison is more convincing.

21 Dio Cassius 68.1.3; Victor 13.10; *Epitome de Caesaribus* 12.10.11.

22 Bennett, *Trajan*, 49, speculated on aspiration of his own vomit, without any evidence. The fever seems quite sufficient.

10 NEW EMPEROR

1 *SHA Hadrian* 2.6; *Epitome de Caesaribus* 13.3.

2 So A.R. Birley, *Hadrian, the Restless Emperor*, London 1997, 38.

3 It is said that Servianus had Hadrian's carriage disabled to prevent him from getting to Trajan before anyone else. But Hadrian – Servianus' own brother-in-law and Trajan's ward – was the obvious man for Servianus to send, as he had been for Marinus a few months before from Moesia: Birley, *Hadrian*, 38, points out that by the time he wrote his memoirs Hadrian and Servianus were enemies, and Hadrian would have reason to justify both his enmity and his forcing Servianus to commit suicide.

4 *SHA Hadrian* 2.5–6.

5 *SHA Hadrian* 2.3–4; Smallwood 109 (= *ILS* 308).

6 *SHA Hadrian* 2.6; Smallwood 109 (= *ILS* 308); Pliny, *Letters* 8.23.5; Eck, 'Statthalter', 328.

7 In comparable circumstances, Harry Truman is said to have commented: '…last night the house, the stars and all the planets fell on me.'

8 Bennett, *Trajan*, 50, provides details, based on Herodian, *Histories*, 4.2. Allowing ten days for the news to reach Trajan and ten for his instructions to reach Rome by return, seven days for the lying in state, two for the journey to the Campus Martius, and the cremation, and several days for the canonisation, one reaches early March.

9 Pliny, *Panegyricus* 21, 57.5, and 84, 6–8; Dio Cassius 68.5.

10 Smallwood 270; he was of equestrian rank, a former cohort commander, with a bravery award, and had been *ab epistulis* for Domitian as well as Nerva: *PIR*(2) O 62.
11 M.F. Speidel, *Riding for Caesar, the Roman Emperor's Horse Guard*, London 1994, 38–41, is the source for this and the next paragraphs.
12 Suggested by Birley, *Hadrian*, 319, note 10, from W. Eck; *AE* 1939, 60.
13 Dio Cassius, 68.5.4.
14 Speidel, *Riding for Caesar* 43.
15 Dio Cassius, 68.5.4.
16 Dio Cassius 68.16.1; Victor 13.9; Pliny, *Panegyricus* 67.8.
17 No reason for his long absence on the frontier is given in any ancient source.
18 For a useful summary cf. Jones, *Domitian*, chs. 6 and 7.
19 Tacitus, *Germania* 29.3; he is somewhat dismissive of the settlers, whom he appears to say came from Gaul.
20 Pliny, *Letters* 1.7.2; cf. Syme, *Tacitus*, app. 6; Syme later changed his mind and accepted the argument that Spurinna was governor of Germania Inferior in 96/97, when he dealt with the Bructeri. This crams far too much into a small space of time; above all, it ignores the fact that the Bructeri were destroyed by their German neighbours almost immediately after their Roman-appointed king was enthroned, if Spurinna performed that deed in 97 or 98 – yet the Romans, with the new emperor on the spot, did nothing about it. Trajan in the circumstances would have had to act, yet did not. It is best to put Spurinna back to the 80s as governor.
21 Tacitus, *Germania*, 38.1.
22 *RMD* I, 6.
23 Dusanic and Vasic, 'Moesian diploma'; R. Lörincz, 'Some remarks on the history of the Pannonian legions in the late first and early second centuries AD', *Alba Regia* 19, 1982, 285–288.
24 Ibid.
25 L.F. Pitts, 'Relations between Rome and German "kings" on the Middle Danube in the first to fourth centuries AD', *JRS* 79, 1989, 54–58; J.J. Wilkes, 'Romans, Dacians, and Sarmatians in the first and early second centuries AD', in B. Hartley and J. Wacher (eds), *Rome and her Northern Provinces*, Gloucester 1983, 255–289. Tacitus, *Germania*, 42, 1– 2, claims these two tribes as having 'Roman backing', but he ignores the two recent wars in 89 and 92, not to mention the war that began in 96.
26 Wilkes, 'Romans, Dacians and Sarmatians', 255–259.
27 Tacitus, *Germania* 39; Dio Cassius 67.5.3.
28 Unless V *Alaudae* was destroyed in the civil war; but Decebalus was certainly reponsible for the defeat of a major Roman force under Cornelius Fuscus in 84.
29 Jones, *Domitian*, 138–138, 141–143.
30 Suetonius, *Domitian* 6.1; Wilkes, 'Romans, Dacians and Sarmatians', 269 and n. 74.
31 Tacitus, *Germania* 41, distinguishes the tribe as '*fida Romanis*', and emphasises the open nature of the Roman–Hermunduran boundaries.
32 Dio Cassius 71.18–19, even implies the existence of a province Marcomannia in 179.
33 Or, as Jones, *Domitian*, 153, puts it: 'Until recently its existence was not even recognised'. In 1974, A. Mocsy, *Pannonia and Upper Moesia*, London, 85, merely noted 'reports of a Suebian war under Nerva'; a dozen years before, P. Oliva, *Pannonia and the Onset of Crisis in the Roman Empire*, trans. I Urwin, Prague 1962, ignored it.
34 His account of the Marcomanni and Quadi contains no indication that a massive Roman army was engaged in a war with them at the very time he was writing.
35 *BMC* III Nerva 50 and 51.
36 *RIC* II Nerva 45 and 46.
37 A diploma of 20 February 98 (*CIL* XVI 42) shows him still in Pannonia; he was not replaced so far as can be seen until 99.

38 Bennett, *Trajan*, 49.
39 H. Schönberger, 'The Roman frontier in Germany: an archaeological survey', *JRS* 59, 1969, 144–197.
40 Pliny, *Panegyricus* 12.2.
41 Pliny, *Panegyricus* 12.3–4 and 16.2.
42 Tacitus, *Histories* 1.4.
43 The standard discussion is J.H. Crook, *Consilium Principis*, Cambridge 1955. Juvenal's fourth satire provides a picture of the *consilium* at work, possibly even accurately.
44 K.H. Waters, '*Traianus Domitiani Continuator*', *American Journal of Philology*, 110, 1970, 385–405, gives a list of probable members at p. 405, abstracted from Crook, *Consilium Principis*; it has only thirty-five names, some of whom can be discarded (e.g. Silius Italicus) and several of whom died early in Trajan's reign (e.g. Corellius Rufus, Julius Frontinus, Verginius Rufus).
45 *AE* 1976, 195; Eck, 'Statthalter', 330.
46 *SHA Hadrian* 4.8.
47 Pliny, *Letters* 8.23.5; Eck, 'Statthalter', 330.
48 His name is omitted from the list in Waters (note 44), and from that of Crook in *Consilium Principis*.
49 As Waters, '*Traianus*' points out.
50 So Bennett, *Trajan*, 51; there is in fact no evidence that Trajan was suggested as consul for 99; since he was essentially responsible for the list he could scarcely 'refuse' the office.
51 Smallwood, p.3, referring to the *Fasti Feriarum Latinarum*.
52 F. Zevi, 'I consoli del 97 D Cr in due framenti gia editi dei Fasti Ostienses', *Listy Filologike* 36, 1973, 125–137.
53 P. Weiss, 'Weitere diplomfragmente von Moesia Inferior', *ZPE* 124, 1999, 287–289; Syme, *Tacitus* 642 and 665 had suggested 97 or 98 as their dates.
54 *PIR*(2) C 1412; Jones, *Senatorial Order* no. 88; Garzetti, *Nerva, certi* 36.
55 *ILS* 1022; Eck, 'Statthalter', 328, with a query; C.P. Jones, 'Sura and Senecio', *JRS* 60, 1970, 98–104.
56 Frontinus had been consul about the year 73, so, if he held the post at the normal age of forty-one (not a necessary condition) he was sixty-eight at the time of Senecio's consulship; he had, of course, been consul for the second time the year before, as one of Trajan's colleagues.
57 Q. Pompeius Falco eventually accumulated thirteen names (cf. Birley, *Fasti*, 95–100).
58 *PIR*(2) M 545 and (1) R 68; Jones, *Senatorial Order* no. 230; Garzetti, *Nerva, certi* 104 and 134; Lambrechts 107.
59 C.P. Jones, *Plutarch and Rome*, Oxford 1972, 54–57.
60 *PIR*(2) D 560.
61 *PIR*(1) S 727; Jones, *Senatorial Order* no. 271; Garzetti, *Nerva, certi* 142.
62 *CIL* XIV 3517; 53; *PIR*(2) M 337; Jones, *Senatorial Order* no. 192; Garzetti, *Nerva, certi* 96.
63 *PIR*(2) F 23; Jones, *Senatorial Order* no. 103; Garzetti, *Nerva, certi* 55. I base my comments on the careers of men who governed Numidia on the list in B. Thomasson, *Fasti Africani*, Stockholm, 1996, and their careers as detailed in Jones and Garzetti.
64 *PIR*(2) C 43; Jones, *Senatorial Order* no. 55; Garzetti, *Nerva, certi* 26.
65 Dio Cassius 68.6.1; Pliny, *Panegyricus* 12.2.
66 Eck, 'Statthalter', 330–338.
67 Eck, 'Statthalter', 334–335; *ILS* 1021a and *CIL* XVI 47.
68 As now appears from a recently published diploma: P. Weiss, 'Neue militärdiplome', *ZPE* 117, 1997, 227–268; the governor's name survives only as 'L POM …' on the fragment; it is expanded to Pomponius and the praenomen corrected to the well-attested 'Q.' by

Weiss; the date (between 1 January and 17 September) 97 brings Pomponius' governorship forward a year from Eck's summary in 'Statthalter', 328–331.

69 *PIR*(1) P 561; Jones, *Senatorial Order* no. 240; Garzetti, *Nerva, certi* 126.

70 *PIR*(2) L 9; Jones, *Senatorial Order* no. 172; Garzetti, *Nerva, certi* 85; Lambrechts, no 81.

71 Dio Cassius 68.3.2 and 68.16.2; *SHA Hadrian* 5.5; Eutropius 8.4; cf. Bennett, *Trajan*, 108.

72 Jones, *Senatorial Order* no. 80; not in *PIR* or Garzetti, *Nerva*; G. Barbieri, 'Pompeio Macrino, Asinio Marcello, Bebio Macro e i Fasti Ostiensi del 115', *Mélanges d'Archéologie et d'Histoire de l'École française de Rome* 82, 1970, 263–287, suggests a consulship in 100; for 101 there is an incomplete name '[...]us Proc[...]' which would fit well; 101 would also suit his career better, for it would be unusual, in settled times, to go straight from a province to the consulship. But – are these settled times?

73 *CIL* III 1699; *ILS* 5863; Smallwood 413; Bennett, *Trajan*, 52; A. Mocsy, *Pannonia and Upper Moesia*, London 1974, 45–48, and 107.

74 Eck, 'Statthalter', 322–332, with several references; Bassus' career is another of those which slowed down under Domitian: praetor before 79, but consul only in 94.

75 Eck, 'Statthalter', 328–336.

76 *P. Oxy* 3022 (= B.W. Jones and R.D. Milns, *The Use of Documentary Evidence in the Study of Roman Imperial History*, Sydney 1984, no. 88); *ILS* 8907.

77 Pliny, *Letters* 10.7.

78 Birley, *Fasti*, 85–91; L. Vidman, 'Die Familie des L. Neratius Priscus', *ZPE* 49, 1981

79 The exact date is disputed: cf. Bennett, *Trajan*, 53 and 235, note 2.

80 Pliny, *Panegyricus* 22 and 23; *Letters* 3.7.6–7.

81 Suggested by Jones, *Domitian*, 149, among others.

82 Pliny, *Panegyricus* 25.2 and 26.1–4; *BMC* III 712.

83 Vidman *FO*, frag Fl and 94–95; the first consul of March–April is only preserved as '...cius Macer', and cannot be securely identified (*PIR*(2) M 14).

84 *PIR*(2) C 732.

85 *PIR*(2) H 126; Jones, *Senatorial Order* no. 126; Garzetti, *Nerva, certi* 63; Lambrechts, no. 273.

86 *PIR*(2) M 92 and 93; Jones, *Senatorial Order* no. 238; Garzetti, *Nerva, certi* 124; Birley, *Fasti* 234–235.

87 *PIR*(2) A 101 for Nerva; Tuscus is not in *PIR* but Vidman *FO* 95 collates some guesses.

88 *PIR*(2) P 490; Jones, *Senatorial Order* no. 225; Garzetti, *Nerva, certi* 118.

89 *PIR*(2) J 273; Jones, *Senatorial Order* no. 158; Garzetti, *Nerva, certi* 70; Lambrechts, no. 68.

90 *PIR*(2) R 93; Jones, *Senatorial Order* no. 247; Garzetti, *Nerva, certi* 133; Lambrechts, no. 119; Birley, *Fasti* 231–232.

91 *PIR*(2) C 1003; Jones, *Senatorial Order* no. 81; Garzetti, *Nerva, certi* 42; he was not merely a *frater*, but *magister* in 101.

BIBLIOGRAPHY

Alcock, S.E. *Graecia Capta, The Landscapes of Roman Greece*, Cambridge: 1993.

Alfoldy, G. *Römische Heeresgeschichte*, Amsterdam: 1987.

—— 'Traianus Pater und die Bauinschrift des Nymphaeums von Milet', *Revue des Études Anciennes* 100, 1998, 367–399.

—— and Halfmann, H. 'M. Cornelius Nigrinus Curiatus Maternus, General Domitians und Rivale Trajans', *Chiron* 3, 1993, 331–373.

D'Ambra, E. *Private Lives, Imperial Virtues, The Frieze in the Forum Transitorium in Rome*, Princeton: 1993.

d'Ambrosio, F.G. 'End of the Flavians: the case for senatorial treason', *Rendiconti dell'Istituto Lombardo, Classe di Lettere, Scienze morali e Storiche*, 114, 1980, 232–241.

Applebaum, S. 'Domitian's assassination: the Jewish aspect', *Scripta Classica Israelica* 1, 1974, 116–123.

Assa, J. 'Aulus Bucius Lappius Maximus', *Akten des IV internationalen Kongresses für griechische und lateinische Epigraphik*, Vienna: 1964, 31–39.

Baldwin, B. *The Roman Emperors*, Montreal: 1980.

Barbieri, G. 'Pompeio Macrino, Asinio Marcello, Bebio Macro e i Fasti Ostiensi del 115', *Mélanges d'Archéologie et d'Histoire de l'École française de Rome* 82, 1970, 263–287.

Barnes, T.D. 'Curiatius Maternus', *Hermes* 109, 1981, 382–384.

Barrow, R.H. *Plutarch and His Times*, London: 1967.

Berriman A. and Todd, M. 'A very Roman coup: the hidden war of imperial succession, AD 96–8', *Historia*, 50, 2001, 312–331.

Birley, A.R. 'The oath not to put senators to death', *Classical Review* 12, 1962, 197–199.

—— *Septimius Severus*, London: 1988.

—— 'Marius Maximus: the consular biographer', *ANRW* II 34.3, 1997, 2678–2757.

—— *Hadrian, the Restless Emperor*, London: 1997.

—— 'Hadrian and Greek senators', *ZPE* 116, 1997, 209–245.

—— 'The life and death of Cornelius Tacitus', *Historia* 49, 2000, 230–247.

Birley, E. 'Septimius Severus and the Roman army', *Epigraphische Studien* 8, 1969, 63–82.

Boulvert, G. *Esclaves et affranchis impériaux sous le haut-empire romain: rôle politique et administratif,* Naples: 1970.

Bowersock, G.W. *Greek Sophists in the Roman Empire*, Oxford: 1969.

—— 'Roman senators from the near east: Syria, Judaea, Arabia, Mesopotamia', *Tituli* 5, 1982, 651–668.

—— *Fiction as History, Nero to Julian*, Berkeley and Los Angeles: 1994.

Breeze, D.J. *The Northern Frontiers of Roman Britain*, London: 1982.

Brunt, P.A. 'Charges of provincial maladministration under the early principate', *Historia* 10, 1966, 189–227.

—— 'The "fiscus" and its development', *Roman Imperial Themes*, Oxford: 1990, 134–162.

—— 'The administrators of Roman Egypt,' *Roman Imperial Themes*, 1990, 215–254.

Bureth, P. 'Le préfet d'Égypte (30 av. J.C.–297 ap J.C.): État présent de la documentation en 1973', *ANRW*, II, 10.1, 1982, 472–502 (with Addenda by G. Bastianini, 503–517).

Buttrey, T.V. *Documentary Evidence for the Chronology of the Flavian Titulature*, Beitrage für Klassische Philologie 112, Meisenheim: 1980.

Calza, G. 'Due nuovi frammenti de Fasti Ostiensi', *Epigraphica* 1, 1939, 151–159.

Campbell, D.J. 'The birthplace of Silius Italicus', *Classical Review* 50, 1936, 56–58.

Campbell, J.B. 'Who were the *Viri Militares*?', *JRS* 65, 1975, 11–31.

—— *The Emperor and the Roman Army, 31 BC–AD 235*, Oxford: 1984.

Carradice, I.A. *Coinage and Finance in the Reign of Domitian*, BAR S 178, Oxford: 1983.

Casson, L. *Ships and Seamanship in the Ancient World*, Princeton: 1971.

Castillo, C. 'Los senadores beticos', *Tituli* 5, 1982, 465–519.

Champlin, E. '*Figlinae Marcianae*', *Athenaeum* 61, 1983, 257–264.

Chastagnol, A. 'Les homines novi entres au sénat romain sous la règne de Domitien', W. Eck, Galstere K. and Wolff, H. eds, *Studien zur antiken Sozialgeschichte, Festschrift Friedrich Vittinghoff,* Cologne and Vienna: 1980, 269–281.

Cheesman, G.L. 'The family of the Caristanii at Antioch-in-Pisidia', *JRS* 3, 1913, 253–266

Crook, J. *Consilium Principis: Imperial Councils and Counsellors from Augustus to Diocletian*, Cambridge: 1955.

Curchin, L.A. *The Local Magistrates of Roman Spain*, Toronto: 1990.

—— *Roman Spain: Conquest and Assimilation*, London: 1991.

Dabrowa, E. *The Governors of Roman Syria from Augustus to Septimius Severus*, Bonn: 1998.

Degrassi, G. *I Fasti Consolari dell'Impero Romani*, Rome: 1952.

de Vita-Evrard, G. 'Des Calvisii Rusones à Licinius Sura', *Mélanges de l'École Française de Rome–Antiquité* 1987.

Devreker, J. 'La composition du senat romain sous les Flaviens', *Studien zur Antiken Sozialgeschichte: Festschrift Friedrich Vittinghoff,* Eck, W., Galsterer, H., Wolff, H. eds., Cologne and Vienna: 1980, 257–268.

—— 'Les orientaux au sénat romain d'Auguste à Trajan', *Latomus* 41, 1982, 492–516.

Duncan-Jones, R.P. 'Age-rounding, illiteracy and social differentiation in the Roman Empire', *Chiron* 7, 1977, 333–353.

—— *The Economy of the Roman Empire: Quantitative Studies*, 2nd edn, Cambridge: 1982.

—— *Structure and Scale in the Roman Economy*, Cambridge: 1990.

—— *Money and Government in the Roman Empire*, Cambridge: 1994.

Eck, W. *Senatoren von Vespasian bis Hadrian*, Munich: 1970.

—— *Die Staatliche Organisation Italiens in der hohen Kaiserzeit*, Vestigia 38, Munich: 1979.

—— *Die Statthalter der germanischen Provinzen vom 1–3 Jahrhundert*, Cologne and Bonn: 1985.

Ehrhardt, C.T.H.R. 'Nerva's background', *Liverpool Classical Monthly*, 12, 1987, 18–20.

Etienne, R. 'Sénateurs originaires de la province de Lusitanie', *Tituli* 5, 1982, 521–529.

Fairon, E. 'L'organisation du palais impérial à Rome', *Musée Belge*, 1900, 5–25.

Fink, R.O., Hoey, A.S. and Snyder, W.F. 'The *Feriale Duranum*', *Yale Classical Studies* 7, 1940.

Frayn, J.M. *Subsistence Farming in Roman Italy*, London: 1979.

French, D. *Roman Roads and Milestones of Asia Minor: 1 The Pilgrims' Road*, BAR S 392, Oxford: 1988.

Gallivan, P.A. 'The *Fasti* for AD 70–96', *Classical Quarterly* 31, 1981, 186–220.

Garnsey, P. *Social Status and Legal Privilege in the Roman Empire*, Oxford: 1970.

—— *Famine and Food Supply in the Graeco-Roman World*, Cambridge: 1988.

Garzetti, A. *From Tiberius to the Antonines: A History of the Roman Empire*, trans. J. Foster, London: 1974.

Geer, R.M. 'Second thoughts on the imperial succession from Nerva to Commodus', *Transactions of the American Philological Association* 67, 1936, 47–54,

Girard, J.-L. 'Domitien et Minerve: un predilection impériale', *ANRW* 2.17.1, 1981, 233–245.

Goodman, M. 'Nerva, the *Fiscus Judaicus* and the Jewish identity', *JRS* 79, 1989, 41–44.

—— *The Roman World 44 BC–AD 180*, London: 1997.

Grainger, J.D. *Hellenistic Phoenicia*, Oxford: 1991.

Greenhalgh, P.A.L. *The Year of the Four Emperors*, London: 1975.

Groag, E. 'Prosopographische Beitrage V: Sergius Octavius Laenas', *Jahreshefte* 21/22, 1924.

Halfmann, H. *Die Senatoren aus dem ostlichen Teil des Imperium Romanum bis zum Ende des 2 Jh. n. Chr.*, Gottingen: 1979.

—— 'Die Senatorien aus den Kleinasiastischen Provinzen des römischen Reiches vom 1 bis 3 Jahrhundert (Asia, Pontus-Bithynia, Lycia-Pamphylia, Galatia, Cappadocia, Cilicia)', *Tituli* 5, 1982, 603–650.

Hammond, M. 'The transmission of the powers of the Roman emperor from the death of Nero in AD 68 to that of Alexander Severus in AD 235', *Memoirs of the American Academy at Rome* 23, 1956, 61–133.

—— 'The tribunician day from Domitian through Antoninus: a reexamination', *Memoirs of the American Academy at Rome*, 19, 1949, 35–76.

Henderson, B.W. *Five Roman Emperors*, Cambridge: 1927.

Holder, P.A. *The Auxilia from Augustus to Trajan*, BAR S 70, Oxford: 1980.

Hopkins, K. 'On the probable age-structure of the Roman population', *Population Studies* 20, 1966, 245–264.

—— *Death and Renewal, Sociological Studies in Roman History 2*, Cambridge: 1983.

Jameson, S. 'Cornutus Tertullus and the Plancii of Perge', *JRS* 55, 1965, 54–58.

Jones, B.W. 'Domitian's advance into Germany and Moesia', *Latomus* 41, 1982, 329–335.

—— 'C. Vettulenus Civica Cerealis and the "false-Nero" of AD 88', *Athenaeum* NS 61, 1983, 516–521.

—— 'Domitian and the exile of Dio of Prusa', *La Parola del Passato* 254, 1990, 348–357.

—— and Milns, R.D. *The Use of Documentary Evidence in the Study of Roman Imperial History*, Sydney: 1984.

Jones, C.P. 'Sura and Senecio', *JRS* 60, 1970, 98–104.

—— *Plutarch and Rome*, Oxford: 1971.

—— 'The Plancii of Perge and Diana Planciana', *HSCP* 80, 1976, 231–237.

—— *The Roman World of Dio Chrysostom*, Cambridge, Mass.: 1978.

Krieler, N. 'P. Valerius Patruinus: Statthalter in Galatien-Kappadokien 83–87 n. Chr.', *Chiron* 4, 1974.

Le Roux, P. 'Les sénateurs originaires de la province d'Hispania Citerior au Haut-Empire romain', *Tituli* 5, 1982, 439–464.

Levick, B.M. *Roman Colonies in Southern Asia Minor*, Oxford: 1967.

—— 'Concordia at Rome', *Scripta Nummaria Romana, Essays presented to Humphrey Sutherland*, ed. R.A.G. Carson and C.M. Kraay, London: 1978, 217–233.

—— 'Domitian and the provinces', *Latomus*, 1982, 50–73.

—— *The Government of the Roman Empire, a Sourcebook*, London: 1985.

—— *Vespasian*, London: 1999.

Lewis, N. and Reinhold, M. *Roman Civilization Sourcebook II: The Empire*, New York: 1966.

Lörincz, B. 'Some remarks on the history of the Pannonian legions in the late first and early second centuries AD', *Alba Regia* 19, 1982, 285–288.

—— and Visy, Z. 'Bemerkunden zu einer Civitasürkunde aus dem Jahre 97', *ZPE* 63, 1986, 241–249.

MacDermott, W.C. '*Stemmata quid faciunt?* The descendants of Frontinus', *Ancient Society* 7, 1976, 229–261.

—— and Orentzel, A.E. *Roman Portraits*, London: 1979.

Magie, D. *Roman Rule in Asia Minor*, Princeton: 1950.

Mann, J.C. 'The raising of new legions during the principate', *Hermes* 19, 1963, 483–489.

—— (ed. M.M. Roxan), *Legionary Recruitment and Veteran Settlement during the Principate*, Institute of Archaeology Occasional Publication no. 7, London: 1983.

Martin, A. *La titulature épigraphique de Domitien*, Beitrage zur Klassischen Philologie 181, Frankfurt on Main: 1987.

Maxfield, V.A. 'C. Minicius Italus', *Epigafische Studien* 9, 1972, 243–245.

—— *The Military Decorations of the Roman Army*, London: 1981.

Merkelbach, R. and Sahin, S. 'Inschriften von Perge', *Epigraphica Anatolica* 11, 1988. 97–170.

Merlin, A. 'Le grand bronze *Tutela Italiae*', *Revue Numismatique* 10, 1906, 296–301.

Millar, F.G.B. *A Study of Cassius Dio*, Oxford: 1964.

—— 'Epictetus and the imperial court', *JRS* 45, 1965, 141–148.

—— *The Emperor in the Roman World*, London: 1977.

—— *The Roman Near East, 31 BC–AD 337*, Cambridge, Mass.: 1993.

Mitchell, S. 'The Plancii in Asia Minor', *JRS* 64, 1974, 37–38.

—— *Anatolia, Land, Men and Gods in Asia Minor*, 2 vols, Oxford: 1993.

—— *Pisidian Antioch*, London and Swansea: 1998.

Mocsy, A. *Pannonia and Upper Moesia*, London: 1974.

Moraviecki, L. 'The symbolism of Minerva on the coins of Domitianus', *Klio* 59, 1977, 185–193.

Notopoulos, J.A. 'Studies in the chronology of Athens under the empire', *Hesperia* 18, 1949.

Oliva, P. *Pannonia and the Onset of Crisis in the Roman Empire*, trans I. Urwin, Prague 1962.

Oliver, J.H. 'The ruling power', *Transactions of the American Philosophical Society* 43/4, Philadelphia: 1953.

—— 'Senators from Greece and Macedonia', *Tituli* 5, 1982, 583–602.

—— 'Roman emperors and Athens', *Historia* 30, 1981, 412–423.

Parke, H.W. *Festivals of the Athenians*, London: 1977.

Parker, H.M.D. *The Roman Legions*, 2nd edn, Cambridge: 1958.

Parsi, B. *Description et investiture de l'empéreur romain*, Paris: 1963.

Pflaum, H.-G. *Les procurateurs équestriennes sous le haut-empire romain*, Paris: 1950.

—— *Les Carrières procuratoriennes équestres sous le haut-empire romain*, Paris: 1960–1984.

Pitts, L.F. 'Relations between Rome and German "kings" on the Middle Danube in the first to fourth centuries AD', *JRS* 79, 1989, 45–58.

Platner, M. and Ashby, T. *A Topographical Dictionary of Ancient Rome*, Oxford: 1929.

Remy, B. *Les Fastes Sénatoriaux des Provinces Romaines d'Anatolie au Haut-Empire*, Paris: 1988.

Reynolds, P.K.B. *The Vigiles of Imperial Rome*, Oxford: 1924.

Rickman, G. E. *The Corn Supply of Ancient Rome*, Oxford: 1980.

Rivet, A.L.F. and Smith, C. *The Place Names of Roman Britain*, London: 1979.

Rogers, P.M. 'Domitian and the finances of state', *Historia* 33, 1984, 60–7.8

Salomies, O. *Adoptive and Polyonymous Nomenclature in the Roman Empire*, Helsinki: 1992.

Saffrey, H.D. 'Un nouveau duovir à Antioche de Piside', *Anatolian Studies* 38, 1988, 67–69.

Schönberger, H. 'The Roman frontier in Germany: an archaeological survey', *JRS* 59, 1969, 144–164.

Scullard, H.H. *Festivals and Ceremonies of the Roman Republic*, London: 1981.

Sherk, R.H. (ed. and trans.), *The Roman Empire: Augustus to Hadrian*, Translated Documents of Greece and Rome 6, Cambridge: 1988.

Sherwin-White, A.N. *The Letters of Pliny, A Historical and Social Commentary*, Oxford: 1966.

Shotter, D.C.A. 'The principate of Nerva: some observations on the coin evidence', *Historia* 32, 1983, 215–226.

Solin, H. and Salomies, O. *Repertorium nominum gentilicum et congnominum Latinarum*, Hildesheim: 1994.

Speidel, M.P. *Roman Army Studies*, vol. 1, Amsterdam: 1984, vol. 2, Stuttgart: 1992.

—— *Riding for Caesar, the Roman Emperor's Horse Guard*, London: 1994.

Starr, C.G. 'Epictetus and the tyrant', *Classical Philology* 44, 1949, 20–29.

Ströbel, K. *Die Donaukriege Domitians*, Antiquitas 1, Bonn: 1989.

Sullivan, R.D. 'The dynasty of Commagene', and 'Papyri reflecting the eastern dynastic network', *ANRW*, II, 8, 1977, 732–798 and 908–939.

—— *Near Eastern Kings and Rome*, Toronto: 1990.

Syme, R. 'The imperial finances under Domitian, Nerva and Trajan', *JRS* 20, 1930, 55–70.

—— *The Roman Revolution*, Oxford: 1939.

—— 'The jurist Neratius Priscus', *Hermes* 85, 1957, 480–493.

—— 'Antonine relatives: Ceionii and Vettuleni', *Athenaeum* 35, 1957, 306–315.

—— 'Consulates in absence', *JRS* 48, 1958, 1–9.

—— 'The Ummidii', *Historia* 17, 1968, 71–108.

—— 'Pliny's less successful friends', *Historia* 9, 1969, 382–379.

—— 'Legates of Moesia', *Danubian Papers*, Bucharest: 1971, 213–224.

—— 'The enigmatic Sospes', *JRS* 67, 1977, 38–49.

—— *Some Arval Brethren*, Oxford: 1980.

—— 'Governors dying in Syria', *ZPE* 41, 1981, 125–144.

—— 'Domitian, the last years', *Chiron* 13, 1983, 121–146.

—— 'Eight consulars from Patavium', *PBSR* 1983, 102–124.

—— *The Augustan Aristocracy*, Oxford: 1986.

—— 'Greeks invading the Roman government', *Roman Papers* IV, 1988, 1–20.

—— 'Prefects of the city, Vespasian to Trajan', *Roman Papers* V, 1988, 608–621.

—— 'Verginius Rufus', *Roman Papers* VII, 518–520.

—— 'Domitius Apollinaris', *Roman Papers* VII, 588–602.

Talbert, R.J.A. *The Senate of Imperial Rome*, Princeton: 1984.

Tansey, P. 'The perils of prosopography: the case of the Cornelii Dolabellae', *ZPE* 130, 2000, 265–271.

Taylor, L.R. *Roman Voting Assemblies*, Ann Arbor: 1966.

Thomasson, B. *Fasti Africani*, Stockhom: 1996.

Townend, O. 'Some Flavian connections', *JRS* 51, 1961, 54–62.

Vidman, L. 'Die familie des L. Neratius Marcellus', *ZPE* 43, 1981, 377–384.

Vitucci, G. *Ricerche sulla prefectura urbi in eta imperiale*, Rome: 1956.

Wacher, J.S. *The Civitas Capitals of Roman Britain*, Leicester: 1966.

—— *The Towns of Roman Britain*, London: 1974.

Waters, K.H. 'The character of Domitian', *Phoenix* 18, 1964, 49–77.

—— '*Traianus Domitiani Continuator*', *American Journal of Philology* 90, 1970, 385–405.

Weaver, P.C. *Familia Caesaris: a Social Study of the Emperor's Freedmen and Slaves*, Cambridge: 1972.

—— 'Two freedman careers', *Antichthon* 14, 1980, 143–156.

Webster, G. (ed.), *Fortress into City*, London: 1988.

Weiss, P. 'Neue militardiplome', *ZPE* 117, 1997, 227–268.

—— 'Weitere diplomfragmente von Moesia Inferior', *ZPE* 124, 1999, 287–289.

Welles, C.B. *et al.*, 'Romanization of the Greek east', *Bulletin of the American Society of Papyrologists* 2, 1964–1965, 42–77.

Wellesley, K. *The Long Year, AD 69*, 2nd edn, Bristol: 1989.

Wilkes, J.J. 'Romans, Dacians and Sarmatians in the first and early second centuries', in Hartley, B. and Wacher, J. (eds), *Rome and her Northern Provinces*, Gloucester: 1983, 255–289.

Winkler, G. 'Norbanus, ein bisher unbekannter Prokurator von Raetien', *Akten des VI internationalen Kongresses für greichische und lateinische Epigraphik*, 1972, 495–498.

Wistrand, E. 'The Stoic opposition to the principate', *Studii Classice* 18, 1979, 92–101.

Woolf, K.A. 'Food, poverty and patronage: the significance of the epigraphy of the Roman alimentary schemes in early imperial Italy', *PSBR* 58, 1990, 197–228.

Wruck, W. *Die Syrische Provincialpragung von Augustus bis Traian*, Stuttgart: 1931.

Yavetz, Z. 'The urban plebs: Flavians, Nerva, Trajan', in *Opposition et Résistances a l'Empire d'Auguste à Trajan*, Entretiens sur l'Antiquité Classique 33, Geneva: 1986, 135–186.

Zevi, F. 'I consoli del 97 D Cr in due framenti gia editi dei Fasti Ostienses', *Listy Filologike* 36, 1973, 125–137.

INDEX

14811829R00107

Printed in Great Britain
by Amazon.co.uk, Ltd.,
Marston Gate.